TAKEDOWN

TAKEDOWN

FROM COMMUNISTS TO PROGRESSIVES,
HOW THE LEFT HAS SABOTAGED
FAMILY AND MARRIAGE

PAUL KENGOR, Ph.D.

 WND Books

TAKEDOWN

Published by WND Books, Washington, D.C. WND Books is a registered trademark of WorldNetDaily.com, Inc. ("WND")

Scripture quotations are taken from the King James Version (public domain).

Book designed by Mark Karis

WND Books are available at special discounts for bulk purchases. WND Books also publishes books in electronic formats. For more information call (541) 474-1776 or visit www.wndbooks.com.

Paperback ISBN: 978-1-942475-10-1   eBook ISBN: 978-1-942475-11-8

Library of Congress Cataloging-in-Publication Data
Kengor, Paul, 1966-
Takedown : From Communists to Progressives, How the Left Has Sabotaged Family and Marriage
/ by Paul
Kengor, Ph.D.
pages cm
Includes bibliographical references and index.
ISBN 978-1-942475-10-1 (paperback : alk. paper)
1. Marriage--Social spects. 2. Marriage--Political aspects. 3. Families--Social aspects. 4. Families--Political aspects. 5. Marxian school of sociology. 6. Political sociology. 7. Radicalism. I. Title.
HQ519.K46 2015
306.81--dc23
2015009444

Printed in the United States of America

15 16 17 18 19 20 LSI 9 8 7 6 5 4 3 2 1

Dedicated to those with the courage to resist redefining the teachings of God, nature, their faith, and their ancestors while liberals/progressives (in the name of "tolerance") denounce, debase, dehumanize, demonize, and seek to destroy them.

CONTENTS

There are forms of ideological colonization which are out to destroy the family. They are not born of dreams, of prayers, of closeness to God or the mission which God gave us; they come from without. . . . The family is threatened by growing efforts on the part of some to redefine the very institution of marriage, by relativism, by the culture of the ephemeral. . . . Every threat to the family is a threat to society itself. The future of humanity . . . passes through the family.

—POPE FRANCIS, JANUARY 16, 2015

Abolition of the family! Even the most radical flare up at this infamous proposal of the Communists.

—KARL MARX, THE COMMUNIST MANIFESTO, 1848

TAKEDOWN

1

FUNDAMENTAL TRANSFORMATION

THAT DISTURBING QUOTATION FROM KARL MARX appears in his *Communist Manifesto*, an enormously influential work that launched a revolution unprecedented in its destruction. Totalitarian movements that envisioned nothing less than the transformation of human nature were inspired by that book. And where is human nature more elemental than in the family and the marital procreative act that produces it?

Even way back then, in the mid-1800s, the far left had its sights on the family, with marriage at the epicenter. And this particular component of the extreme left—the communist left—was devoutly atheistic in its orientation, ambition, and mission. It rebelled against God, a rebellion against the Creator that was central to its new direction and fundamental transformation.

Generally speaking, such rebellion is not new at all; it is as old as the Old Testament, even as communists had a new, perverse rebellion in mind. The revolt against God is an ancient battle that circles back to the Garden of Eden, where a sinister force first tried to separate man and woman from the will of Divine Providence and tear asunder the male-female union that the Creator had ordained. Fortunately for the long scope and history of humanity, better angels prevailed, as did natural law and common sense, all of which, by practice and experience, enabled civilization to hold the bonds of matrimony and the traditional family together.

Nonetheless, the far left has remained undeterred, faithful to its rebellious roots. It has long been hell-bent on taking down the family, especially over the last two centuries. In that objective, leftists have made their arguments and tried different tactics, but they at long last have the vehicle to make it happen: this entirely novel phenomenon called "gay marriage." It is their Trojan horse. Once advocates of same-sex marriage succeed in redefining marriage as anything but one man and one woman, there will be no end to the redefinition. The current liberal/ progressive standard that consenting adults who love each other ought to be entitled to "marriage rights" cannot, by sheer logical consistency, prohibit polygamous marriages, group marriages, interfamily marriages (mother married to son or daughter or stepson or stepdaughter, dad to son or daughter or stepson or stepdaughter, married uncles and nieces, aunts and nephews, etc.), and numerous other innovative arrangements. By the left's new insistent standard for what rises to the level of "marriage," any and all of these variations are fair game for consideration if not implementation. Liberals in their hearts know this; it is undeniable.

Gay-rights activists certainly know it. "Being queer means pushing the parameters of sex, sexuality, and family, and, in the process, transforming the very fabric of society," explains Paula Ettelbrick, former legal director of Lambda Legal Defense and Education Fund. "We must keep our eyes on the goals of providing true alternatives to marriage and of radically reordering society's view of reality."[1] Likewise, here is a candid admission by Masha Gessen, an accomplished writer, author, and gay-rights activist:

> It's a no-brainer that [homosexuals] should have the right to marry,
> but I also think equally that it's a no-brainer that the institution of
> marriage should not exist. . . . Fighting for gay marriage generally
> involves lying about what we are going to do with marriage when
> we get there—because we lie that the institution of marriage is not

going to change, and that is a lie. The institution of marriage is going to change, and it should change. And again, I don't think it should exist. And I don't like taking part in creating fictions about my life. That's sort of not what I had in mind when I came out [of the closet] thirty years ago.

I have three kids who have five parents, more or less, and I don't see why they shouldn't have five parents legally. . . . I met my new partner, and she had just had a baby, and that baby's biological father is my brother, and my daughter's biological father is a man who lives in Russia, and my adopted son also considers him his father. So the five parents break down into two groups of three. . . . And really, I would like to live in a legal system that is capable of reflecting that reality, and I don't think that's compatible with the institution of marriage.[2]

In short, when "marriage" becomes everything to everybody, it ceases to be marriage, and likewise for family. It's a no-brainer that what Gessen is saying will come to fruition once the stalwart, steadfast institution of one-man-one-woman marriage is taken down. That is the breach in the dam that opens the floodgates.

Liberals/progressives should also understand, or might understand if they moved beyond the emotion of the moment and gave the issue deeper thought, that redefining marriage cracks the door for the polygamy/polygyny of fringe religious cults that the left despises and ridicules. For this or that wacky, weird religious group that allows a man to marry multiple wives, the mad liberal/progressive push to redefine marriage is a gift from the heavens. It is exactly what is needed. For that matter, it will be viewed as a gift from Allah by rising Muslim populations in America that follow the Koranic belief that a man is permitted up to five wives. Advocates of sharia law, some of whom favor death for homosexuals, are surely astonished at how such a generous redefinition of historic Western-Christian marriage by liberals might help them in their most fundamentalist interpretations of Islamic marriage—an interpretation that Western progressives find cruelly sexist and misogynistic. So be it. Liberals/progressives will have been the ones who unlocked the door by resetting the boundaries of marriage to begin with. Sure, when the moment comes that an American Muslim man asserts the legal right to five wives, these same leftists will cry foul and busily try to reestablish some (obliterated) boundaries—fluidly reversing and contradicting themselves as they often conveniently do—but the mold will have been broken. They will have smashed it.

That is the real danger at work here. The problem is less same-sex marriage than the legal redefining that will enable much more. That is the bottom line. That is what this is really all about. It is a shame that the battle must entail such acrimony between, say, faithful Christians and gay-rights groups, especially given the undeniable cruel discrimination that so many homosexuals have struggled with for so long—unfair treatment that was unacceptable and uncharitable and (when leveled by Christians) notably un-Christian. Christians should feel guilt for a measure of that mistreatment, and should feel a measure of repentance. But repentance cannot, of course, lead them to violate their faith's teachings on the sanctity of marriage, any more than they should violate the theological virtue of charity. Faithful Christians have no right to arrogantly redefine their God's standard for marriage. The typical liberal/progressive, however, apparently harbors no such fears.

In the end, this redefining will make a mess—a mess of marriage.

A mess of marriage, of course, means a mess of the family. And as families fall apart, so does society. Research has confirmed time and time again that the best situation for a child is a two-parent home with a mother and a father, which should always be the goal of any culture or polity. Sociologists know this; their own studies show it.[3] Common sense and experience show us. Children who grow up with the presence of a mother and father are less likely to be poor, to end up in prison, or to get addicted to drugs. Also, they are generally healthier, stronger and more successful. The most common denominator among men in prisons is not racial or ethnic background, not income or class distinction, not high school or college diploma, but whether or not they grew up with a father in the home.

In a speech for Father's Day 2008, Senator Barack Obama was emphatic in championing fatherhood: "We know the statistics—that children who grow up without a father are five times more likely to live in poverty and commit crime; nine times more likely to drop out of schools and 20 times more likely to end up in prison. They are more likely to have behavioral problems, or run away from home, or become teenage parents themselves. And the foundations of our community are weaker because of it. . . . Of all the rocks upon which we build our lives . . . family is the most important. And we are called to recognize and honor how critical every father is to that foundation." If "we are honest with ourselves," said Obama, "we'll admit that . . . too many fathers are . . . missing—missing from too many lives and too many homes."

Obama summed up: "We need fathers."[4]

Nary a single anti-Obama Republican would disagree with any of this—a rare moment of complete conservative agreement with Barack Obama. For that matter, few liberals would have disagreed—until now. Liberals have been compelled to reverse themselves because of the political gyrations in which they must engage to accommodate their ideological marriage to gay marriage. Now, liberals (Obama among them) are suddenly pushing relentlessly for fatherless families—or, more specifically, for a new form of American family that is fatherless. With their embrace of gay marriage, a massive shift not only within America, American culture, and human civilization, but also within the Democratic Party, liberals/progressives nationwide are simultaneously advocating a redefinition of family that embraces fatherless families. Married female-female parents will be households without dads.

In so doing, liberals are shattering a rare, precious consensus they had nurtured with conservatives, including as recently as the 1990s, when Bill Clinton and other Democrats championed the excellent National Fatherhood Initiative. There are few things that liberals and conservatives have agreed upon, but one of them was the central importance of children being raised in a home with a dad and a mom. Kids need dads. Sons need dads. Daughters need dads. Families need dads.

That principle remains unchanged. What has changed, however, is liberals' fierce acceptance and advancement of gay marriage. In this rapid push, they are jettisoning this national consensus on fathers, demanding a category of parenting that excludes fathers. As for those who disagree with this new paradigm, they are derided as cruel, thoughtless, backward bigots, with no possible legitimate reason for their unenlightened position.

Actually, what today's liberals are advocating is far worse than that. They are pushing not only for fatherless families but also, conversely, motherless ones. Married male-male parents (the other half of gay marriage) will be households without moms. There will be a new generation of children deliberately raised without moms and with the sanction and celebration of the state and culture.

The process is well under way. Since July 2006, a group instructively called Beyond Marriage has pushed a statement titled, "Beyond Same-Sex Marriage: A New Strategic Vision for All Our Families & Relationships." The group has actively circulated a petition led by self-described "lesbian, gay, bisexual, and transgender (LGBT) and allied activists, scholars, educators, writers, artists, lawyers, journalists, and community organizers" who "seek to offer friends and colleagues everywhere a new vision for securing governmental and private institutional recognition of diverse kinds of partnerships, households, kinship relationships and families. In so doing, we hope to move beyond the narrow confines of marriage politics as they exist in the United States today." The statement candidly admits that "the struggle for same-sex marriage rights is only one part of a larger effort"—albeit the seminal breakthrough to make other arrangements possible. The group's openly professed goal is "much broader than same-sex marriage," and the numerous proposed forms of new marriage it lists are so sweeping as to seemingly accommodate practically any sort of configuration.[5] Prominent members of the group include Chai Feldblum, Georgetown University law professor and EEOC commissioner under President Barack Obama.[6]

In the past, such a group of leftists would have loudly raised their voices but not caused any real damage. They would have been dismissed as left-wing cranks and minor irritants and agitators with no serious concern. But now, with formal legalization of same-sex marriage afoot—i.e., traditional marriage redefined—they are getting what they want. And what they want will change everything.

So, what will have initiated this fundamental transformation of this onetime pillar of human civilization? The answer is this twenty-first-century novelty called "gay marriage." It is entirely new, entirely untried, entirely untested over time or even one generation; it isn't as old as the cell phone. Its antecedents, however, go back much further.

This is not to say that readers of this book will discover receptivity toward gay marriage or homosexuality by Marx and Engels in the 1850s or by Communist Party USA (CPUSA) in the 1950s. Yes, there were certain Marxists in groups like CPUSA who challenged sexual convention and the bounds of the traditional family, but they were not advancing or remotely contemplating gay marriage—a notion that was utterly unthinkable until only very recent times. The mere fleeting contemplation, the mere momentary notion, the slightest passing fancy of a man legally marrying another man (with widespread cultural acceptance) in the 1850s or 1950s, or as recently as the 1980s or 1990s, would have been scoffed at as inanely incomprehensible; its proponents would have been deemed certifiably insane. Public authorities might well have hauled them away as menaces to society.

Nonetheless, along the road that prodded civilization toward this historically extremely unusual spot, there were some influential forces on the far left and communist left that cannot and should not be ignored. Among certain extreme-left elements, there was a pronounced sexual radicalism that arguably helped surface the road, or at least broke the ground. One such element was the neo-Marxists of the Frankfurt School, which had an especially strong impact on the universities, particularly in the 1960s. Individuals in this school were not orthodox Marxists or CPUSA types; they were not even economists. They were *cultural* radicals—from sociology, psychology, outside of economics departments; they were devotees of Freudian thought more zealous than Sigmund Freud. Of course, not that all of these men—Georg Lukács, Herbert Marcuse, and Wilhelm Reich were especially prominent—were vocally and explicitly pro gay marriage or pro-gay (again, to support gay marriage would have been viewed as a form of madness), but they were sexually extreme, and they peddled practices conspicuously contrary to traditional morality and marriage, to normal sexual relations, and to the nuclear family. Their aggressive notions of equality were not income-based, like the traditional Marxists were, but culture-based. And they influenced many of the '60s student radicals, especially on exceptionally detrimental campuses like Columbia University, and with figures like Marxist feminist Kate Millett and unhinged organizations like the Weathermen, or the Weather Underground Organization (WUO). With the accompanying advent of the '60s' sexual revolution, these youthful enthusiasts (and future educators) helped thrust forward the corrosive ideas of certain Frankfurt neo-Marxists, extending stances like open marriage into the new realm of open homosexuality. The Frankfurt School did not achieve this as an organized, cohesive, hand-in-glove conspiracy, but neo-Marxists speaking and publishing and lecturing from within that school of thought initiated certain sexual ruptures against marriage and family, which other leftist activists anxiously took further decades later.

The ideology of these leftists steadily drove their reconfigurations of marriage and family from the 1800s to recent times. To borrow from Pope Francis, their relativistic conceptions fostered their "ideological colonization" of marriage and family.[7] In some cases, as we will see in this book, they spawned literal ideological communes that endeavored to reinvent married and family life, from the old-left colonies of Robert Owen and Charles Fourier in the heartland to the Red Family and other New Left communes on the West Coast in the 1960s, where traditional familial mores were systematically taken down.

In short, what we have here, and what I intend to show, is not an early embrace of homosexuality or gay marriage by the early Marxist movement, but a long, slow progression that has ultimately helped move the culture in that direction. Today, in a fascinating but telling development, Communist Party USA and its flagship publication *People's World*, are totally and equivocally pro–gay marriage. They are completely on board. With gay marriage, today's communists thus have the straw to crack the once-unbreakable back of the traditional-natural-biblical family, allowing a redefinition that forever changes the boundaries of how marriage and family have been long understood.

Same-sex marriage is hardly a Marxist plot, a latent communist conspiracy.[8] It is, however, a crucial final blow to marriage—the only blow that is enabling a formal, legal redefinition that will unravel the institution. It has distinct origins traceable to the far left's initial thrusts at this once unassailable monogamous, faithful male-female institution.

To reiterate, this is not a grand communist conspiracy, or any kind of conspiracy. I am not laying the entirety of the culture's collapse at the feet of communists. I am not asserting that Marxists have given us gay marriage. I want to be clear on these points. It is a mistake to exaggerate and boil down complex things to handy, binary, black-and-white caricature. We can be prone to hyperbole, especially when politics and agendas get involved. Yet, just as we can easily overstate things, we can also easily understate them, and to do the latter likewise would be a mistake. What the left has steadfastly said and written and done to marriage and the family over the last two centuries cannot be ignored. Those actions have been undeniable contributing factors—along with many other undeniable factors—that at least in part help explain why and where we are today.

The current state is the end road of a steady evolution that should not be viewed entirely separate from or totally unrelated to early attacks by the communist left. The journey had many prior destinations. A people do not just one morning wake up and ditch the sacred and natural character of the male-female marital union that served their parents, grandparents, great-grandparents, great-great-grandparents, great-great-great-grandparents, great-great-great-great-grandparents (perhaps I do indeed need to belabor this point) and the ongoing long line of ancient ancestors who preceded them. All of these relations of ours surely were not mere wild "hatemongers." A people do not arise one morning and, after coffee, ham, and eggs, casually dismiss this thousands of years' worth of prior wisdom, experience, and opinion—what G. K. Chesterton called "the democracy of the dead"—without some busywork by some factions in the years before. Ground had been plowed to ready this soil. Much deconstruction and desensitizing to the sanctity of marriage had to be done over a long haul to arrive at this final destination.

Yet, if there is one source of clear commonality from the early nineteenth to early twenty-first centuries, it is this: as modern liberalism/progressivism and the Democratic Party have become increasingly secular, often antireligious, or certainly dismissive of traditional notions of morality, the embrace of same-sex marriage has become possible. For communists, two centuries ago and still today, that requisite antireligious secularism has been there all along. Much of the wider American culture, outside of the far left, has also become secular and dismissive of traditional religious teaching on matters such as family and marriage. That disregard if not outright rejection of Christian ethics has brought all of these forces full circle in a joint willingness to permanently alter the historic Western/Christian understanding of male-female matrimony.

Alas, here is the ultimate kicker, and really a rather stunning development: The radical left could never have achieved this ultimate takedown of marriage without the larger American public's increasingly broad acceptance of gay marriage. The wider gay marriage–supporting public has been the indispensable handmaiden to the radical left's ability to at long last redefine marriage and the family. Sure, those mainstream Americans have no idea that they have unwittingly aided and abetted that process; they are fully oblivious to it, but they have. That is a realization that ought to give them pause, if they ever became aware of it.

And finally, what do we mean by "takedown," or making a mess of the family? Gay activists and same-sex marriage proponents assert that heterosexuals have done a bang-up job ripping apart the family themselves: marital infidelity, single-parent homes, divorce, abandonment, abortion, and a litany of other maladies. Heterosexuals, they insist, have undermined marriage and the family quite adequately on their own. Christians likewise, they argue, have made a mockery of the sacred character of their marital vows. They are, of course, exactly right. No question. But still, such very recent plagues against marriage did not dent the fundamental understanding of marriage and how it always was and (it was assumed) must remain, as between one man and one woman, which has worked for millennia as a blueprint for civilization. The excessive divorce and abortion rates over the last forty to fifty years are a recent blip on the historical radar. The male-female base remained intact, surviving all of these self-inflicted wounds. The foundation was still there, firm, unshakable, unquestioned, despite threats and self-generated poxes. Heterosexuals embarrassed and gravely hurt their sacred institution, yes, but they had never theretofore resolved to redefine it, to boldly assume that marriage is something they have the right to redefine.

Here too, however, the cultural Marxists/neo-Marxists must be taking a measure of supreme satisfaction. These modern sicknesses that have impaired marriage are largely a latter-twentieth-century phenomenon. What caused them was a lack of moral restraints and checks, a trashing of common ethics and virtue, a complete misunderstanding of freedom that degenerates into license (i.e., licentiousness)—a "confused ideology of liberty," as Pope Benedict XVI put it,[9] which harms others, especially the violated spouse and children. Well, it was precisely such unrestrained "free love" and selfish sexual behavior (and so-called sexual communism) that many Marxists and socialists had badly wanted for so long. They wanted those rules broken.

All of these vectors arrayed at the end of the twentieth century to puncture marriage and family but not mortally wound it. All were mere pinpricks that hurt marriage but could not redefine it. To redefine it required another means altogether; it required "gay marriage." With that, at the start of the current century, we are alas witnessing a truly watershed event in cultural-social-human history, and most of those living through it, or advocating it, have no idea just how significant it is. It is a fundamental transformation, to borrow from our "fundamental transformation" and first Gay Marriage President, Barack Obama.

For Marx and Engels and Lukács and Marcuse and the others, direct, barefaced appeals to classic Marxism or neo-Marxism or cultural Marxism or communal "free love" could never have worked to take down marriage and the family. Neither could radical feminism. But gay marriage, with its appeals to tolerance and diversity and love and freedom, has worked masterfully. It is the nuclear trigger for the nuclear family that the likes of Lukács and Marcuse and Reich could not find elsewhere in the arsenal.

Only now, unlike any time in history, can one encounter bizarre insistences that it "doesn't matter" if a home is parented by two dads or two moms or a dad and a mom, as if the blatantly obvious gender differences and complementarity between husbands and wives and fathers and mothers is somehow no longer relevant or even discernible. "Good parenting" is reduced to the functional ability of getting the kids to and from soccer practice, out of bed and on the bus, washing their dishes and clothes, and paying for their college, not modeling traditional notions of virtue, chastity, purity, motherhood, fatherhood, or manhood. This is a surreal societal-cultural earthquake so shattering that people seem to have lost their levelheadedness, with their elected representatives blithely going along in the process. It is absolutely unprecedented. It is not passive but active, and, given the sheer speed, hyperactive.

And that is something that even the Marxist patriarchs at the forefront of this longer marriage/family takedown would be shocked to assimilate. Nonetheless, they leveled some of the most bruising initial chips and swings at the foundation. Shoving their revolutionary ideas at aghast citizens, these leftists questioned the basic morality of marriage, scandalizing their populations with their harebrained theories and suggestions, but they could never succeed in legally changing its very definition. Only the advent of same-sex marriage—with now, remarkably, the support of mainstream populations—has this fundamental redefinition and transformation been made possible.

Readers will wonder if I am looking to halt the redefinition and transformation, if I am endeavoring to help change the mind of American culture on gay marriage with this book, to which I respond: *Are you kidding?* America has entered a protracted phase of post-Christian thinking and ethics, a dismal state where individualism and a dictatorship of relativism reign supreme, fostered by a long line of incredibly naïve parents who marched their children in wide-eyed cadence through the educational system at giant costs both financial and moral. Nothing short of a major religious revival will save it. My task with this book is diagnostic: to simply help explain how America slowly but steadily walked to the marriage-family precipice where it now stands. My expertise is communism, communists, and their work, not redefinition and fundamental transformation.

Let us now look at some of the roots of where this extraordinary progression started to take place.

2

EARLY COMMUNIST AND SOCIALIST
MOVEMENTS AGAINST FAMILY AND MARRIAGE

THE HISTORY OF VARIOUS COMMUNIST AND socialist movements[1] on family and marriage is an uneven one, with myriad wrinkles and manifestations, but one thing is sure: they have challenged if not targeted our understanding of human nature. These movements have sought to alter our most basic conventions.

Throughout the nineteenth century, varying communists, socialists, and assorted utopians wrote about the glories of "free love" and cogitated on the inherent ills of the traditional family. Some became so brash and boisterous that governments viewed them as a growing peril to society; in Prussia and Germany, for instance, legislation was enacted to try to protect the family from these forces. Even before Marx and Engels came along, or agitators like Clara Zetkin, the leading German Marxist feminist, the likes of August Bebel (a German socialist), the English utopian-socialist Robert Owen (who held a special contempt for the family as an institution), and Charles Fourier (a French socialist), were busy laying an intellectual foundation for the rejection of traditional family relationships.

Among these characters, Owen (1771–1858) and Fourier

(1772–1837) were especially influential on American soil, establishing numerous communes that would become a staple of the left's ideological colonization of the family. Daniel J. Flynn, in his history of the American left, refers to Owen and Fourier and (more specifically) their disciples as "Yankee Utopians."

Robert Owen certainly left his collectivist footprint. On July 4, 1826, as Thomas Jefferson and John Adams, the geniuses of the Declaration of Independence, both dramatically breathed their last gasps of life on the fiftieth anniversary of their eloquent achievement on behalf of life, liberty, and the pursuit of happiness, Robert Owen stood in front of his new ideological colony in New Harmony, Indiana, and delivered his "Declaration of Mental Independence." It was, in effect, an anti–Declaration of Independence, and somewhat of a precursor to the *Communist Manifesto*. "I now declare to you and to the world," proclaimed Owen, "that man up to this hour has been in all parts of the earth a slave to a trinity of the most monstrous evils that could be combined to inflict mental and physical evil upon the whole race." What were these monstrosities? "I refer to private property, absurd and irrational systems of religion and marriage founded upon individual property, combined with some of these irrational systems of religion."[2] Property, religion, marriage—Robert Owen's unholy trinity.

Like Maximilien Robespierre's totalitarian, guillotining Jacobins of the French Revolution (and Pol Pot's later Khmer Rouge in Cambodia), Owen's acolytes began their new civilization by scrapping the Christian Anno Domini calendar, marking 1826 as their new Year One, just as the Jacobins had done with the year 1794 in France amid their blood-curdling de-Christianization of France. Owen's communes pooled not only profits but people, replacing the nuclear family with the collective family. Children were removed from parents into separate parts of the collective for proper "education." As Dan Flynn rightly put it, "Owen declared war on marriage, private property, and the family."[3]

Flynn argues that Robert Owen "would feel more at home" today in a world of gay marriage, easy divorce, and public squares and court-houses stripped of manger scenes and the Ten Commandments.[4] This is surely true. But for now, in the 1820s and 1830s, it is interesting that he did not feel fully at home in the ideological colony of his own making—a common trait among the left's leaders. As the New Harmony colony floundered within just two years, Owen was curiously absent from his creation for sustained periods, setting the standard for future socialist-communist utopians: they rarely live according to the rules and systems they create for others. Socialism and communism have always been for "the people," "the masses," the ruled, but rarely for the rulers. Castro, Stalin, Pol Pot, Mao—given the choice, they never lived the same way with the same rules and equal salaries as the serfs. Indeed, how could they? Their communist cocoons were always intolerable because they were bankrupt and unnatural.

But the unnatural is what so many leftist utopians pursued then and in the years and centuries ahead. Even as Robert Owen's New Harmony commune quickly collapsed, a dozen or so imitators sprang up around the country. Rarely did any of them last more than four years. Owen squandered most of his personal fortune on his failed colony, but his leftist vision remained alive and undeterred. "The social system is now firmly established," he asserted.[5]

An uphill stream of Owen-like dreamers on the left would keep the flame alive, from the 1820s to the 1960s in their own communes, and into the twenty-first century with their own versions of marriage and family. Never learning from failed projects of the past, they would always convince themselves that the previous project simply wasn't done quite right—not yet. When they implemented *their* commune, *their* utopia, *their* more enlightened and modern view of marriage and the family, it would surely work this time around. Such is the faith.

Indeed, almost immediately after Owen's scheme failed, Charles Fourier's new human blueprint rapidly followed. Fourier died and never actually made it to America. His enthusiasts would enact his ideas in his absence.

Fourier likewise detested private property and traditional marriage and religion. He, too, saw communes as the new world panacea for a more progressive humanity. In the 1830s, two centuries before

Chai Feldblum and friends were planning to move Beyond Marriage, Fourier was openly advocating the termination of monogamous marriage in order to allow extramarital license among spouses. His chief implementer in America, Albert Brisbane, who in addition to three illegitimate children (very unusual for the period) maintained several mistresses, tried to keep a lid on some of Fourier's more unpalatable sexual ideas, given that the masses in the heartland were not quite ready to take up polygamy, homosexuality, and just about every other kind of tantalizing "free love" that the Frenchman recommended.[6] Collective schools were created for the children generated by Fourier's protocommunists; they could be taught more *sophisticated* notions of what was right and wrong; they would be separated from antiquated notions of morality.

The Fourier-Brisbane communes worked about as well as Owen's ideological colonies. And when they fell into disgrace, more American leftists generated more communes with more ideas on marriage and family. There were probably forty-some such communes that sprang up around the country in this period.

One of the longer-lasting and more idiosyncratic was started by John Humphrey Noyes (1811–86), one of the few communists who was also a Christian—a "free love"–wheeling "Bible Communist" educated by the Ivy League. The communist tendency to reinvent and make up one's own morality got the better of Noyes's Christian ethics. Taking family into his own hands, and moving beyond marriage, or at least beyond the traditional Christian understanding of holy matrimony between one man and one woman, he conjured up a communal arrangement that he called "Complex Marriage," where he married hundreds of his ideological colonists together in collective marriages.[7]

Noyes governed a group of some three hundred men and women who divined that monogamy was impure. They were probably the first serious practitioners of what the 1960s' New Left would call "smashing monogamy." They pursued "group love." They deemed monogamy a sin, whereas the '60s radicals—who blanched at the very notion that there was sin—would deem it a form of constrictive fascism. The Noyes gang saw itself as pursuing a divine plan linking all of the commune's men and women. Their new sex for their new ideological colony included forced arrangements of unhappy young teens paired with older and less-desirable adults (some in their fifties and sixties).[8] Babies that were produced in the process were raised communally in designated children's sections of the commune. There was collective parenting as well as collective sex, collective property, collective exchange of bodily fluids, and the collective pooling of children and their education. Marriage was a truly open affair.

Most of this ideological fancy took flight at Noyes's commune in Oneida, New York. The Puritans had booted Noyes from New England, where he first ramped up his vision, leading him to relocate westward. The Oneida experiment actually lasted longer than most communes, perhaps in part because of its strong faith component that convinced many of the followers that they were doing God's will, but it, too, eventually collapsed.

If only Noyes could have known that he was about two hundred years too early to reconfigure marriage. The marriage redefiners were awaiting him in the twenty-first century. They are starting with "gay marriage," of course, but that convenient device will enable new "Bible Communists" like Noyes with new cults/communes to resurrect their own innovative models as well. When they do, these new religious cultists should not expect sympathy from the secular left. The left will malign them as new Jim Jones cultists. But it will not matter, because these liberals/progressives will have produced the possibility with their unyielding, unhesitating, *absolutely-no-second-thoughts-whatsoever*, *anyone-who-disagrees-is-a-hater* push to redefine marriage as anything but one man and one woman.

Unfortunately for John Humphrey Noyes, it was the nineteenth century, not the twenty-first, and the fundamental transformation he had planned for marriage did not pan out.

Nevertheless, the utopian wheel would keep turning, always in search of yet another brave new world. The left remained vigilant, ever on the lookout.

As for Karl Marx and Friedrich Engels, they did not merrily endorse all of these assorted ideas on marriage and family by this panoply of utopian planners. Quite the contrary, some of their writings excoriated (they excelled at excoriating) these earlier utopians. They had their own fundamental transformations in mind.

To that end, Marx's and Engels's positions are often hard to unpack. There was an evolution/progression in their thinking from the 1840s through the 1880s. But even then, Marx and especially Engels would pick up the leftist-utopian slack and drag it forward in a way not healthy to the family.

"Although Marx and Engels were not the instigators of the anti-family trend among socialists, they—especially Engels—contributed mightily to it," wrote Professor Richard Weikart in his journal article "Marx, Engels, and the Abolition of the Family." Weikart cited a contemporaneous report to the Prussian minister of the interior (there were many of these), which noted that German communists were "so unusually dangerous for the state, the family and the social order." The authorities warily had their eyes on them. There were, said Weikart, "no doubts in the minds of Marx's and Engels' contemporaries that socialism was a threat not only to the state, but also to the family."[9]

It was widely understood that communist ideas were antagonistic toward the family. As noted in the epigraph to chapter 1, Marx in the *Communist Manifesto* wrote of the "abolition of the family" as not only "radical" but as an "infamous proposal of the Communists." In their own time, their ideas were infamous. Weikart emphasized:

Some recent commentators on Marx's and Engel's view of the family cast doubt on their radicalism. Some construe their attacks on the family as a call for reform, as an expression of a desire to sweep away abuses, while retaining the basic family structure intact. Others discover in Engels' writings on the family naturalistic elements that allegedly vitiate his radical pronouncements on the abolition of the family. . . . These interpretations of Marx's and Engels' position on the family, while often raising important points, tend to obscure somewhat the radicalism of their views. . . . While Marx once alluded to a higher form of the family in communist society, he and Engels usually wrote about the destruction, dissolution, and abolition of the family. The relationships they envisaged for communist society would have little or no resemblance to the family as it existed in nineteenth-century Europe or indeed anywhere else. Thus it is certainly appropriate to define their position as the abolition of the family. Only by making the term *family* almost infinitely elastic can they be said to have embraced merely a reformulation of the family.[10]

One fact beyond debate is that like so many writers on the left, Marx and Engels had an evolving conception of family that was not based on a fixed structure stemming from an absolute rendering of Scripture, God, or any Christian church or denomination. For Marx and Engels, their structure was economic, materialistic, and relativistic, based on their interpretation of historical cultures and nature. "Even during the time they assumed that the family was a natural institution of society," wrote Weikart, "Marx and Engels were clear that it was not a fixed entity." In *Das Capital*, Marx dismissed as "silly" the idea of absolute norms for the family. In their 1845 work, *The German Ideology*, Marx and Engels asserted that "it is not possible to speak of *'the'* family." They argued that the family played an important but malevolent role in human history.[11] It had to be changed.

Marx and Engels, in fact, chided fellow socialist Hermann Kriege for not insisting that the family be destroyed. "Therefore after, for example, the earthly family is discovered as the secret of the holy family," wrote Marx, "the former must itself be theoretically and practically destroyed."[12]

These particular Marx-Engels thoughts were expressed prior to their *Communist Manifesto* in 1848, where the family rhetoric was amplified a few decibels. "Abolition of the family!" yelped Marx in the *Manifesto*. "Even the most radical flare up at this infamous proposal of the Communists."

Marx and his comrades scoffed at what they dismissed as the "bourgeois family." "Bourgeois marriage is in reality a system of wives in common," Marx snarled. Bourgeois marriage and the bourgeois family

comprised a "dirty existence" of "domestic slavery" and "general hypocrisy."[13] It was a "system" he and fellow communists would in some form
endeavor to change, even if "reproached" in the process.[14] He hoped and
predicted that "the bourgeois family will vanish as a matter of course,"
as would "bourgeois marriage." These should go, vanish, averred Marx,
along with all morality, eternal truths, and religion, which was the
"opiate of the masses." Marx, of course, was no champion of religion,
which was a particularly obstinate obstacle to his vision. "Communism
begins where atheism begins," he said in another context. They were all
interconnected: communism, atheism, abolition of religion, abolition
of marriage, abolition of the family—all peas in the same pod.

Overall, stated Marx, "the communist revolution is the most radical
rupture with traditional relations; no wonder that its development
involves the most radical rupture with traditional ideas." Yes, no wonder.

In all, stated Richard Weikart, Marx and Engels "never masked their
contempt for present family relationships and their hope for radically
new social relations in communist society."[15]

Weikart dealt at length with academic disputes over what Marx
and Engels meant by these things. Likewise, I recently had a series of
lengthy email discussions on the subject with a colleague, Dr. D. Vance
Smith, a thoughtful professor of English at Princeton University who
responded to an article I wrote on this subject and then dialogued with
me in several follow-up emails. On the word *abolition* as used by Marx,
Professor Smith makes the legitimate point that the original word
Marx used in German was *Aufhebung*. Given Marx's Hegelian understanding of dialectic, Marx (says Smith) was suggesting not a destruction or abolition of marriage, "but rather the much more complex
idea of surmounting, or transcending, or moving forward and upward
with the past not negated but preserved." Stated Smith: "The idea of
Aufhebung is pretty basic in Hegel, and rather important for Marx, too.
A further point: Marx does not talk about the abolition of marriage
strictu sensu, only the sublation (one of the more precise words you
could use to translate *Aufhebung*) of bourgeois marriage, not of all marriage." Thus, argued Smith, "it's not exactly right to say that Marx . . .

was 'looking' to abolish marriage. Marx only said that bourgeois marriage (again, not all marriage) will disappear at a certain historical stage. He makes an observation, not a recommendation."[16]

Professor Smith has a valid point, though translators of Marx have opted to use the word *abolish* or *abolition* rather than *transcend*. Should they be using the word *transcended* instead of *abolished*? Or should they use a phrase like *moving beyond marriage*—which, interestingly, is the slogan of today's Beyond Marriage movement of Chai Feldblum and friends?

A Google search on the word *Aufhebung* first displays a *Wikipedia* definition that appears to accurately reflect most definitions retrievable from other sources. It states: "*Aufheben* or *Aufhebung* is a German word with several seemingly contradictory meanings, including 'to lift up,' 'to abolish,' 'cancel' or 'suspend,' or 'to sublate.' The term has also been defined as 'abolish,' 'preserve,' and 'transcend.' In philosophy, *aufheben* is used by Hegel to explain what happens when a thesis and antithesis interact, and in this sense is translated mainly as 'sublate.'"[17]

Richard Weikart, who has studied Marx's (and Engels's) position on marriage perhaps closer than anyone, repeatedly opts for the words *abolish* and *abolition*, including in the title of his article (published in a refereed academic journal) on the subject. And yet, Weikart likewise stated that Marx envisioned a kind of "supersession" of family in communist society. As Weikart puts it, Marx and Engels believed that the abolition of private property and the integration of socialism would bring in their wake an inevitable dissolution of the family. It was as if communism would come first and then the disappearance, or "abolition," of the family would naturally follow in due course. Weikart contrasts this with Charles Fourier and Robert Owen, who saw abolition of the family as a precursor to their utopian vision "as part and parcel of their socialist proposals to ameloriate society."[18]

Still, this does not fully reconcile Marx's phraseology, nor does it mean that Marx was not calling for something altogether radically different. He and Engels regardless harbored radical views on marriage and what it should be and how it should be understood and reshaped.

As to the point on Marx making an "observation" rather than a "recommendation:" If Marx was proffering an observation and not personally endorsing the abolition of marriage, then why did he couch his line in the form of a blanket statement from others—namely, from communists, of which he was not only one but the leading theoretician? He stated explicitly that this "abolition" was an "infamous proposal of the Communists." Note the word *proposal*.

The excitable, aggressive tone of Marx in the *Manifesto* suggests more than just a passive observation. He seems enthused by the prospect of this abolition or transcendence. And for the record, Marx showed blatant contempt for marriage not only in his public writings but in his private actions—a personal point that seems relevant to this discussion on how he perceived marriage (more on this later).

Even if Marx and Engels thought that marriage and family would "wither away" in their utopia, this was something that pleased them. They wanted this withering away, this vanishing. It was an outcome they welcomed with great enthusiasm. They intended to promote the outcome.

Another valuable academic voice to add to this discussion is Professor H. Kent Geiger, who in 1968, through Harvard University Press, published *The Family in Soviet Russia*, probably the seminal scholarly work on the subject. "There is room for argument on how important the family is in modern life," wrote Geiger in the opening words of his book, "but few today feel that the family is slated for disappearance. Yet Karl Marx and Friedrich Engels did entertain this view."[19]

Also citing the original German language, Geiger noted of Marx and Engels: "Again and again they stress that the bourgeois family is in a state of de facto dissolution (*Auflosung*)."[20]

That said, there is support for Professor Smith's preference for the word *transcendence* over *abolition* in one particular line in the *Manifesto*, which is part of Marx's extended diatribe against the family: "The bourgeois family will vanish as a matter of course when its complement vanishes, and both will vanish with the vanishing of capital." By "its complement," Marx (as usual) was not entirely clear, though he seemed to be referring to the scourges of "capital" and "private gain." These, too, would vanish in the final stage and achievement of the communist utopia.

What else so fundamental to the family would go away? In the *Manifesto*, Marx and Engels added the "exploitation" and "home education" of children by their parents. "Do you charge us with wanting to stop the exploitation of children by their parents?" Marx asked rhetorically. "To this crime we [communists] plead guilty. But, you will say, we destroy the most hallowed of relations, when we replace home education by social."[21]

To this, too, Marx pled guilty. He wanted abolition here, for sure. He fulminated against "the bourgeois claptrap about the family and education" and sniffed at "the hallowed correlation of parent and child," both of which he found "disgusting." The tenth and final point of Marx's crucial ten-point plan in the *Manifesto* called for "free education for all children in public schools."[22] He wanted those children out of the harmful reach of their parents' home education and corralled instead into the public-education collective. Of course, numerous leftists, most of all Columbia University professor John Dewey—whose work was adored and implemented by the Bolsheviks in establishing the Soviet education system[23]—would enthusiastically seek to do just that, fully agreeing with Marx on the vital "social" thrust of education.

This thinking on education would dominate communist societies. One Soviet official, writing in the 1980s, would state emphatically that under communism, the "school becomes literally a home."[24]

This was also what Charles Fourier and Robert Owen desired. They wanted public schools and communal enclaves to replace the father and mother as the primary educators and shapers of society's children. (This, of course, would be forcibly done in brute fashion in certain Asian communist experiments, such as China and Cambodia, where it produced unprecedentedly deadly results.) Weikart noted: "Owen's continual emphasis on the role of education in shaping an individual's character and outlook lent urgency to his appeal for the abolition of the family, since only by removing children from their supposedly irrational and deleterious influence of parents could he hope to alter society."[25]

This thinking is very much alive today. The atheist philosopher/

educator Richard Rorty—who, not coincidentally, was raised a Red diaper baby[26]—candidly stated that the job of professors like him is "to arrange things so that students who enter as bigoted, homophobic religious fundamentalists will leave college with views more like our own" and "escape the grip of their frightening, vicious, dangerous parents." Many leftists in the education field despise homeschooling for similar reasons—often sexual-cultural reasons. They want sex education, including their leftist views on marriage and family, to be taught not at home (where parents differ) but in public schools, where they can manipulate classroom content. And if they fail to get hold of the minds of those students in the K–12 years, they eventually get them in the universities, where the parents hand over the child and pay huge fees for a reeducation completely contrary to what they carefully inculcated at home for eighteen years.

Getting back to Marx and Engels, they thus wanted "free education" for every child in "public schools." No more of this "hallowed correlation of parent and child" and "bourgeois claptrap about the family and education." Again, this was the tenth and final point of their plan.

Another of their ten crucial points that was explicitly family related was their insistence on ending "all right of inheritance." Marx and Engels saw inheritance as a menace that perpetuated the role of traditional family.[27] How could a classless society guarantee equality of income when some persons at birth were *unjustly* handed more income from their parents than others? (Ironically, both Marx and Engels existed and operated off Engels's inheritance, which subsidized their work, especially after Marx sucked as much money as he could from his own financially drained parents, who were very bitter at how he exploited them.) This point from the *Manifesto*, Marx's third point, is translated succinctly as "Abolition of all right of inheritance." Here, "abolition" seems to mean nothing but that, an actual termination of the "right" to inheritance. With this, too, Marx was looking to dramatically affect the family. Such proposals would change family.

Of course, inheritance was about private property, and as Professor Geiger noted, "Marx and Engels hated private property." Here, too, they were not about to wait to transcend anything. They would advise flat-out abolishing forms of property ownership. As Geiger stated, both writers "were logically forced into the position of opposing the family mainly because it was a basic property-holding institution." He noted that this would become a major thrust within the revolutionary Soviet Union.[28]

Generally, overall, there is no question that Karl Marx, whether he was talking about "abolition" or "transcendence," was looking to seriously alter the family—through completely reversing inheritance, home education, or any number of other means. Yes, Marx envisioned all of this happening in a matter of course, hoping the family would "vanish" in the process, or be transcended by these new forces. And yet, in the meantime, Marx seemed to be prescribing some specific actions to get there pretty darned quickly.

Clearly, this can become a technical academic debate, made worse by Hegel's and Marx's notorious ambiguity, but it is not irrelevant. It is worthwhile in trying to get a handle on exactly what Marx meant. Indeed, to that end, perhaps more important is how Marx had been interpreted, by both his supporters and critics, by his disciples and detractors—and by his partner, Engels.

As Professor Weikart has noted, while it still sometimes remains "not at all clear" what form Marx envisaged for marriage in communist society, Engels filled in the details. He did so a year after Marx's death in his 1884 book, *The Origin of the Family*, which, Engels explained in the preface, reflected Marx's views. Engels there stated that Marx himself had wanted to undertake this particularly important work and had produced extensive extracts up until his death, which Engels had reproduced in the book "as far as possible." Professor Geiger noted that "many of the ideas" in *The Origin of the Family* can be found in the first joint work by Marx and Engels, *The German Ideology*, which was not published during their lifetimes. "Quite clearly," wrote Geiger, *The Origin of the Family* "was in the main a joint work of the two founders of Marxism and points to an impressive unity and continuity over four decades in the basic outlines of their thoughts."[29]

Here, the vision on marriage and family was much more specific, not blurred by Marx's frequent habit of ambiguity. Engels reiterated a position earlier advanced by him and Marx, namely, that a woman's/ wife's private housework would be supplanted by social labor in the communist state. Women would not only be channeled into factories, to work there, but private housework would be nationalized by the state. Housework would become a public industry, with communal child care, cooking, cleaning, and so forth. This was intended to liberate mothers and wives from the chains of conventional family *economic bondage*. Children would be raised communally.[30]

Engels saw this as a plus for children of unwed mothers as well as married ones. But more than that, he also saw it as a huge benefit to women's sexuality. He hoped this vision could unleash "unconstrained" sexual behavior among women (which would redound to his own pleasure). He urged wider public *tolerance* in this regard. He wrote with great excitement:

> With the transfer of the means of production into common ownership, the single family ceases to be the economic unit of society. Private housekeeping is transformed into a social industry. The care and education of the children becomes a public affair; society looks after all children alike, whether they are legitimate or not. This removes all the anxiety about the consequences which today is the most essential social-moral as well as economic factor that prevents a girl from giving herself completely to the man she loves. Will not that suffice to bring about the gradual growth of unconstrained sexual intercourse and with it a more tolerant public opinion in regard to a maiden's honor and a woman's shame?[31]

The nurturing, care, and education of children would become a public affair, a social industry. Society would look after all children. This would free the woman, especially to give herself more fully (i.e., sexually) to the man she "loves."

Professor Geiger noted that Engels and Marx seemed to have "little to say" about the relationships between parents and children beyond the crucial recommendation that "they would not continue to live together, because society was to rear and educate" (Geiger's words). This was encompassing enough. It was not clear how much or even whether at all parents and children would see one another in the communist system. The authors stated merely that this communal rearing of children would bring "real freedom" to all members of the family. Geiger stated that Marx and Engels were "clearly willing" to consider "a certain abolition of parental rights" (with abolition meaning true abolition/elimination), given that under communism the rearing of children would be the right and responsibility of society as a whole; that is, of the state.[32]

This was quite a vision for any time, but especially in the nineteenth century, where it was particularly progressive. Sadly, it signaled a vast change not only in sexuality but in married and family life. This drastic communal aspect of raising society's vast pool of children would be seized upon by later communist writers and theorists and even implemented by communist governments, always via coercion and with tremendous trauma and dislocation.

In *Origins* and other writings, Engels favored that marriage should not be a legal relationship but a purely private affair—ironically, one of the few areas where he or Marx favored privatization, likely because it served his own interests. Engels in his writings revealed a highly promiscuous attitude toward sexual morality and marital relationships. In one key chapter of *Origins*, titled "The Monogamous Family," Engels argued that "monogamous marriage" in the past had meant not "reconciliation of man and woman" but "subjugation of the one sex by the other." His attitude toward monogamy, more than any of his family teachings, would become a staple among 1960s communists in America.

This laissez-faire view of fidelity was symptomatic of what Engels vigorously practiced in his own life. He had many mistresses, particularly during his sexually active 1840s, when he and Marx were compiling the *Manifesto*. Engels refused to marry these women, but at one later point in the 1850s seemed to refer to one of his longer-term, live-in women as his "wife," even though they were not legally or technically married. After her death, he apparently married another paramour, the late woman's sister, but only on her deathbed.[33]

Engels was no poster boy for marital fidelity. He was a proponent of promiscuity and, most of all, easy divorce—which communist regimes of the twentieth century implemented with vigor, and with subsequent huge divorce rates that dealt unprecedented blows to families.

As for Marx, his own marriage and family life were a wreck. It would not be a harsh judgment to call Marx a bad family man.[34] This is not the place to visit all the sordid details, but a few seem relevant to this discussion:

From his own mother and father, Marx had a parasitical relationship, leeching as much money from them as he could, until they had no recourse but to cut him off. He refused to secure income for his own family. His mother expressed the wish that "Karl would accumulate capital instead of just writing about it." For this, he was so bitter that he cut off his parents and refused to attend his father's funeral. He then drew yet more cash from Engels and Engels's inheritance, as Marx himself refused to work, leaving his family in chronic destitution, hunger, and lacking for medical attention, which his truly suffering wife blamed on his laziness and selfishness.[35]

In November 1849, Marx and his family were evicted from the rooms they rented because of his refusal to earn money and pay the landlord, not to mention his rampant uncleanliness and resistance to grooming or bathing. The family took refuge in a squalid German boardinghouse, where the weakened baby, Guido, died that winter. British historian Paul Johnson wrote of Marx's wife: "Jenny left a despairing account of these days, from which her spirits, and her affection for Marx, never really recovered."[36]

Any affection withdrawn by Jenny seemed no big deal to Marx, who apparently subscribed to Engels's and his later disciples' (especially the 1960s New Left) rejection of monogamy. He had a sexual relationship with the family's longtime young nursemaid, whom he allegedly impregnated, though he refused to ever concede that the unfortunate child was his—and certainly refused to provide a penny of child support. His wife, Jenny, suffered a broken heart from this and from Marx's many other considerable character flaws as a husband and father.

Paul Johnson stated that as Marx's daughters grew, he denied them a satisfactory education, if any education at all, and vetoed careers for them—another irony given Marx's stature among later Marxist feminists. Four of Marx's six children died before he did, and at least two of the daughters committed suicide, one of them reportedly in a suicide pact with her husband—a son-in-law that Marx ridiculed.[37] Marx detested both of his sons-in-law, writing, "To hell with both of them!" One of them, Paul Lafargue, his daughter Laura's husband, came from Cuba and had some "Negro" blood in his veins, prompting Marx to denigrate him as "Negrillo" or "the Gorilla," and to sardonically judge that Paul was thus ideally suited to work as a zookeeper. Karl Marx was brutally racist, with horrible epithets aimed at blacks, at Jews (Marx was an ethnic Jew, ironically), and especially at those he considered "Jewish [Negroes]" (Marx used the other N-word).[38]

It was an unpleasant family situation. It was surely no surprise that in 1862 Marx wrote a letter to Engels noting that every day his wife expressed a wish to die; such was her misery.[39] In another letter to Engels during one of Marx's many financial crises, Marx asserted to his partner, "Blessed is he who has no family."[40] In all, it seems no surprise that Karl Marx's writings on the family and marriage and parenting were so negative, or that he would look to the state for child-rearing responsibilities.

In so many ways, Marx's personal lifestyle redounded to the kind of revolutionary state that he not only wanted but needed for his own lifestyle—which is also true for Engels and many of these revolutionaries. A trenchant insight in this regard comes from Aristotle, a classic observer of human nature: "Men start revolutionary changes for reasons connected with their private lives."[41]

Whatever Karl Marx and Friedrich Engels lived and meant with their writings, their ideological inheritors would not hesitate to seek to alter or abolish the family, marriage, the parental function, home education, and anything and everything else that stood in the way of their new utopia. The two centuries following their words have been all about the wider left's aggressive actions on all those fronts.

That brings us to the main point of this book: certain Marxists, various communists dedicated in some way to Marx, and many on the secular left generally, have sought to abolish or radically restructure the family, traditional marriage, religion, and conventional morality. In Bolshevik Russia, Mao's China, Pol Pot's Cambodia, Fidel Castro's Cuba, and other communist tyrannies, they did not wait to "transcend" anything. Quite the contrary, they aggressively sought to abolish these timeless institutions, often with violent force. Here in America in the 1960s, various Marxists, communists, and leftists likewise targeted these "bourgeois" values, especially in the universities. Even if and when Marx himself did not always seek to literally abolish these things, his disciples did, with gusto.

3

MARX'S DISCIPLES

THE DISCIPLES OF KARL MARX AND Friedrich Engels were committed to a revolution in family life, to a radical rupture in traditional relations between husband and wife and parents and children. Their first and most ardent practitioners, the Bolsheviks, followed the new faith with reckless abandon.

Implicit to the Bolsheviks' fundamental transformation of Russian society was a fusillade aimed at the despised foe, religion. After the October 1917 revolution, Vladimir Lenin and his cabal immediately forbade religious instruction to anyone younger than eighteen, by parents or the church. Children were encouraged to turn in their parents if they taught them about God, and all education was removed from the Russian Orthodox Church and turned over to public schools. The parental/husband-wife relationship was infringed upon in multiple intrusive ways. Marriage was transformed into a strictly civil ceremony; weddings, as well as baptisms and funerals, were converted into bizarre "communist" ceremonies. Soviet officials substituted secular ceremonies infused with communist ideology, pejoratively labeled by outsiders as "red weddings," "red baptisms," and "red funerals." In red baptisms, infants were given social "god-parents" who undertook to ensure the child was brought up to become a worthy "builder of communism." The parents of newborn children would promise to raise their children "not as slaves for the bourgeoisie, but as fighters against it." Young mothers would declare: "The child belongs to me only physically. For his spiritual upbringing, I entrust him to society."[1] The "spiritual" upbringing here would be the new and only approved faith of Marxism-Leninism.

Note that there was no sublation or superseding or transcending at work here by Lenin and Leon Trotsky and Joseph Stalin and cohorts. This was pure abolition.

The Russian Orthodox Church's long-standing prohibition against divorce was lifted by the Bolsheviks, leading to an explosion in divorce rates and utter havoc upon the Russian family.[2] The dramatic combined effect of an immediate full liberalization of divorce laws and institution of "red weddings" became especially acute with the corresponding complete legalization of abortion in 1920, which was an unprecedented action anywhere in the world at the time. With those changes and the squashing of the Russian Orthodox Church and its guidance in marriage and families and children and education and more, Lenin and his allies dealt a severe blow to marital and family life in traditionally religious Russia. Right out of the gate, within the first months and years after they seized power, the Bolsheviks had initiated these jolts to society.

Worse, through their Communist International (the Comintern), the Bolsheviks militantly pursued the global revolution that they and Marx and Engels envisioned. They sought to export these policies worldwide. They wanted all other communist parties around the world, which swore a loyalty oath to Moscow, to follow similar practices. The Comintern, based in Moscow and headed by Lenin crony Grigory Zinoviev, was the literal headquarters of what Lenin and Marx called "the worldwide revolution."

In the Soviet Union and other subsequent communist countries that followed suit, the effect on marriage and the family was nothing short of catastrophic. The divorce rate skyrocketed to levels unseen in human history. In short order, it seemed as though everyone in Moscow had a divorce. One Russian man, painfully recalling his boyhood years from the late 1920s, stated, "The years 1929 to 1932 were the unhappiest period for my family. At that time there were many cases of divorce. Many of our acquaintances got divorced. It was like an epidemic."[3]

The numbers grew worse decade by decade. As one study reported in the late 1960s, "it is not unusual" to meet Soviet men and women who had been married and divorced upwards of fifteen times.[4]

The world certainly took notice of this domestic carnage. It looked to outsiders as if these communists really were looking to abolish marriage. In fact, it is instructive that the influential American magazine the *Atlantic* published a 1926 piece with the title "The Russian Effort to Abolish Marriage."

If divorce was an epidemic in the USSR, abortion was a black plague.

The Bolsheviks legalized abortion shortly after they seized power. Like divorce, it was a rare area where the communists allowed for individual freedom. Here they enacted full privatization. So long as the family went up in flames, it seemed, the communists would eagerly allow full and free private ownership of gasoline and matches—with no rationing. You weren't free to own a farm or factory or business or bank account or go to church or print your own newspaper, but if you wanted a divorce or abortion, the sky was the limit in Bolshevik Russia.

Having overthrown the ship of state and murdered the entire Romanov family in July 1918—a fitting symbol to the coming war on the family—Vladimir Lenin made good on his June 1913 promise for an "unconditional annulment of all laws against abortions."[5] By 1920, abortion was fully and legally available and provided free of charge to Russian women. The number of abortions skyrocketed.

By 1934 Moscow women were having three abortions for every live birth, shocking ratios that American women, in the worst, wildest throes of *Roe v. Wade*, never approached. The toll was so staggering that an appalled Joseph Stalin, the mass murderer, actually banned abortion in 1936, fearing a vanishing populace. He seriously contemplated that there would be no future Russia, let alone Russian families. But Stalin was just one Bolshevik yelling halt. Too many other Soviet planners were dedicated to this new thing that American progressives would one day christen "abortion rights."

As Stalin sought to crack down on abortion, his primary antagonist in exile, Leon Trotsky, the more intellectual leftist of the two, was urging its continuation. In chapter 7 of his classic, *The Revolution Betrayed*, Lenin's old sidekick affirmed that "revolutionary power gave women the right to abortion" as "one of her most important civil, political and cultural rights." Trotsky's chapter was titled "Family, Youth, and Culture," where he addressed the "new family" and how "the old family continues to dissolve far faster." "You cannot 'abolish' the family," lectured Trotsky. "You have to replace it."

Eventually, the Trotsky view prevailed, literally outliving Stalin. A more progressive Nikita Khrushchev put things back in order in 1955, reversing Stalin's abortion ban (and ramping up religious persecution), thus allowing rates to ascend to heights heretofore unwitnessed in human history. One authoritative source from the late 1960s reported, "One can find Soviet women who have had twenty abortions."[6]

By the 1970s, the Soviet Union was averaging 7 to 8 million abortions per year, annihilating whole future generations of Russian children. (America, with a similar population, averaged nearer 1.5 million abortions per year after *Roe* was approved in 1973.) Only recently, under Vladimir Putin, who faced a projected population plunge from 140 million Russians in 2000 to roughly 100 million by 2050 (with abortion and abortion-induced infertility the chief culprits) has Russia put restrictions on abortion and created policies to encourage fertility.

This compulsion for legal abortion was in no way merely a Bolshevik aberration. Communists generally aggressively advocated abortion. Long before American pro-choice liberals were touting slogans like "This is my body" —which, chillingly, is an inversion of the precise sacrificial words of Jesus Christ—or "My body, my choice" or "Keep your hands off my body," communist women in Germany in the 1920s were urging abortion under the slogan "Your body belongs to you."[7] In so many areas, including radical changes in sexuality, communists were simply a few decades ahead of American liberals/progressives, with the latter eventually catching up to the communists or evolving to their position. Abortion is a painful example.

To this day, the countries with the highest abortion rates remain communist or recently communist countries: Russia, Cuba, Romania, and Vietnam. Cuba had been a devout Catholic country before Fidel Castro's takeover in 1959, with a special devotion to the Virgin Mary, venerated as a symbol of motherly sacrifice and purity. Leading sites of Marian veneration in Cuba, such as Our Lady of El Cobre, once attracted pilgrims worldwide. But then, Castro, like all good communists, declared war on religion, immediately opening up divorce laws and abortion clinics—all in the name of "women's rights"—and then watched a corresponding death eruption once utterly unimaginable in Cuba. Though reliable statistics are hard to find, the vast majority of Cuban marriages end in divorce, making America's sizable divorce rate seem tiny by comparison. Cuban children who survive divorce and the abortion clinics are herded into the grand communist collective that is the Cuban public school system, where they are steeped in Marxist-Leninist indoctrination.

Red China cannot be excluded from this analysis. Many if not most of China's abortions are compelled by the regime's one-child policy, one of the most severe infringements on family life ever inflicted by a government on its people. It is difficult to find a greater imposition on the male-female marital bond than a state limiting the procreative will and capacity of its citizens. In China, communism has so directly impacted the family that it actually regulates the permissible size of the family, a size capped for most Chinese at the lowest possible limit: three people.

China's one-child policy was implemented not by the murderous tyrant Mao Zedong but by the more moderate and reform-oriented Deng Xiaoping. As for Mao, his revolutionary dagger into the heart of China's family already had been repeatedly inserted throughout his Great Leap Forward (1957–60) and Cultural Revolution (1966–69). Under Mao, the familial masses were steered into omnipresent communes, cultural-administrative units that oddly would find curious appeal among many "hippie"/communist emulators in the United

States in the 1960s. Families were balkanized into these communes and children pulled from their parents. As recorded by John King Fairbank, the renowned Red China watcher and admirer, all parents were to work twenty-eight days of each month and were to eat in large mess halls while their children went into day nurseries. This would bring all of China's labor, including its "womanpower," into "full employment."[8]

Consistent with communist philosophy, this was seen as an emancipation of mothers and families—as was the Bolshevik-like liberalization of divorce laws in Red China. Mao was allowing China's women to at long last have their way. And meanwhile, Mao had his way with China's women. Like many communists, he advanced in private the sexual frontiers he unloaded upon the public. His personal physician, Li Zhisui, noted that during the Cultural Revolution, the aging despot was constantly serviced by a harem of handpicked young girls, always the most desirous virgins plucked from nearby villages for the Marxist master's full-time satisfaction. Dr. Li says that his patient, who refused to bathe and brush his teeth, and who had chronic venereal disease, was "sometimes in bed with three, four, even five women simultaneously." The girls' parents were expected to cheerfully support this family contribution to the communist revolution. Mao had himself an "uncountable" number of fresh young women whom he found physically preferable to his older wife. And that wasn't all. Mao showed himself to be a sexual progressive; he reportedly took some young men for himself as well.[9]

What Chairman Mao did to these young people is a metaphor for what he did to China. Call it Mao's Sinification of Marxism, his own adaptation, though with one faithful commonality to other communist theorists: an obliteration of traditional sexual morality and married and family life, rooted foremost in an attempted obliteration of religion.

4

THEORISTS AND PRACTITIONERS

THOSE ARE SOME REAL-WORLD MANIFESTATIONS OF communism's direct effect on marriage and the family, shared by the world's most proficient communist regimes and practitioners.

Throughout the twentieth century, a new generation of theorists and practitioners chimed in with recommendations and extensions, further elucidating the reflections of Marx and Engels, Fourier and Owen, and others. Here, any number of thinkers could be cited, from Lenin to Trotsky to Clara Zetkin, the feminist-communist who in 1920 made the extraordinary claim to the Third Comintern Congress that "as long as capitalism rules, the stronger sex will threaten to deprive the weaker of livelihood and the means of life."[1]

One of the most influential Bolshevik theorists on the family was Aleksandra Kollontai, the regime's leading feminist. A sort of Soviet version of Eleanor Roosevelt, Kollontai was appointed people's commissar for social welfare by Lenin. She became the most prominent woman in the regime. In 1919, she founded Lenin's "Women's Department." An early sexual feminist, Kollontai was an advocate of so-called free love, which spread like wildfire among American progressives of the day, including Planned Parenthood matron Margaret Sanger.

Kollontai joined up with the Bolshevik Party in Russia in 1915, and would spend the next years as one of its most fiery feminist agitators. A cheerleader for "housewives uprisings," urging on her communist sisters in Russia, Austria, England, France, Germany, and elsewhere, Kollontai sought liberation for "captive housewives." This, she said, only Russian communism could offer. "The shackles of the family, of housework, of prostitution still weigh heavily on the working woman," stated Kollontai. "Working women and peasant women can only rid themselves of this situation and achieve equality in life itself, and not just in law, if they put all their energies into making Russia a truly communist society." She insisted that "only the overthrow of capitalism and the establishment of soviet power will save them from the world of suffering, humiliations, and inequality." She thus sought to organize and mobilize through a more "excellent method of agitation among the less political of our proletarian sisters."[2]

For Kollontai, the communist revolution was a revolution not only for factory workers but for home workers, not only for economic roles but gender roles, not only for trade unions but for nuclear families. She became the leading Bolshevik spokeswoman for the housewife front. In the new utopia, the family would be not merely transcended but would cease to be a necessity. The family "deprives the worker of revolutionary consciousness."[3]

In her 1920 Marxist classic, *Communism and the Family*, Kollontai wrote: "There is no escaping the fact: the old type of family has had its day. The family is withering away not because it is being forcibly destroyed by the state, but because the family is ceasing to be a necessity." She dismissed "the old family," "the typical family," which, she celebrated, "is changing before our very eyes." Kollontai asked: "Will the family remain in the same form? These questions are troubling many women of the working class and worrying their menfolk as well. Life is changing before our very eyes; old habits and customs are dying out, and the whole life of the proletarian family is developing in a way that is new and unfamiliar and, in the eyes of some, 'bizarre.'"[4]

Venerable traditions were bizarre to the communists. Marx saw the old nostalgia for traditional family life as a bunch of bourgeois "claptrap," and so did Kollontai. "The worker-mother must learn not to differentiate between yours and mine," the Bolshevik feminist said of the child of the new communist world. No, the worker-mother "must remember that there are only *our* children [emphasis added], the children of Russia's communist workers." In full keeping with the communist-socialist writings of Marx and Engels and others, Kollontai insisted that, "Communist society will take upon itself all the duties involved in the education of the child." She did, however, add this motherly touch: "but the joys of parenthood will not be taken away from those who are capable of appreciating them."[5] That is, from those mothers (and fathers) who happily accept that the best educators are not the parents but the collective, not the sanctuary of the home but the supremacy of the state. The children would be reared by "society." Children would be wards of the state.

We should pause here to note that as shocking as this idea is, it has currency among progressives in America today, many of them products of Deweyan views of education and culture in our universities. Professor Melissa Harris-Perry, for instance, regrets that, "We have never invested as much in public education as we should have because we've always had kind of a private notion of children." Kollontai-like, Harris-Perry laments that "we haven't had a very collective notion" of our children. "We have to break through our kind of private idea that kids belong to their parents, or kids belong to their families," says Harris-Perry, "and recognize that kids belong to whole communities."[6]

Notably, Perry is no village idiot. She is an influential writer and television commentator on the political left, with a doctorate from Duke. She has been a professor at Princeton and Wake Forest and has run or served in several academic centers and studies. Perry's comments were not overheard among some faculty-lounge banter. They were recorded as an advertisement for MSNBC's "Lean Forward" campaign, and backed by educators and psychologists. Of course, her comments certainly had detractors. Fox News quoted one: "The notion that children belong to a state government rather than their own flesh and blood is the most disturbing statement made in recent political times," complained one parent.[7]

It may be disturbing, but it isn't new. Harris-Perry's wistful gaze toward the collective landscape is consistent with leading theorists of Lenin's and Stalin's totalitarian-communist state—which brings us back to Aleksandra Kollontai.

In Marxist fashion, Kollontai believed that the family would eventually wither away once full communism (and thus utopia) was ushered in. The family, like marriage, like property, would be transcended and thus abolished as a matter of course. In this new and better communist world, men and women and their children would be one with the masses, the state, society, the collective, not with their bourgeois families. But in the meantime, she and her Bolshevik comrades were more than happy to provide a not-so-gentle nudge or two or three or four, just in case the "transcendence" that was to come in "due course" was not coming quick enough. Indeed, Professor Geiger, in his work, pointed to Kollontai in helping resolve the scholarly debate as to whether institutions like the family and religion would in course "wither away" in communist society or whether the Party and its followers should take an active role in bringing about the process. Kollontai, he affirmed, responded with a "vigorous yes" on both scores.[8] She was more than happy to vastly accelerate the *withering* process.

For her work for the revolution, Kollontai would be awarded the prestigious Order of Lenin by Joseph Stalin's regime.

Also a prominent voice in the revolution was Leonid Sabsovich, who by the Stalin period became perhaps the leading Soviet urban planner. Of course, in the communist world, "urban planning" had an altogether different and frightening meaning. It entailed totalitarian dreams and methods involving the fundamental transformation of the human family.

In a series of influential writings published by the Kremlin in the late 1920s, Sabsovich brandished his Bolshevik notions for a cultural revolution via a revamping of marital and family relations. He argued for a total separation of children from parents starting in the earliest years of child development. As for those who disagreed with him, Sabsovich, betraying the attitude and tactic of a diehard leftist, excoriated them. Those who found his suggestion of full child-parent separation unnatural and unwelcome were unprogressive cretins "soaked in petit bourgeois and 'intelligentsia-like' prejudices."[9] They were prejudiced bigots. And likewise befitting a die-hard leftist, he advocated absolute state power to steamroll those in his way.

Sabsovich insisted that because the child should be and was the property of the state, rather than the family, the state had the right to compel parents to turn over their offspring to specially designed "children's towns." These towns needed to be built "at a distance from the family." Remember that Sabsovich's province was urban planning, and thus this fell within his domain. Such extreme family proposals by this urban communist would be incorporated within his plans for creating the ideal "socialist city."[10]

For the record, Marx and Engels recommended mass relocations of families, or at least have been (understandably) so interpreted by their disciples. Point 9 in their ten-point plan in the *Manifesto* called for "gradual abolition of all the distinction between town and country by a more equitable distribution of the population over the country." For communist regimes in nations like Cambodia, this "gradual abolition" took the form of immediate overnight mass deportations at the tips of automatic rifles, a sickeningly drastic action that was vividly captured in the 1984 film *The Killing Fields*.

As for Sabsovich, in his wondrous "socialist city," everything would be redistributed and collectivized, not only economic life and consumption but also leisure and family. The family dwelling would be completely abolished—not transcended or withered away or allowed to vanish over time as a "matter of course." Families would be balkanized into living quarters where communal peoples had individual rooms for individual peoples, though married couples would be permitted to have adjoining rooms. This was "truly socialist," insisted Sabsovich, and it should be implemented immediately: "Down with so-called 'transitional forms!'" he shouted.[11]

Keep in mind: this was one of Stalin's top urban planners. Here was another communist bomb-thrower eagerly launching grenades at the edifice of marriage and the family.

Who were other Marxist voices on marriage and the family? Were all Marxists about radical reshaping of families? Were they all about "free love" and sexual license and jettisoning moral restraints? No, not all of them. This was something that varied, particularly among American communists. Addressing it properly requires some nuance.

Bella Dodd (1904–1969) is a case worth briefly considering as a transition from a Soviet female communist like Kollontai to an active American one. Though a dedicated communist for a time, Dodd always seemed more conflicted about its demands on motherhood and family than did the resolute Kollontai.

Born in Picerno, Italy, in October 1904, Dodd was baptized Maria Assunta Isabella. Her family immigrated to America. She eventually attended Hunter College. But what really began Bella's political wreckage was the day she and her friend Ruth Goldstein enrolled in summer session at Columbia University. Her "work at Columbia" was pivotal to her sharp turn left, as it would be for many young Americans. She "discovered the John Dewey Society and the Progressive Education Association" and, of course, the Columbia Teachers College. She soon realized "what a powerful effect Teachers College would have on American education." She was especially influenced by Dr. George Counts, a John Dewey pal who had made a political pilgrimage to Moscow to pay homage to the Motherland.[12]

She also discovered what a powerful effect the Communist Party could have, as Bella moved into the education front and joined the Party. She became a self-described "card-carrying Communist," and in March 1943 consented to become "an open Party leader" to untether her ideological activities. In no time, those activities became a major hindrance to her married and family life. As she made clear, "marriage for the intellectual proletariat" was always problematic. She and her husband, John, had a civil marriage, given that John was "bitterly anti-clerical." Their marriage did not last.[13]

"The Party did all it could to push women into industry," noted Dodd. "The bourgeois family as a social unit was to be made obsolete." In March 1943, as she gave herself totally to the Party, she longed for family life. "I often talked of adopting children," she wrote later. "But the comrades dissuaded me."[14]

In later testimony to the US Senate, after she broke with the Party, Dodd said that "Communism is an all-embracing philosophy which embraces everything you do, which determines the kind of marriage you have, your relations with your children, your relationship to your community, your relationship with your profession."[15]

As a teacher who was a leader in the teachers' union, she was especially concerned about how communists were manipulating children through the educational system. "There is no doubt in my mind that the Communists will use the schools and every other educational medium," she told the US Senate. "They will use every educational medium . . . from the nursery school to the universities." The teachers, said Dodd, "were used on many different fronts" by the Party. This was fundamental, she said, "to establish a Soviet America," the designation used by CPUSA leaders to describe their new Comintern-directed country upon their "victory in America."[16]

Dodd became very disillusioned. She could only take so much. But before she could leave the Party, her comrades expelled her in June 1949. Fundamental to her putting the Party behind her was a rediscovery not of Marx or Dewey or Columbia but her Catholic faith. She was brought back into the Church by Bishop Fulton Sheen.[17]

Bella Dodd longed for motherhood, for stability, for monogamy in a sound marriage. But that was not the desire of every Communist Party organizer.

Sexual libertinism was not unusual among homegrown Marxists in the United States, as embodied in the escapades of carefree playboys like John Reed (1887–1920), namesake of the John Reed Clubs and one of the earliest founders of the American communist movement. The communist cad and philanderer hopped from bed to bed, woman to woman, torpedoed marriage after marriage, and disseminated the venereal disease that made him urinate red and left at least one of his temporary girlfriends with inflamed ovaries requiring surgical removal.[18] Reed, who died young, was so influential and so esteemed by Moscow that his body was literally interred in the wall of the Kremlin. To this day he is celebrated among the American left, so much so that in 1981 he was the protagonist of the epic film *Reds*, where he was played by Hollywood liberal Warren Beatty, who was so taken by Reed that he produced, directed, and cowrote the film.

Reed was not uncharacteristic. A brave public witness to this period was Ben Gitlow, who had been such a leading figure in Communist Party USA that he twice ran as the party's candidate for vice president of the United States (1924 and 1928). Gitlow was so high up that he served on the Executive Committee of the Comintern. Disillusioned, he left the Party in 1929 and, after a long silence, emerged to testify before Congress (1939) and to write two major books, *I Confess* (1940), and *The Whole of Their Lives* (1948),[19] where he laid out a litany of disturbing facts on CPUSA's fully subservient relationship with Moscow, its financial dependence on the Kremlin, and its members' "fanatical zeal" for the Soviet Union and Communist Party. Gitlow ultimately spoke to just about everything that American communists ever did. Among them, he noted that leading communists changed wives as often "as one does an overcoat."[20]

To be fair, other American Reds in the rank and file could be fairly staid in their sexual conduct. David Horowitz, raised a Red diaper baby by communist parents in New York, told me that his mother and father were conventional in their tastes and behavior. "While it's true that the Communist left was always open to bohemianism," said Horowitz, "it's my impression that this was a limited phenomenon. My parents and their friends were very middle class. People on demonstrations wore suits. They were law abiding. They were proper." Even though the *Communist Manifesto* attacked the family, conceded Horowitz, the American communists that he saw interacting with his parents "were quite bourgeois."[21]

This would change, said Horowitz, with the New Left of the 1960s, which will be covered at length later in this book.

Speaking of that '60s New Left, Ron Radosh, a longtime friend of Horowitz who was also raised a Red diaper baby in New York, added that the Trotskyists of the Socialist Workers Party in the 1940s and 1950s were "much more bohemian" in their conduct. Many of them, particularly in top leadership posts, had "open marriages," taking in "lovers" other than their own spouses. By contrast, Radosh stated that Communist Party USA at the time, which was committed to Stalin and thus anti-Trotsky, was "much more of a traditional institution."[22]

That said, many communists through the first half of the twentieth century, before the sexual revolution of the '60s exploded upon the national landscape, often had a reputation for being revolutionary not only in their politics but also in their sexual adventurism. And many of them fully earned that reputation.

5

"COMMUNIST MARRIAGE"

TO PICK A HIGH-PROFILE CASE, CONSIDER Whittaker Chambers, who, along with Alger Hiss, stood at the epicenter of the trial of the century (1948–50) on the matter of communist infiltration of the US government. About the time that Aleksandra Kollontai (who Chambers would have read) was being considered for her Order of Lenin, Chambers was being tugged from his editorship of *New Masses* toward the Soviet GRU as an official spy for the Kremlin. In his gripping work *Witness* and elsewhere, Chambers wrote all about that period. He included not only details on the spy intrigue but also the lifestyle choices he experienced and engaged in.

Here, a lot of sordid details could be shared, but, in a nutshell, Chambers acknowledged that many American communists had open marriages, rampant divorce, and very libertine views of sexuality, and embraced abortion as a means of birth control, long before such things were common to American progressives and modern culture. It was the communist way.

In *Witness*, a Random House best seller published in 1952, Chambers wrote of his comrade Sam Krieger's breakup with his wife, Carol, and talked of marriage being considered a "bourgeois convention" among the Kriegers and other Marxist faithful. "They regarded marriage as a 'bourgeois convention' and loathed it with the same intensity with which many middle-class persons loathe sin," wrote Chambers. "Theirs was the first 'party marriage' that I observed."[1]

He should have added that it was the first such marriage of which he felt the pain. It is very telling that Chambers saw clearly that when these marriages broke up, they "sometimes led Communists to emotional upsets as shattering as any suffered by the bourgeoisie."[2]

Indeed they did. Despite all their grandiose, arrogant claims to a more sophisticated higher theory, communists could not escape the natural law that burned in their hearts. Sam and Carol Krieger, like other communists, had loved each other. So when they parted, it hurt. No matter how desperately they tried to dismiss marriage as a mere bourgeois convention, their own separation tore them up. The tugs of a dead nineteenth-century German philosopher's political theory could not extinguish the fire of marital love instilled in their hearts and minds and souls by a Creator in whom they professed to not believe. Marx and Engels's pompous blather on bourgeois marriage offered no solace from the heartache.

Chambers did not simply sit back and take notes on Sam Krieger's escapades as an object lesson in what not to do. He lived much the same lifestyle. Before meeting the woman who would become his wife and lifelong partner (even then, only after much tumult), Chambers slept with, lived with, and dated several women with whom he shared "party marriages." In June 1927, Gertrude Hutchinson, the wife of one of Chambers's old Columbia University comrades, separated from her husband and invited Chambers to move in with her in a small house she rented in Queens, New York. Though this was not an unusual step by today's standards, such a move was odd in the 1920s, unless one was a communist. Chambers stayed with Hutchinson for about a year in his first extramarital "party marriage."[3]

Sam Tanenhaus, editor of the *New York Times Book Review* and the outstanding Chambers biographer, explained that this arrangement was condoned by the communist movement precisely because it represented another blow to the weakening walls of the bourgeois state. Then, to further attack one-man-one-woman marriage—creating a communist polygamy of sorts—Chambers brought a buddy into the relationship, a friend named Bub Bang, who he felt needed a little consoling after losing his mother. The three jammed into their tight quarters, a kitchen plus two other rooms, and Chambers prevailed upon his communist "wife" to give herself to Bub for his needs. She did as requested, but found the arrangement unnaturally "intolerable and tense." Once again, for all the sniffing at "bourgeois values," devotions to communist theory could not override the deeper bonds between one woman and one man. Chambers soon ended the ideological "marriage" to Gertrude.[4]

Besides, by then Chambers had already sauntered into a second "communist marriage," this time to a divorced Jewish woman named Ida Dailes. The same age as Chambers, Ida had worked as a stenographer for a Manhattan-based communist agency called the Workers International Relief and had taught with Chambers at the Workers School in New York. Chambers taught journalism there, whereas Ida taught a course called "Fundamentals of Communism." With Chambers, Ida practiced the fundamentals of communism by shacking up and scoffing at traditional notions of marriage. They bounced from house to house, including a period of bedlam in the home of Chambers's mentally unstable mother, who soon bounced Ida.

Chambers and Ida lived together in various residences in New York for a while.[5] It was indeed a communist marriage not only in the sense that the two participants were communists, but in that they were defying the traditional "restrictions" on a man and woman joined together in matrimony. They also did the communist thing when Ida found herself pregnant. Chambers pressured the mother of his unborn child to get an abortion, which she did, and then he dumped her.[6]

Besides, Chambers was again already in another communist marriage, his third, this time to a woman named Esther Shemitz. They had first met in 1926 when agitating together at a textile strike. She had been a quite an activist in her own right, one of fifty charter members of the John Reed Club. He moved in with her and her roommate, the leftist writer Grace Lumpkin, who along with Esther was described as a "warm fellow traveler" (an understatement of their far-left politics). Soon a fourth participant moved into the household, Michael Intrator, another Chambers comrade. Michael had his way with Grace, whom he married several years later, and then divorced several years after that.[7]

It would take a few years, including extricating himself from the Communist Party and its practices and behaviors, but Chambers eventually came to deeply love Esther. As he did, and only slowly pulled away from his ideological hedonism, he had to reconcile communism's unnatural teachings on marriage with his natural feelings and inclinations toward Esther. He also had to survive the intrusion of Grace Hutchins, an obnoxious communist operative who interceded on behalf of the Communist Party to inform Esther that the Party had ordered that she never again see Chambers, who at the time was considered too "anti-Party." Nonetheless, their attraction was undeniable, with natural love again transcending the unnatural fiats of the Party.[8]

Chambers later wrote in *Witness* that from the outset he had been drawn to Esther, particularly her ability to (he claimed) remain "uncontaminated" by the sexual promiscuity that he said the Communist Party had elevated to the level of a "Marxist principle."[9] (This is a curious characterization by Chambers, who surely was not implying that Esther had been a virgin before their marriage in April 1931, after apparently having lived together for several years.)

Sexual nihilism was so common among many communists that it was also not unheard-of to find homosexuality among some of them in this strongly antihomosexual era (1930s). Unbeknownst to many conservatives, who rightly consider Chambers an icon to their movement, Whittaker Chambers himself engaged in homosexuality for a period and had been (in effect) bisexual. (Chambers's father, who was not a communist, was also bisexual.)

Sam Tanenhaus quoted claims and speculation by some sources that Chambers; his wife, Esther; and their communist friends Grace Lumpkin and Michael Intrator may have all at one time engaged in sexual relations with members of the same gender. Chambers himself said no such thing in Esther's case, though he was forthright on his own same-sex feelings. Chambers later confessed to engaging in "numerous homosexual activities both in New York and Washington, D.C." between roughly 1933–34 and 1938, which was precisely the same period during which he betrayed his country, and during which he was married to Esther. Chambers was surprisingly candid about this in his statements to Congress.[10]

Interestingly, when Chambers left the communist movement and moved toward God and yearned for a family, he also forever left the homosexual lifestyle. He said that when he broke with communism, he also "managed to break" himself of his homosexual tendencies. Even some ten years after ceasing such activity, he said he was still not "completely immune to such stimuli," but nonetheless had acquired the "self-control" to live a "blameless and devoted life as husband and father." As Tanenhaus put it, Chambers had mastered his desires once he committed himself to God and his Christian faith.[11]

That said, while Chambers's homosexuality was not unconnected to his communism, it was not a by-product of anything pro-gay in the teachings or practices of the American Communist Party or Moscow or Marx or Engels or Lenin. Quite the contrary, many in the Party would have been appalled at his sexual practices. One of his comrades in the Party described him as a "pervert" because of his same-sex attraction.[12]

(Congressional investigators considered whether Alger Hiss and Whittaker Chambers, who shared an apartment for a time, might have been homosexual partners, but found no such evidence. It is telling that investigators considered the possibility not out of character for communists.)

Nonetheless, for Chambers, like certain other communists, much of his nontraditional sexual behavior was consistent with a communist lifestyle that rejected traditional God-fearing notions of sexuality, marriage, and family.

For instance, so common was abortion among many hard-core communists even in America (where it was illegal until *Roe* in 1973) that

Chambers simply assumed that his wife would abort their first child when the pregnancy was discovered. To the contrary, they resisted that choice and had the child, a beautiful little girl who profoundly altered their lives, including Chambers's evolutionary-atheistic views. In *Witness*, Chambers marveled one morning studying the intricacies of his infant daughter's ear, which conveyed to him signs of design rather than evolutionary happenstance. The old ex-communist was so moved by this epiphany that he devoted an eloquent chapter to the subject, titled simply "The Child."[13]

Not so fortunate were Alger Hiss and his wife. In 1929 Priscilla Hiss, before she was married to Alger and during a time when she had several boyfriends, did the communist thing and aborted her child. It is not clear to what degree that abortion damaged Priscilla's fertility, but it unquestionably marred her emotional stability. Psychologically, it devastated her, and she never fully recovered. Sam Tanenhaus says that Priscilla's abortion was "the great shame of her life."[14]

6

MARGARET SANGER'S RUSSIAN ROMANCE

NO DISCUSSION OF THE SHAME AND devastation of abortion would be complete without the mention of Margaret Sanger, founder of Planned Parenthood, America's most proliferate and proficient abortion mill, which has performed countless millions of abortions since 1973. Some readers might balk at this book's focus on communism, Marxism, Soviet Russia, and how those subjects relate to abortion and the family and marriage. Surely this would not involve Sanger. Think again.

Margaret Sanger was born Margaret Louise Higgins in September 1879 in Corning, New York. Her devout Catholic mother had eleven children in addition to several miscarriages. Margaret looked at her mother pitifully as an overburdened birth machine. She might have held a grudge against her father, Michael, if not for the fact that he was a "freethinker," a gene he passed along to his daughter. Michael Higgins was an Irish immigrant and Catholic-turned-atheist who touted progressive causes, including "free" public education.

Upon leaving home to become a nurse, Margaret met William Sanger, who would become father to her children—three of them. Biographers say that she loved her children, but did not love assuming responsibility for them. Her son Grant would later bitterly state, "Mother was seldom around. She just left us with anybody handy, and ran off we didn't know where."[1] Child rearing was a burden she would rather leave to her husband and, more preferably, to the state. This desire she held in common with communists, including pro-Moscow friends like John Reed and Bill Haywood, and would longingly admire upon a visit to Moscow—yet another of her long absences from home.

Before that, however, Margaret also came to admire the "free love" movement spearheaded by radicals such as Russophile Emma Goldman, who was deported from the country by the administration of President Woodrow Wilson, the progressive's progressive who (to his unappreciated credit) saw Bolshevism as politically insane and outright criminal.[2] The victim of Sanger's embrace of free love was her loving husband, who had no choice but to suffer his wife's voracious sexual appetite and seemingly insatiable taking of other lovers. Margaret and her pal Emma would discuss radical politics and radical sexuality, imbibing in both as natural ideological companions. In the summer of 1913, when visiting Emma, Margaret had her first of innumerable affairs, which, she claimed, "really set me free."[3]

Margaret declared what she deemed "a woman's duty: To look the whole world in the face with a go-to-hell look in the eyes." She claimed many "rights" for "rebel women" such as herself: "The Right to be Lazy. The Right to be an Unmarried Mother. The Right to Destroy." She destroyed her marriage, demanding a divorce from her reluctant husband, who did his best to hold the family together. Margaret would have none of that nonsense, again fleeing the family for an extended jaunt, this time for a year in Europe, where she became lovers with married "sexologist" Havelock Ellis and other left-wing intellectuals, including Stalin dupe and writer H. G. Wells.[4] "I've never met a man more candid, fair, and honest," marveled Wells after meeting Stalin in 1934, at the start of his Great Purge. "Everyone trusts him." (Wells had likewise been impressed by Vladimir Lenin, whom he called a "frank," "refreshing," and "amazing little man," who "almost persuaded me to share his vision.")[5]

Sanger was a champion of not only extramarital but also premarital sex. As an elderly woman, she wrote a letter to her sixteen-year-old granddaughter, endorsing "kissing, petting and even intercourse." "As for intercourse," the insatiable grandmother told the minor, "I'd say three times a day was about right."[6]

This was a vision and lifestyle that demanded birth control. And if there was anything that *really* set Margaret Sanger's passions free, it was birth control. For Sanger, birth control was a golden key to a new universe. It allowed women not only to space their children and prevent unwanted births but, for her personally and professionally, it jarred the bedroom door to her sexual license outside the restrictions of her marital bond and—further—enabled her to pursue another love: "racial health" in the form of racial eugenics.

To that end, Sanger in 1921 would launch the American Birth Control League not long after the Soviets launched the Comintern. It would eventually become Planned Parenthood.

The passionate racial eugenicist expressed her wish to rid America of its "idiots" and "morons" and "imbeciles" and "mentally and physically defective" as part of her crowning vision for "race improvement." The Planned Parenthood founder lamented America's "race of degenerates." The nation's landscape needed to be purged of its "human weeds" and "the dead weight of human waste." This included the "feeble-minded" and the "insane." Sanger shared the disparaging perception of humanity held by another progressive icon, Supreme Court Justice Oliver Wendell Holmes, who declared that "three generations of imbeciles are enough." Like Holmes, she hoped to finesse and refine the "gene pool."

Margaret Sanger maintained that "the most urgent problem today is how to limit and discourage the over-fertility of the mentally and physically defective." One of her favorite slogans, which even adorned the masthead of her *Birth Control Review*—founded in 1917, the same year that Bolshevism became the masthead of Russia—was "Birth Control: To Create a Race of Thoroughbreds." Progressives today dare not raise the grim specter of Sanger's Negro Project or her related correspondence with Dr. Clarence Gamble, whom, in a remarkable December 10, 1939, letter today held in the Sanger archives at Smith College (I have a photocopy), Sanger urged, "We do not want word to go out that we want to exterminate the Negro population."

It is not entirely clear what Sanger meant there, with interpretations differing. The letter was within the context of the Negro Project, however, which inclines one to a negative interpretation, whereas her liberal defenders again rush to her defense.[7] My negative assessment is influenced by other revolting Sanger race-related actions, such as her May 1926 speech to the Ku Klux Klan in Silver Lake, New Jersey.

Though liberals have done backflips to avoid this elephant in the progressive living room, Sanger openly wrote about the KKK speech on pages 366–67 of her 1938 autobiography published by W. W. Norton, one of the leading New York publishing houses. She was eager to speak to the group, which had kept her waiting for nearly three hours while it engaged in its incendiary routine. She recalled that she was "summoned at last and entered a bright corridor filled with wraps. As someone came out of the hall I saw through the door dim figures parading with banners and illuminated crosses. I waited another twenty minutes. It was warmer and I did not mind so much. Eventually the lights were switched on, the audience seated itself, and I was escorted to the platform, was introduced, and began to speak."

Sanger relayed little of what she shared with the Klanswomen at their rally, though apparently she was extremely successful and satisfied with herself: "I believed I had accomplished my purpose. A dozen invitations to speak to similar groups were proffered. The conversation went on and on, and when we were finally through it was too late to return to New York. . . . I could not even send a telegram to let my family know whether I had been thrown in the river or was being held incommunicado. It was nearly one before I reached Trenton, and I spent the night in a hotel."

The Planned Parenthood founder's KKK talk was a smash hit. Not only did it go very late, after a very long wait, but she received numerous invitations to speak to other groups like the Klan.

Why would the KKK be so interested in Ms. Sanger? The reasons are obvious, a natural fit. It was because Sanger was a passionate racial eugenicist with grandiose dreams of "race improvement."

Sanger found eugenics refreshing. She also found Bolshevism refreshing. No, Margaret Sanger was not a communist, though she was very critical of capitalism, of religion, of Christianity generally, and especially of the pope and the Roman Catholic Church, which she openly mocked in published writings. She scoffed at Catholic teaching on birth control as "illogical, not in accord with science, and definitely against social welfare and race improvement." She scorned the claims of the Church and the pope as "authorized guardian and interpreter of 'divine law' applying to marriage." She was incredulous at how the pope could instruct the faithful on regulating their conjugal life "without the benefit of science and according to theories written by St. Augustine, also a bachelor, who died fifteen centuries ago."[8]

Sounding not unlike a writer for *Pravda* in a typical rant against Rome, Sanger found Bolshevik Russia ever more appealing. She became a fellow traveler to the Soviet Union, making pilgrimages, like her lover H. G. Wells and associates such as John Dewey and George Bernard Shaw. Shaw became the ignominious owner of some of the most egregious remarks ever made on Stalin and his killing machine, a fact ignored by his fawning fans who stage his plays. I have recorded those at length elsewhere,[9] and this is not the place to revisit them, but his remarks on marriage are likewise alarming—and Sanger-like. In his 1928 work, *The Intelligent Woman's Guide to Socialism, Capitalism, Sovietism and Fascism*, Shaw wrote, "At present a married woman is a female slave chained to a male one; and a girl is a prisoner in the house and in the hands of her parents."[10]

Such sad words were music to Margaret Sanger's ears, or at least to her goals. Like Shaw and Wells and many other Potemkin village progressives, she went to the USSR in the summer of 1934 to soak in the glorious triumphs of the communist Motherland. Each progressive who made that pilgrimage had his or her own reasons. John Dewey, for instance, hailed the Bolsheviks' "Great Experiment" in public education. He was there finding harmony between America and Soviet public schools. As for Sanger, she was enticed by Lenin's and Stalin's reportedly wondrous advancements for women, which she eagerly shared in the June 1935 edition of her *Birth Control Review*, in an article titled, "Birth Control in Russia."

That article was highly positive, though Sanger was taken aback by the sudden proliferation of abortions in the Soviet Union, which seemed to have spun out of control so quickly that Bolshevik central planners did not even know how many were taking place. "The total number is not known," she reported, "but the number for Moscow alone is roughly estimated at 100,000 per year."

Sanger seemed initially perturbed by this sudden surge in death of the unborn. At this point in her work, she had favored birth control mainly so that women could space their births, and for purposes of eugenics. She had not yet embraced abortion, or certainly not publicly— that, too, was something that American progressives needed to warm up to. Nonetheless, she allowed her concerns to be assuaged by Stalin's officials. She confidently told her readers: "All the officials with whom I discussed the matter stated that as soon as the economic and social plans of Soviet Russia are realized, neither abortions nor contraception will be necessary or desired. A functioning Communistic society will assure the happiness of every child, and will assume the full responsibility for its welfare and education."

That, in a statement, is progressive utopianism, an absolute faith in central planners. Contrary to the Planned Parenthood founder's optimism, abortions ultimately skyrocketed to seven million annually in the USSR.

Something else, however, more than impressed Sanger, making up for any disappointment. She was bowled over by the birth-control bonanza she found in Moscow. Again in her article "Birth Control in Russia," she reported approvingly, "Theoretically, there are no obstacles to birth control in Russia. It is accepted . . . on the grounds of health and human right. . . . [W]e could well take example from Russia, where there are no legal restrictions, no religious condemnation, and where birth control instruction is part of the regular welfare service of the government."

What really strikes me in reading this assertion today is how modern liberal/progressive Democrats in America have arrived at Sanger's Bolshevik ideal, where Planned Parenthood's services have become, in their mind, "part of the regular welfare service of the government," just like in Stalinist Russia. Fast-forwarding, note that even in the face of record deficits and national debt, Democratic responses to Republican efforts to cut taxpayer funding of Planned Parenthood in 2011 were comically frenzied. Senate majority leader Harry Reid (D-NV) said that Republicans had placed "a bull's eye on women in America," and it was keeping them from getting the "health services they need."[11] And Chuck Schumer (D-NY) warned that "the dangerous, ideological cuts to Planned Parenthood that passed the House are never, never, never going to pass the Senate."[12]

Democrats were united in such vitriol: "The real reason that the right-wing extremists in Congress orchestrated this outrageous government shutdown is to try and defund Planned Parenthood as part of their ideological assault on women's health care," said Rep. Diana DeGette (D-CO).[13] Congresswoman Barbara Lee (D-CA) insisted, "This is a war on women. They're trying to inject their politics and their religion into local family planning."[14] Senator Dianne Feinstein (D-CA) blasted defunding efforts as "nothing more than an opportunity for the right wing in the House to sock it to women."[15] Former House Speaker Nancy Pelosi (D-CA) called it a "very dangerous situation for the health—the reproductive health—of women across our country." Pelosi told reporters: "It's degrading to women; it's disrespectful; it doesn't make any sense; and if you want to reduce the number of abortions in our country, you must commit to supporting contraception and family planning." The lifelong Roman Catholic and mother of five said Republicans were using Planned Parenthood as a "whipping boy."[16] Finally, Senator Barbara Boxer described Republican efforts as a "vendetta" against women, asserting, "Behind each of these Republican proposed cuts, there are thousands, maybe millions of people who would be hurt."[17]

All of this is getting way ahead of the timeline in this book and seems somewhat off topic, though it is not unrelated. Indeed, for "progressives," this is how "progress" proceeds. It took Democrats a while to get there, but, finally, almost a century after the launching of the Bolshevik Revolution and of Margaret Sanger's organization, they have finally arrived at where Sanger and the Soviets found common ground. They indeed act as if, as Sanger said about Stalin's Russia, "birth control . . . is part of the regular service of the government."

That same "progress" is evident in abortion itself.

It is vital to understand that one of the only things that can really be known about progressives, and that they know about themselves and their ideology, is that they favor constant "change," "reform," an ever-shifting, ongoing "evolution." And therein is an inherent, significant difficulty: progressivism offers no clear, definable end. For nonprogressives, this ambiguity is troubling bordering on maddening, as we cannot, by the very nature of progressivism, get an answer from progressives as to where, exactly, they intend to stop.

Take for example Sanger's Planned Parenthood. It took off in the 1920s, initially as the American Birth Control League. At first, Sanger and friends wanted birth control and eugenics, not abortion. It will shock modern pro-lifers and pro-choicers alike to hear this, but Margaret Sanger initially denounced abortion. "It is an alternative that I cannot too strongly condemn," wrote Sanger in the January 27, 1932, edition of the *Nation*, two and a half years before her pilgrimage to Moscow. "Some ill-informed persons have the notion that when we speak of birth control we include abortion as a method. We certainly do not."[18]

Nonetheless, for these progressives, what began as birth control and eugenics—aimed at halting life at conception—needed only a few decades to snuff out life after conception. As with much of what progressives do, where they started was not enough. And naturally, once legalized abortion came along, it, too, was not enough. Today, progressives tell us abortion should be funded by taxpayers.

In fact, we have now arrived at another new stage in the progressive death march. Just twenty years ago, it was unthinkable that an overwhelming consensus of progressives/liberals would compel everyone, including conscientious objectors invoking their sacred First Amendment religious freedoms, to forcibly pay for others' contraception, sterilization services, and abortion-inducing drugs—via the Obama HHS mandate or whatever other vehicle. "Pro-choice" liberals once assured us that they would never be so crude as to ask others to pay for their abortions. That would be completely over the line. And to pay for their contraception, too? *No way!* they scoffed. They merely wanted pro-lifers "out of their bedroom" to allow them their "safe, legal, and rare" abortions.

Well, here we are today, and the unfathomable is now the unwavering position of liberals/progressives.

How did they change so much so fast? The short answer is that they had to *progress*, to evolve to this current understanding that they consider more enlightened. As for those of us who have not changed, who once shared a similar position as these liberals/progressives did, we are now deemed the extremists, the intransigents. We are said to favor a "war on women." In pleading with liberals/progressives to not force us to violate our sacred beliefs on human life by subsidizing their abortions, we are told that we are "imposing" our religious beliefs, and also "denying" women the contraceptives they remain fully free to purchase with their own money.

Alas, this is where progressives have progressed on unborn life. It is the next stage. It is, yet again, a new stage that furthers death. It uses force not only against the victims, the unborn, but against those pleading not to be party to the victims' destruction.

Still, that, likewise, will not be enough. What might be next in the progression? We do not know, just as progressives themselves do not currently know—even though it serves us all, including unborn future generations, to want answers to some hard questions as far as ultimate objectives are concerned. We can beg progressives for some contours, a vague estimate: *Could you please, this time around—where human life is concerned—establish some boundaries, set an end goal or two, offer an inkling of predictability, a modicum of expectation, some flicker of a suggestion as to where you want to take us?*

Unfortunately, they cannot, as such is the crux of their ever-changing philosophy.

Again, all that we really know about progressives, and that they know about themselves, is that they are always changing. Because of that, neither we nor they can tell us where they will stand on issues X and Y in twenty years. We can't know because they don't know. They will tell us when they get there.

But we do know this much: what is seemingly inconceivable to all of us right now, including to progressives themselves, may become the dogmatic position of progressives in a generation. The once-inconceivable absurdities become reality, and when they do, the progressive shrugs and then shouts—at you. If you suggest that a certain impossible position might become progressives' position in, say, the year 2034, they will laugh, insisting they could never hold such an intolerable position. Alas, when they arrive at that position in 2034, they will tell you that you are the crazy one; more than that, you are the vile extremist for disagreeing with their newfound position. And they will attempt to force your compliance under the coercive power of the state.

Again, this discussion here might seem like a digression, but it is not. This abortion "progression" by secular progressives who started as sympathetic to certain goals of Soviet communism, such as Margaret Sanger, would directly and devastatingly impact the family. And it also applies to how the wider left and progressives have "progressed" in redefining marriage, creating their newest *rights*, "marriage rights," on the heels of their "abortion rights."

Just twenty years ago, the entire Democratic Party, from its leadership in the House and the Senate to Bill and Hillary Clinton in the White House, supported retaining the definition of marriage as between one man and one woman. Just five years ago, Barack Obama and Hillary Clinton held that same position. And by 2012, that was completely gone. Now, anyone who opposes redefining marriage—and who stands now where virtually all Democrats stood a mere two decades back—is derided as a bigoted extremist. It is telling that in the opening line to his 2012 book, *What Liberals Believe*, Professor William Martin wrote,

"Liberals value equality. . . . We are unequivocally pro-choice . . . and pro-marriage equality."[19]

Fine, but when were liberals so unequivocally for these two things? They were not just two decades ago, or even five years ago. When did it change, and why, and how? And under what situation will it presumably change again? If the only certainty is *change*, and the only real definition is *progression*, then how can the positions not change again? By what defining standard of change and progression can a liberal/progressive say that these things will stay the same? The only thing they can say is that it will not stay the same.

Where is the progressive goalpost for marriage and family? What does it look like? What shape and form? Progressives literally cannot answer that most basic question. They can tell you only that the goalpost will be different from whatever and wherever it is today.

If you are confused, you have plenty of company. This is a confused train wreck of an ideology than cannot stay on the tracks and can only careen to disaster, with humanity the crushed victims.

This is a radical individualism and moral relativism where all "rights" and "freedoms" and the very definitions of things—some of them ancient things—are simply redefined according to the political-ideological currents and sentiments and needs of the moment and of the tasks at hand. It is all done apart from God or any religious contours. This, in its essence, is what Marx and Engels and Owen and Fourier and the others had done from the outset.

Finally, to bring this back to Margaret Sanger and Stalin's regime, Sanger was impressed by the new world that Lenin and Stalin had created for Soviet women, with birth control the pinnacle of her infatuation. The "attitude of Soviet Russia toward its women," stated Sanger, "would delight the heart of the staunchest feminist," which of course described her. "Equal rights are a settled and accepted fact," she continued. "Woman is equal to man in every occupation, in sports, in the arts, in marriage." Interestingly, Sanger identified a moment when "this equality ceases," wherein women were allegedly given even better treatment by men, a favoritism she unequally favored. What was this area?

"When pregnancy begins this equality ceases," she wrote. "Then the woman becomes a protégé of the State. Both the mother and the child are under the protection and care of the government, to an extent perhaps never before equaled in history."[20]

Sanger approved of this mother ship of the Soviet Motherland, of this nannydom of the Bolshevik nanny state. The idea of "woman [as] protégé of the State" warmed the blood of Planned Parenthood's founding mother.

Sanger had many friends and associates and fellow believers who were similarly enamored with the Soviet experiment. They thought maybe the Soviet Union held the bright light to the new future, and that maybe the USSR had simply moved there faster than progressives and socialists (and Fabian socialists, for that matter) were willing to go. But perhaps most important, from an American perspective, is that Sanger and friends were part of a wider left that would nudge America toward altogether new horizons for women and for married and family life.

7

MARGARET MEAD AND FRIENDS

AS WE SEE IN THE CASE of Margaret Sanger, a wider swath of leftists, liberals, progressives, and fellow travelers progressively reinforced communists in their steady radicalization of the family and sexuality. This concentric circle was not composed of doctrinaire Party members but often sympathizers or people frequently headed in the same direction with critical areas of commonality. They included the likes of Margaret Mead, Clarence Gamble, Alan Guttmacher, and (among others) the sadomasochistic sexologist Alfred Kinsey.[1] These individuals were labeled "the Sex Planners" by Donald De Marco and Benjamin Wiker in their excellent work, *Architects of the Culture of Death*. De Marco and Wiker also pointed to a separate category called "the Pleasure Seekers": Helen Gurley Brown, Sigmund Freud, and Wilhelm Reich, a Marxist of special interest whom I will detail later.

Many of these individuals would merit reflection in a lengthy book fully chronicling the wider left's attack on marriage and the family, among them, famed anthropologist Margaret Mead.

Born in Philadelphia in December 1901, Mead was raised in nearby Doylestown, Pennsylvania. Her father was a finance professor at Wharton School of Business, and her mother, Emily Fogg Mead, a sociologist born of refined Philadelphian stock. Her upbringing seemed fairly stable. As a young woman, she met a theology student named Luther Cressman, and they were married in an Episcopal church. It is said that both were virgins.

Things began to unravel when the couple pursued their graduate educations at Columbia University. They got there about the time that Columbia was turning Whittaker Chambers into a communist, en route to his becoming a Soviet spy, and shortly before Elizabeth Bentley got there and turned into a communist en route to becoming a Soviet spy. Margaret Mead surely encountered the unavoidable Young Communists at Columbia. I cannot say that Margaret became a communist (I know of no indication that she did), but she certainly was tugged far to the left.

There, too, at Columbia, something else tugged at Margaret's heart. She met Ruth Benedict, with whom she seems to have probably had a physical relationship. Benedict was also a fellow aspiring researcher who would become a successful academic.

Overall, Columbia University was responsible for molding the Margaret Mead of history, as it was so many of the figures in this book, ruining yet another political soul.

Within just a few short years of her marriage, the twentysomething Margaret penned a farewell letter to her husband. She also boarded a ship off the West Coast for the island of Samoa to launch the research that made her famous. She portrayed the natives of the island as living a primordial but sublime human existence, a kind of Rousseau-like peace in nature. She positively presented them as obsessed but liberated sex freaks craving almost any kind of interchangeable intercourse. Progressives lapped it up. Samoa seemed to represent the kind of sexually idyllic "free love" world that repressed America so desperately ached for. *If only America could be like Samoa.*

Mead became very well known in her time. If there could ever be such a thing as an anthropological rock star, she would have been it. From the 1950s to the late 1970s, she was one of the most-admired and recognized women in America. For two decades she wrote a popular regular column for the women's magazine *Redbook*. In 1969, *Time* magazine crowned her "Mother of the World." This was truly a breathtaking move by *Time*, astonishingly bold either in its arrogance or ignorance, or both.

Yet another product of Columbia University graduate schools unleashed upon American culture, the celebrated Mead was much further to the left than the people who sang her hosannas in the media ever bothered to report to the housewives awed by her scientific pedigree. Many of those who admired her would not have emulated her practices in real life. Not many June Cleavers in the 1950s were sending their children to the Downtown Community School, a supplement to the left's iconic Little Red School House, which was founded in the early 1920s by New York communists and progressives. There, Margaret Mead stood shoulder to shoulder with other left-wing parents (not to mention trustees, like Lillian Hellman), such as Franklin Folsom, a writer for TASS, the official Soviet news agency; Simon Gerson, editor of the *Daily Worker*; V. J. Jerome, editor of the Communist Party's theoretical journal, *Political Affairs*; and the Boudins, whose little daughter Kathy was fated to become one of the convicted and imprisoned Weather Underground terrorists and bombers. She was convicted for murder—after she completed her studies at Columbia University, which had been properly prepared for by a fifteen-month stint in Moscow.[2]

It is hard to imagine Beaver Cleaver and Whitey and Judy and Larry Mondello reciting passages from Marx with Miss Canfield at their idyllic public school in the suburbs.

It is likewise difficult to say just how many hard-core Marxists, Stalinists, Leninists, Trotskyists, and assorted "progressives," liberals, liberal dupes, Soviet admirers, Soviet sympathizers, Kremlin agents of influence, fellow travelers, and various other purveyors of leftist propaganda that Margaret Mead ran with and worked with. The problem in adequately documenting them is that Mead in death is protected as Mead was in life by sympathetic liberal sources—then journalists, today academic biographers—who reflexively dismiss any suspicions of pro-communist work as loathsome McCarthyite innuendo and smear mongering. I will leave the full task to some enterprising future researcher who does not mind being blackballed and denied tenure by the agents of "tolerance" in today's academy. But for the sake of the interests of this book, one Mead cohort who easily eludes the radar even of highly knowledgeable historians of communism is Kurt Lewin. A few words on Lewin are worthwhile here.

Kurt Lewin (1890–1947) was a Freudian Marxist who hailed from Germany. He got his doctorate from the University of Berlin and became a lecturer at its Psychological Institute. He quickly connected with the extraordinary group of cultural neo-Marxists of the University of Frankfurt and their Institute for Social Research. Many if not nearly all of them (Lewin included) were Jewish Marxists forced to flee Germany in the 1930s under Hitler.

They found a welcome home in American academia, with Columbia University rolling out the red carpet. As for Lewin, he ended up lecturing and teaching at a number of colleges, from Cornell to Harvard, with a long-term podium awaiting him at the University of Iowa, smack-dab in the middle of the American heartland. He was also a regular haunt at the Columbia University Faculty Club, and was almost hired permanently at the New York–based New School for Social Research.[3]

Lewin became a highly successful left-wing academic, credited as a founder of the field of social psychology, of so-called change theory, of "field theory," and notably, as the founding father of "sensitivity training." The left admires his work on "collective decision-making" and combating "religious and racial prejudice," both for which he is prominently remembered today in his biographical entry at Marxists. org.[4] One of his legacies, the Kurt Lewin Foundation, seeks to foster Lewin's promotion of "tolerance."

Of course, it is crucial to understand that Kurt Lewin understood tolerance and prejudice and sensitivity training in a way that a cultural Marxist interprets them. He understood them in ways understood by the modern left, which has misused and abused such notions in ways that advance the current takedown of the traditional culture.

Among these, particularly odious has been the modern application of "sensitivity training," which has become a vehicle for leftists to herd together assorted groups ranging from reluctant workplace employees to college freshmen, to browbeat and embarrass them into accepting whatever prevailing cultural-sexual rot du jour the liberals are serving at the moment, and nearly always in opposition to traditional-biblical beliefs and mores. Conservative journalist Ralph de Toledano noted that Lewin's work in this regard has been a gift to leftists and feminists who have sought to emasculate the American workplace and entrepreneurial class. More than that, Toledano referred to Lewin as the undisputed intellectual guru of the group "that brought brainwashing to American education."[5]

Toledano listed Margaret Mead among Lewin's "worshippers." No doubt, she deeply respected the man. Lewin and Mead worked closely together, to the point that in October 1943 they coauthored and published an academic paper.[6] Far more scandalous, during World War II both Lewin and Mead worked for the Office of Strategic Services (OSS), the wartime predecessor to the CIA. On the surface, this seems impossible, shocking, and amazing, but in truth, OSS was among the most heavily penetrated wartime offices of the US federal government. It was rife with communists and communist sympathizers, including literally countless dedicated to Stalin's goals in Europe.

After the war, both academics, particularly Lewin, would be rewarded with all sorts of fat research grants for their work, especially from the Rockefeller Foundation, which, unbeknownst to countless millions of American innocents, has been a horrendously destructive force in subsidizing some of the worst work and researchers ever to tread US soil.

Toledano saw Lewin, much in the mold of Wilhelm Reich, as a cultural Marxist whose personal behavior toward women in his own life could be "domineering" and "antagonistic," but who, nonetheless, found feminists to be ideal allies in the "war against the family" and against patriarchy.[7] In this, argued Toledano, Lewin and Mead were kindred spirits who found common cause.

As for Margaret Mead, the famed anthropologist's highly unorthodox 1950s views on sexuality were another skeleton in the closet not rolled out by her fawning liberal media to the Ozzie-and-Harriet-Nelson world. Mead was a disenchanted Anglican, one of America's most liberal denominations, but not liberal enough for her. The Anglicans were the first major denomination to sign on to birth control, which pleased Mead's friend Margaret Sanger, and likely thrilled her as well, but it was not enough to keep her in the flock. It seemed fitting that Mead once had an uncle who had been booted out of the Unitarian Church for heresy, a seemingly impossible task. The Unitarians are literally more liberal than any denomination. But they were not left-wing enough for Margaret's uncle or, for that matter, her Philadelphia high-society mother.[8]

Mead's move toward agnosticism and eventual departure from religion conveniently helped her leave three marriages in favor of alternative arrangements. The self-appointed expert in human nature declared that "rigid heterosexuality is a perversion of nature" and wanted Americans to "come to terms with the . . . normal human capacity to love members of both sexes." Like Margaret Sanger, her professional and personal views were all about easy love and easy divorce, with husbands suffering the consequences.[9]

There is no question that Margaret Mead today would be a leading same-sex-marriage advocate, even as unthinkable as the notion was in her day. She had all the ancillary ingredients to allow for that evolution. This includes singing the left's rendition of "tolerance." Children "must be taught tolerance," said Mead way back in 1928, a mother who sent her child to a school that taught that Stalin's Soviet Union was the pinnacle of human advancement.[10]

And like Margaret Sanger, she believed "that our abortion laws should be changed," a position she took in 1963, ten years before *Roe v. Wade*.[11]

Margaret Mead was very much the progressive. She argued that society lived "in a period of transition." She said that society had been terribly hindered and shackled by the belief that "only one standard can be the right one."[12] She applied those relativistic standards to marriage and the family.

8

FIGHTING THE "SATANIC SCOURGE"
OF COMMUNISM

THE SEXUAL IDEAS AND PRACTICES OF leftists from Marx and Engels, to Mead and Sanger, to Kollontai and Chambers, were not atypical, nor were they completely concealed from the "masses." The licentious life-styles and beliefs of communists, many progressives, and related radicals were not a secret to the wider population. Their various escapades were sometimes pointed to by God-fearing Americans as evidence of the hedonistic danger they posed to respectable society.

Though the term has vanished today, the phrase "sexual communism" was once used in certain quarters, much like the term "free love," and sometimes synonymously. (In an Internet search at the time of the writing of this book, I found no references at all to the term, including on *Wikipedia* or the Urban Dictionary, the latter of which requested that I write an entry.) The term was still known well enough by the late 1960s that Professor H. Kent Geiger, in his Harvard University Press work, could write almost interchangeably of "the 'free love' or 'sexual communism' that horrified the nineteenth century."[1] Yes, *horrified*; such behavioral antics advocated and espoused by certain communists were notorious to polite culture.

Certainly, the Marxist message on morality did not escape the notice of the world's largest Christian denomination, which decided to fight back, not standing idle against this threat to family, faith, and the globe. To that end, the most relentless adversary of communists from the outset of their agenda was the Roman Catholic Church, which looked to shed light on this dark presence plaguing the world. Since the time of Marx, the Magisterium, the teaching body of the Church, had been on the case.

This is starkly evident in Pope Pius IX's early condemnation in the encyclical *Qui Pluribus* (On Faith and Religion), released in November 1846—two years before the publication of the *Communist Manifesto*. The first of many Pius IX statements during an unprecedented thirty-two-year reign as pope, it eviscerated "the unspeakable doctrine of Communism, as it is called, a doctrine most opposed to the very natural law."

Here we should pause for a moment to briefly explain natural law, which will be invoked many times in this book, and which is essential to understanding the fundamental impediment to redefining marriage. Numerous sources from Augustine to Aquinas could be cited. Here, I would like to start by quoting a colleague, Dr. Robert Barker, professor emeritus of law at Duquesne University, and an eloquent expert on the subject, particularly on how natural law influenced the American founders and the US Constitution.[2]

Barker defines natural law thus: "God, in creating the universe, implanted in the nature of man a body of law to which all human beings are subject, which is superior to man-made law, and which is knowable by human reason." Such law, notes Barker, has been for over two millennia a "traditional and essential" element of Western civilization. To illustrate the point, he marshals the likes of Aquinas, Sophocles, Aristotle, and Cicero. He cites Sophocles's play *Antigone*, where the heroine (of the same name), condemned to death by an unjust king, informed the king that he was violating a superior, natural law. "I had to choose between your law and God's law," she told the king, "and no matter how much power you have to enforce your law, it is inconsequential next to God's. His laws are eternal, not merely for the moment. No mortal, not even you, may annul the laws of God."

As Aristotle put it, the natural law is a universal law that transcends earthly regimes and stands common to all human beings, "even when there is no community to bind them to one another." Cicero, too, saw natural law as true law. He wrote: "True law is right reason in agreement with nature; it is of universal application, unchanging and everlasting. . . . It is a sin to try to alter this law . . . and it is impossible to abolish it entirely." He added that "whoever is disobedient" to the natural law "is fleeing from himself and denying his human nature."

Note that Cicero insisted it is a "sin" to try to alter that law. Such is a dire warning to religious people today who seek to advance ideas and laws that alter natural law.

Notably, Aristotle, who was Greek, and Cicero, who was Roman, both of them among the greatest philosophers, preceded Christianity. One need not be a Christian to believe in natural law. A modern atheist can believe in natural law in the sense of believing that nature, through whatever origin or mechanism, either design or sheer evolution, has biologically ordered things to be the way they are. As applied to sexuality, a strict evolutionist could examine the male and female sexual organs and discern from nature alone that they are compatible for purposes of procreation and conjugal union between a man and a woman; the distinct but complementary parts go together in a way that the private parts of a male and male or female and female cannot. That is why these sexual organs are known as *reproductive* organs. Whereas an atheist could make this obvious observation from a strictly natural perspective, a religious person would take the observation a step further, arguing that this naturalness was instilled by a Creator, who "made them male and female" for such complementarity, and that no man should tear asunder this design that God conceived for nature.[3]

Christianity has affirmed the natural law from the very beginning. Here, so many church fathers are often quoted, from Augustine to Aquinas. Augustine said that natural law is, simply put, "the truth"— the "light we call the truth." Aquinas agreed that "God has given this light or law at the creation."[4] In his classic *Summa Theologica*, Aquinas maintained that natural law is "nothing else than the rational creature's participation in the eternal law."

A lesser-known insightful (but by no means obscure) source is a renowned contemporary of Augustine, Gregory of Nazianzus, whose soaring orations on the Trinity in the fourth century earned him the title "the Theologian." This was a pivotal time in church history, when the Trinity was being defended and defined by the early church councils. Gregory had some words, too, on the "unwritten law of nature": "God has been merciful in the greatest ways, giving us in addition to everything else law and the prophets and, before these, the unwritten law of nature, the watchdog of our actions, by way of pricking our consciences and advising and directing us."[5] This natural law helps guide us, advise us, navigate us; it is nothing less than a heavenly watchdog to help keep us and our consciences in line.

Of all the faith traditions, none has a library of understanding of natural law like the Roman Catholic Church, which almost seems to have a corner on the subject—an assertion the Church would dispute, contending that nature and nature's God have that corner. One of the richest compilations elucidating natural law is the *Catechism of the Catholic Church* (paragraphs 1954–60). It calls natural law "immutable and permanent throughout the variations of history," a universal "rule that binds men," is "written and engraved in the soul of each and every man," and is "present in the heart of each man and established by reason." Even when this law is rejected, "it cannot be destroyed or removed from the heart of man."

To this day, the Church refers to the idea of a man and a man or a woman and a woman marrying or even having sexual relations with each other as an unequivocal violation of the natural law, an arrangement it has condemned as "gravely contrary" to human nature and "objectively disordered" and "morally wrong."[6] Not coincidentally, the Catholic Church would place both same-sex "marriage" and communism under the same leaky roof: both violate natural law.

That brief overview of natural law brings us back to Pius IX's 1846 encyclical *Qui Pluribus*,[7] which castigated the doctrine of communism for standing in stark opposition to natural law: if this doctrine were accepted, warned the pontiff, "the complete destruction of everyone's laws, government, property, and even of human society itself would follow." Pius IX predicted severe destruction from communism, including moral collateral damage. Communism was among "the most dark designs of men in the clothing of sheep, while inwardly ravening wolves." These men peddled their nostrums "by means of a feigned and deceitful appearance of a purer piety, a stricter virtue and discipline; after taking their captives gently, they mildly bind them, and then kill them in secret. They make men fly in terror from all practice of religion, and they cut down and dismember the sheep of the Lord." Not mincing words, the pope blasted the writings of communists, saying that their "books and pamphlets . . . teach the lessons of sinning" and generate a "widespread disgusting infection."

"These works, well-written and filled with deceit and cunning," continued the pontiff, "are scattered at immense cost through every region for the destruction of the Christian people. They spread pestilential doctrines everywhere and deprave the minds especially of the imprudent, occasioning great losses for religion." The Church saw the "imprudent" as vulnerable to communist cunning and deceit, and might well have expected the intellectual carnage to come in the universities. With this depraving of minds comes the lowering of morals and undermining of the faith that produces the morals:

> As a result of this filthy medley of errors which creeps in from every side, and as the result of the unbridled license to think, speak and write, We see the following: morals deteriorated, Christ's most holy religion despised, the majesty of divine worship rejected, the power of this Apostolic See plundered, the authority of the Church attacked and reduced to base slavery, the rights of bishops trampled on, the sanctity of marriage infringed, the rule of every government violently shaken and many other losses for both the Christian and the civil commonwealth.

Yes, noted Pius IX, "the sanctity of marriage" would also be violated. Again, this encyclical was released two years before Marx and Engels published the *Manifesto*. Clearly, communism as a threat to marriage and the family must have been already apparent—or the Church was indeed guided (as it claims to be) by the Holy Spirit and thus able to foresee such things (or both).

Pius IX was succeeded by another long-serving pope, Leo XIII, who would hold the chair of Saint Peter for twenty-five years (1878–1903). Likewise in the first year of his pontificate, even before classics like his *Rerum Novarum*, this pontiff wasted no time zeroing in on the scourge of communism and its predicted wreckage. On April 21, 1878, he released his first encyclical, titled *Inscrutabili Dei Consilio* (On the Evils of Society), and then three days after Christmas, on December 25, 1878, released the second, *Quod Apostolici muneris* (On Socialism).

In *Quod Apostolici muneris*, Pope Leo XIII excoriated communism as "the fatal plague which insinuates itself into the very marrow of human society only to bring about its ruin."[7] From start to finish, the encyclical denounced communism's pernicious effects, including on marriage and family life.[8] The opening passage of the encyclical could not be more unmistakable: "At the very beginning of Our pontificate, as the nature of Our apostolic office demanded, we hastened to point out in an encyclical letter addressed to you, venerable brethren, the deadly plague that is creeping into the very fibers of human society and leading it on to the verge of destruction." These evils, the pope feared, "have so rapidly increased." What evils? Leo XIII did not waste words: "We speak of that sect of men who, under various and almost barbarous names, are called socialists, communists, or nihilists, and who, spread over all the world, and bound together by the closest ties in a wicked confederacy, no longer seek the shelter of secret meetings, but, openly and boldly marching forth in the light of day, strive to bring to a head what they have long been planning—the overthrow of all civil society whatsoever."

This was a damning indictment of the writings of Marx and Engels and friends. Leo XIII did not bother naming them, but there was no question to which forces he was referring. Just how destructive were they? "They leave nothing untouched or whole which by both human and divine laws has been wisely decreed for the health and beauty of life," stated the encyclical. "They refuse obedience to the higher powers, to whom, according to the admonition of the Apostle [Paul], every soul ought to be subject, and who derive the right of governing from God."

Among the beauties of life they foul up, said the Church, are marriage and the family, as the encyclical underscored in the next sentence: "They debase the natural union of man and woman, which is held sacred even among barbarous peoples; and its bond, by which the family is chiefly held together, they weaken, or even deliver up to lust."

The encyclical continued:

> Even family life itself, which is the cornerstone of all society and government, necessarily feels and experiences the salutary power of the Church, which redounds to the right ordering and preservation of every State and kingdom. For you know, venerable brethren, that the foundation of this society rests first of all in the indissoluble union of man and wife according to the necessity of natural law, and is completed in the mutual rights and duties of parents and children, masters and servants. You know also that the doctrines of socialism strive almost completely to dissolve this union; since, that stability which is imparted to it by religious wedlock being lost, it follows that the power of the father over his own children, and the duties of the children toward their parents, must be greatly weakened. But the Church, on the contrary, teaches that "marriage, honorable in all," which God himself instituted in the very beginning of the world, and made indissoluble for the propagation and preservation of the human species, has become still more binding and more holy through Christ, who raised it to the dignity of a sacrament, and chose to use it as the figure of His own union with the Church.

The Church defended "parental and domestic authority" in teaching children over the authority of the state. That was how God had ordained it: "the authority of our heavenly Father and Lord is imparted to parents and masters, whose authority, therefore, not only takes its origin and force from Him, but also borrows its nature and character." According to the Church, the extreme left, these socialists and communists and nihilists spread throughout the world and bound in this wicked confederacy, threatened these precious things.

Is it any wonder these groups so despised and demonized the Catholic Church and so viciously targeted and smeared and persecuted its officials?

And yet, the Catholic Church was just warming up. More anticommunist pronouncements followed from the Magisterium, in 1924, 1928, 1930—particularly Pope Pius XI's February 1930 *The Soviet Campaign Against God*, the major portion of which dealt with prayers for Russia—then another statement in 1931, two in 1932, and another in 1933, with the harshest still yet to come.[9] In March 1937, Pope Pius XI issued the Church's most scathing and incisive attack on communist ideology, *Divini Redemptoris*, precisely as Joseph Stalin was ramping up his killing machine. The encyclical accurately stated that the Church had called public attention to the perils of communism "more frequently and more effectively"—and more timely, it might have added—than "any other public authority on earth." It was about to go even further.

Grounding its analysis in Augustine, Aquinas, and other Church fathers, in faith and reason, in revelation, and on a rich tradition of Church critiques of communism in numerous previous encyclicals, *Divini Redemptoris* described communism as nothing short of a "satanic scourge." It was not only "godless" and "by its nature anti-religious," but also a form of "perversity" and "trickery" and "poison" and "fury" that was "intrinsically wrong." Communism was "violent, deceptive," an "extreme danger," a "deluge which threatens the world," a "collectivistic terrorism . . . replete with hate," and a "plague" that leads to "ruin" and "catastrophe." This diabolical scourge "conceals in itself a false messianic idea." It was a false faith rooted in a form of "class-warfare which causes rivers of blood to flow," a "savage barbarity" that "has not confined itself to the indiscriminate slaughter of bishops" and the destruction of churches and monasteries. The Marxists were "the powers of darkness," orchestrating a battle against "the very idea of Divinity."

"The evil we must combat," said the Church in maybe the strongest denunciation in the entire encyclical, "is at its origin primarily an evil of the spiritual order. From this polluted source the monstrous emanations of the communistic system flow with satanic logic."

The powerful encyclical has been remembered for its influence and unbridled refutation of communism generally speaking, but largely forgotten were sections 10 and 11 of the encyclical, which took specific aim at communism's attack on marriage and the family, and particularly motherhood and education.

"Communism," said the encyclical, "strips man of his liberty, robs human personality of all its dignity, and removes all the moral restraints that check the eruptions of blind impulse. . . . No natural right is accorded to human personality, which is a mere cog-wheel in the Communist system. In man's relations with other individuals, besides, Communists hold the principle of absolute equality, rejecting all hierarchy and divinely-constituted authority, including the authority of parents."

This was indeed precisely the core of the problem with communists, socialists, and assorted radicals. Their views on marriage and the family were entirely of their own doing, answering to no one or no thing, and certainly no divine or church authority, no Bible or book, no Protestant denomination, no Catholic Church Magisterium, no bishop or cardinal or pope or pastor. In the end, the statements that undergirded their declarations were really just their own self-made and self-based opinions. Who or what was to settle who was exactly right in their ongoing conceptions of marriage and family? Who or what was the ultimate arbiter? The only answer that these far-left elements had was that the arbiter would not be God or any earthly religious body.

Really, communists were their own gods. Whittaker Chambers noted precisely this, as would President Ronald Reagan years later in his "Evil Empire" speech, where Reagan quoted Chambers on the point. Chambers declared that Marxism-Leninism is actually the world's second oldest faith, first proclaimed in the garden of Eden with the words of temptation, "Ye shall be as gods."[10]

Divini Redemptoris continued its refutation of this false messiah,[11] saying of communist man: "What men call authority and subordination is derived from the community as its first and only font. Nor is the individual granted any property rights over material goods or the means of production, for inasmuch as these are the source of further wealth, their possession would give one man power over another. Precisely on this score, all forms of private property must be eradicated, for they are at the origin of all economic enslavement." This thinking was directed at communist reformulation of family and married life. In the next passage, the encyclical again struck at the core of the problem:

> Refusing to human life any sacred or spiritual character, such a doctrine logically makes of marriage and the family a purely artificial and civil institution, the outcome of a specific economic system. There exists no matrimonial bond of a juridico-moral nature that is not subject to the whim of the individual or of the collectivity. Naturally, therefore, the notion of an indissoluble marriage-tie is scouted. Communism is particularly characterized by the rejection of any link that binds woman to the family and the home, and her emancipation is proclaimed as a basic principle. She is withdrawn from the family and the care of her children, to be thrust instead into public life and collective production under the same conditions as man. The care of home and children then devolves upon the collectivity. Finally, the right of education is denied to parents, for it is conceived as the exclusive prerogative of the community, in whose name and by whose mandate alone parents may exercise this right.

This was spot-on in its analysis, unfailingly correct in each of its points. A well-read communist would agree that the Church had its facts in order, disagreeing only on the encyclical's condemnation of these ideas. In the communist world, who or what would determine the family and marriage? *Divini Redemptoris* had it right then, and (for the record) has it right still today in modern America and the West, where the state and society think they know best. Today in America, modern men and women are remolding marriage and family in whatever image they prefer, disregarding the authority or even input of a religious or church authority, refusing any sacred or spiritual character.

Finally, equally notably is the closing reference to the family in section 28 of *Divini Redemptoris*: "Just as matrimony and the right to its natural use are of divine origin, so likewise are the constitution and fundamental prerogatives of the family fixed and determined by the Creator. In the Encyclical on Christian Marriage and in Our other Encyclical on Education,[12] cited above, we have treated these topics at considerable length."

Here we have an even older affirmation of family and marriage by the Catholic Church, one that long predates the aberration that is communism. Here, in addition to a further affirmation of family-led education, was a recognition of marriage as "matrimony" between man and woman, divinely ordained by the Creator. This was both "fundamental" and "fixed."

Thus, contained within this 1937 document was not only a condemnation of communism's attack on the family in 1937 but, applied many decades henceforth, condemnation of the left's attack on family through same-sex "marriage" today, which violates the Creator's *fixed* and *fundamental* prerogative.

Today's liberals/progressives, like their leftist forebears, have taken it upon themselves to reinvent our very order in their own image: *Ye shall be as gods.*[13]

9

THE VOICE OF SHEEN

THE UNIVERSAL ROMAN CATHOLIC CHURCH WAS far and away the dominant international voice of opposition to the communist movement and its tumultuous machinations. No single group of spokesmen was as influential, and I have not addressed supernatural elements, such as the warnings against communism's many "errors" and persecutions by Our Lady of Fatima, an extraordinary voice that was formally approved by Rome as literally miraculous in its outreach.

But not to be neglected was the significant role of the American church generally, both Catholic and Protestant. A list of those players would be long, from the likes of Dr. Fred Schwarz and his Christian Anti-Communist Crusade,[1] which attracted the likes of a young Hollywood actor named Ronald Reagan, to the Reverend Richard Wurmbrand, the tortured Romanian pastor who wrote the shocking international best seller *Tortured for Christ*; the Reverend Billy Graham;[2] and (among Catholics) well-known Church officials such as Cardinal Francis Spellman of New York and Archbishop Fulton J. Sheen, as well as laypersons as diverse as James Burnham, Clare Boothe Luce, and William F. Buckley Jr.

Among them, few were as widely listened to, read, and watched in the critical period of the 1930s through the 1950s as Fulton Sheen.

Sheen (1895–1979) attracted untold millions of Americans on radio (during its heyday) and then television (at its zenith). He became one of the most recognized faces in America—a household name. This was especially true with the advent of his TV show, *Life Is Worth Living*, which began in February 1952, coming on the heels of Sheen's immensely popular *Catholic Hour* radio broadcasts that started in 1928, and on top of his innumerable newspaper columns, speeches, and books. The TV shows were sophisticated, integrating philosophy, psychology, and various other disciplines. One today marvels that network television (NBC) was willing to run such a cerebral and unapologetically and overtly religious primetime program. The brilliant bishop never talked down to his audience and spoke without notes or teleprompter.

Life Is Worth Living was given a Tuesday night spot against Milton Berle on one channel and Frank Sinatra on the other: known in the industry as an "obituary spot." Sheen knocked them out. By April 1952, the priest from Peoria was on the cover of *Time* magazine. He won the 1952 Emmy Award for "Most Outstanding Television Personality," beating out Jimmy Durante, Edward R. Murrow, Lucille Ball, and Arthur Godfrey. (In his acceptance remarks, he said, "I wish to thank my four writers: Matthew, Mark, Luke, and John.") A nationwide poll of radio and television editors named him TV's "Man of the Year." Vice President Nixon thanked him for his "outstanding contributions to a better understanding of the American way of life." President Eisenhower invited him to the White House.[3]

This is a short list in a long line of accolades. A poll taken at the end of the twentieth century by the Internet's *Catholic Daily*, with 23,455 respondents, listed the top four Catholics of the century as Pope John Paul II, Mother Teresa, Padre Pio, and Sheen. *The Catholic Almanac* for the year 2000 rightly described Sheen as "perhaps the most popular and socially influential American Catholic of the twentieth century."[4]

A snapshot of Sheen's most significant period opposing communism is the late 1940s. This could be a long and detailed snapshot, but for the purposes of this book, consider just two Sheen anticommunist works that bear on our marriage-family focus. In 1948 and 1949 (respectively), Sheen published two best sellers, *Communism and the Conscience of the West* and *Peace of Soul.*

Published by Bobbs-Merrill, *Communism and the Conscience of the West* is now out of print, and accessible chiefly through libraries. It ought to be required reading for anyone studying the Cold War, Soviet history, communism, and even the twentieth century. It is a profound work that demonstrated the staggering breadth of Sheen's integration of various disciplines: theology, philosophy, politics, science, history, literature. He cited scholar after scholar, discussed competing theory after competing theory, and clarified term after term, while remaining eminently readable. One would never know that the book was written for public consumption, and that the public consumed it. The endnotes were reflective not of a TV preacher but of an exhaustive academic. Many notes took up full pages; one particular endnote carried a forty-work, three-page bibliography on the subject of "fallacies of communism in the philosophical order." Among his sources, because Sheen was fluent in multiple languages, he incorporated significant works on Marx and communism that were never translated into English.

Communism and the Conscience of the West relied on Marx and Lenin in making Sheen's point: "The truth on the subject is that communism and atheism are intrinsically related and that one cannot be a good Communist without being an atheist and every atheist is a potential Communist." He quoted Marx himself, from an original French edition that Sheen translated: "Communism begins where atheism begins." Sheen dedicated the book to Russia's conversion, and advised that Christians pray daily for Russia: "It is not Christian to wish for the extinction of Communists, though it is most Christian to pray for the evaporation of communism." He distinguished between ordinary Russians and the horrific system of apparatchiks that enslaved them, greatly respecting Russia's culture and rich religious heritage.

In *Communism and the Conscience of the West*, Sheen cleverly turned Marxist phrases on their heads. He showed how *communism*, rather than religion, was an opiate of the masses. He laid out the religious-like nature of Soviet communism, the "preaching" of Lenin, the "apostles of Marx," and the manner in which Stalin was treated like a god.

Sheen paused to emphasize that the Church played an unwavering role in confronting atheistic communism. "The Catholic Church is sometimes praised for its opposition to communism," wrote Sheen. "This compliment is deserved, for the Church is the only solid moral force in the world that has been consistently opposed to the new barbarism."

This was a point that no less than Whittaker Chambers (not a Catholic) would make after his conversion out of communism. "No matter what critics might say," wrote Chambers, "it is scarcely deniable that the Church Apostolic, through the encyclicals and other papal pronouncements, has been fighting against totalitarianism more knowingly, devoutly and authoritatively, and for a longer time, than any other organized power."[5] Chambers typed those words five years earlier in a remarkable August 1943 cover feature on Pope Pius XII for *Time* magazine, five years before Chambers himself would become a household name in his gripping showdown with Alger Hiss. Chambers was impressed with the consistency of both the Church and its pope, and surely also with Sheen (who met with Pius II to discuss communism), whose face and voice were simply unavoidable in the America of the 1940s.

Sheen's *Communism and the Conscience of the West* is one of the single most sophisticated dissections of communism. Sheen responded to Marx and Engels without straw man arguments, dealing with them on their own terms. While most who study Marx's motivations look to Hegel, Sheen looked also at the neglected influence of German philosopher Ludwig Feuerbach, which is essential to understanding Marx's unbelief.

All along, Sheen's wit, master of the metaphor, and unique parallels shined through. For example, he pleaded that people not be deterred from the cross because of personal suffering: "Christianity," wrote Sheen, "comes to optimism through pessimism; to a resurrection through a passion, and to a crown of glory through a crown of thorns; to the glory of

Easter Sunday through the ignominy of a Good Friday." Tying that to the suffering wrought by Soviet communism, Sheen advised that the Russian people—for whom, he rightly said, "atheism is not natural"— take heart that Christ's tomb is empty, while Lenin's tomb is not.

But most relevant to this book here was chapter 7 of *Communism and the Conscience of the West*, which carefully exposed the attitude toward family and marriage by communism and Soviet Russia. This chapter must have been a wake-up call to the huge numbers of Sheen followers. The entire chapter merits a close reading, but here are a few highlights:

"Communism in its philosophy and its early practice was so anti-moral and antihuman," began Sheen in his opening to the chapter, "that it was necessarily opposed to the family as the unit of society." Sheen went straight to the words of Marx and Engels and Alexandra Kollontai. Citing Engels's *The Origin of the Family*, he quoted this passage from Marx's partner: "Only a union based on love is moral; hence the union should last only as long as love lasts. When love ceases to exist, or when it is succeeded by a new passion, divorce becomes a benefit."[6]

That teaching of Engels, which is really an *attitude* above all else, succinctly describes Margaret Sanger's view of her marriage to William Sanger and when and why she felt the need to cease their union. Here, too, in Engels's words we see a rejection of marriage as having a lifelong, sacred, 'til-death-do-us-part component. Engels's pronouncement stood contrary to the Western/Christian understanding of marriage. It can really only exist and flourish in a post-religious culture and nation that rejects Christian conceptions in devising new definitions of marriage— as Americans are doing today.

Sheen next unveiled the Bolshevik state's policies and laws enacted against marriage and the family. He cited the Matrimonial Codes of 1918 and 1927, which affirmed that "all children belong to the state," as opposed to the mother and father. He pointed to the Soviet state's family code of October 22, 1918, almost one year to the date after the launch of the revolution. It ordained that all church marriages were thereby invalid, and therefore could be freely dissolved by the will of either party. The process for this was amazingly simple, one of the easiest things to do in an otherwise immensely bureaucratic communist state: the spouse who wished to terminate the marriage for whatever reason merely needed to send a postcard to the local registration office, which, in turn, sent a new postcard formally dissolving the union. Divorce became a breeze, with no pesky church obstacles. The Soviet state's attitude was captured in the Thirteenth Congress of the Communist Party of the Soviet Union, which decried the family as a "formidable stronghold of all the turpitudes of the old regime."[7]

A key word in that phrase is *formidable*. Being so formidable, the family, like the church, was subjected to special and fierce persecution by Soviet communists. Its dissection and annihilation required concentrated attention.

Core to the family's liberation from its reactionary "turpitudes" was the liberation of the wife and mother. Sheen listed another early Bolshevik decree that declared all women ages seventeen to thirty-two to be likewise deemed "property of the State," with the "rights of husbands" to consider them their wives "abolished." Whether these married women considered themselves married was entirely up to them and their continuation. The husbands' right to object to their spouses' termination of marriage was "abolished."[8]

Sheen quoted a Soviet statement from 1935 that equated "women's labor" (a vaunted concept) not with housework but strictly with factory work. The Bolshevik regime boasted that during Stalin's first of his hideous five-year plans, there had been an estimated six million housewives in nearby Moscow towns. In an almost militaristic sense, these women were considered "reserves" for factory production in the revolution. Said the statement: "All the local Communist organizations received orders to call up the reserves and attach them to production."[9]

Many on the political left to this day saw this as "progressive" and a form of "women's liberation." (A recent high school civics text used in American public schools states that under the Bolsheviks, "legally speaking, Russian women were better off than women anywhere in the world."[10]) It may have been "progressive," by the left's employment of the term, but it most certainly was not liberation. What is compulsory is not freedom. Countless scores of these women did not desire leaving their homes to work in sewers and mines. Sheen listed data reporting that an estimated 23 percent of Russian coal miners by the 1940s were women. Worse, these women were assigned to their positions and expected to unquestioningly and happily accept them as good communists. The communist state, which was the sole employer, often assigned the wife to work in one town and the husband in another, further straining the marriage bond and the family—with children housed in full-time nursery facilities. If the strain on the marriage became too hard, noted Sheen, the Soviet Labor Board decreed that either spouse could find a new partner in the new place of occupation. And why not? Marriage was to be transcended by the new faith: the communist utopia that would usher in a new form of happiness altogether.[11]

And if the strain on children—and especially would-be children—seemed too hard, the Soviet state took care of that inconvenience as well: it opened abortion clinics throughout the country.

Sheen detailed that disaster as well. Citing data consistent with my own longtime research on this subject, he reported that in Moscow in 1934 there had been 154,000 abortions versus 57,000 births—as noted earlier, a stunning ratio of nearly three to one. In surrounding villages that year, there were 324,194 abortions versus 242,979 births. Likewise, by the mid-1930s, there were 44 percent more divorces than registered marriages in Moscow, a number that by the 1970s would skyrocket to levels unprecedented in the history of humanity.[12] The communists had set out to "abolish" marriage and the family, and by golly, they were doing it in spades.

Sheen could not begin to imagine in 1948 just how bad it would get in Russia, especially the abortion travesty. Quite the contrary, he had good reason to be optimistic. As Sheen noted, these new communist family policies quickly became so deadly that Joseph Stalin, one of history's greatest mass murderers, was forced to ban abortion (and seek to prohibit divorces) or risk a massive reduction in his population, which would be catastrophic not only to communist production levels but also to any invasion by the likes of Hitler and his Nazis. Sheen chronicled the actions that Stalin took to reverse and even stop abortions in the country as well as to curtail the runaway divorce rate, with the Soviet government going so far as to manufacture wedding rings, in addition to imposing hefty fines for divorce. In an almost hilarious irony, the Soviet Commission of Jurists and Sociologists in April 1936 found itself essentially invoking natural law on behalf of motherhood: "The Soviet woman is the equal of man, but she is not dispensed from the great duty which nature has conferred about her, namely, that of motherhood; her health is double precious, first as a human being, and then as a mother." It added: "Abortion is inadmissible."[13]

The Roman Catholic Church itself could have written that one. As Bishop Sheen noted, with full appreciation of the irony, "Thus Russia, after 20 years of communism in practice, rejects its entire Communist philosophy of the family, and without it even intending to do so, proves that when we fail to obey God's laws, expressed in rational nature, we defeat ourselves, just as the man who uses a pencil to open a can, not only does not open the can but even destroys the pencil." He grimaced that those women Lenin ordered "to leave the hearth and the home for the mines and monkey wrench" are now told to reconsider. Those who glorified "free love" were thinking again. Communists, averred Sheen, were essentially reaffirming the family as the unit of society.

Yes, they were, but not for long, as the bonds to godless communism proved more enduring than God-centered natural law. After Stalin's death in March 1953, many of the dictator's welcomed changes on marriage, the family, and even religion (where Stalin eased up the persecution during the perilous war years) were reversed by Nikita Khrushchev and his successor Leonid Brezhnev.

In 1955 Stalin's successor, Nikita Khrushchev, reconstituted legalized abortion. By 1958 there were 5 million abortions per year in the Soviet Union. (This contradicted Margaret Sanger's optimistic prediction that "neither abortions nor contraception will be necessary or desired" once a "functioning communistic society" was in full bloom in the USSR.) By 1965, abortions peaked at 8.2 million, dwarfing the worst years in America post–*Roe v. Wade*. By 1970, some three thousand full-time abortion doctors were performing roughly 7.2 million abortions per year. By the 1980s, Soviet citizens comprised 5 to 6 percent of the world's population but 25 percent of the world's abortions.

The Cold War and communism ended in Russia in the 1990s, but the runaway abortion rates did not. An illuminating article in the *Washington Post* in February 2003 reported that 13 percent of Russian couples were infertile, with more on the rise. "In nearly three out of four cases," said the article, "infertility is attributed to the woman, typically because of complications from one or more abortions." The Russian Health Ministry reported 1.7 abortions for every live birth,[14] which was actually an improvement from previous decades, but only because contraception was being more widely used. Either way, it added up to a decline in population.

Sheen did not foresee this resurgence in 1948, though had he known that genuine Soviet communists would retreat to genuine Soviet communism, he could have predicted the dire consequences.

In short Fulton Sheen's 1948 book revealed the calamitous effect that communist ideology was having on marriage and the human family. He followed *Communism and the Conscience of the West* with an equally interesting book, *Peace of Soul*, published in 1949 by McGraw-Hill. The book likewise had a major impact. Notably, William P. Clark, who would become President Ronald Reagan's most crucial adviser in the takedown of the Soviet Union in the 1980s, would call *Peace of Soul* one of the two books that most influenced his discernment of the priesthood and his ultimate decision to fight communism and defeat the USSR.[15]

Sheen wrote *Peace of Soul* at a time when Marxism, psychoanalysis, and Freudian sexual psychobabble were a prevailing part of the culture. He focused not on a "peace of mind" that psychoanalysis promised but could not deliver, nor a Marxist utopia that communists tried to conjure up, but a "peace of soul" that only faith could bring. "Unless souls are saved," said Sheen, "nothing is saved; there can be no world peace unless there is soul peace."

But especially interesting from *Peace of Soul*, and a crucial segue to the next section of this book and the next critical manifestation of

Marxism in its takedown of marriage and family, is what Sheen wrote in just a few pages about Marxism and Freudianism, which I will note here only briefly.

Sheen shuddered at the impact of Marx and Freud on the modern mind. He noted that neither man would have dared written or even had an audience in earlier times, especially in, say, the Elizabethan era. Only by the mid-twentieth century was the climate of the world favorable to entertaining their snake-oil solutions. There had to be a proper "materialist preparation"—and corresponding spiritual separation—for their individualistic ideas on god and man. For Freud especially, there had to be a "cult of sex" and "sex deification" connected to the loss of belief in God, just as Marx's ideas required a parting from belief in God.[16]

Sheen saw that an age of "carnal license" would be an age of political anarchy and revolution just as Marxism was, with the family left on the ash heap of history. "The foundations of social life are shaken at the very moment when the foundations of family life are destroyed," wrote Sheen. "The rebellion of the masses against social order, which Marx advocated, is matched by the rebellion of the libido and the animal instincts, which the sexists [i.e., Freud] advocate within the individual."[17] Both systems, said Sheen, deny responsibility; they do so "either because history is believed to be economically determined or because man is called biologically determined." What they agree upon is that man is not spiritual determined.

Both Freudianism and Marxism elevated the material above the spiritual, with the focus on (respectively) sex and economics, to the negation of man as a religious being.

Fulton Sheen was onto something. Though he gave no indication of any awareness in *Peace of Soul*, just down the street from his New York television studio was a ruinous institution called Columbia University, where the leftist professoriat were devouring the ideas of Freud and Marx, and where some of their colleagues were concocting a noxious fusion of these two adverse ideologies. They were opening up a whole new Marxist door, one with major inroads into the culture, and with further major fissures in store for marriage and the family.

10

CULTURAL MARXISM AND
THE FRANKFURT SCHOOL

IN HIS WRITINGS ON COMMUNISM AND sexuality, Fulton Sheen obviously never broached the unthinkable historical-cultural absurdity of same-sex "marriage," which both he and his communist opponents (especially in Russia) would have seen as beyond bizarre. In retrospect, perhaps the most sardonically prophetic of Marxist assessments on marriage was Aleksandra Kollontai's 1920 statement that "old habits and customs" were "dying out" and "developing in a way that is new and unfamiliar and, in the eyes of some, 'bizarre.'" And yet, Kollontai and crew helped pave the way by advancing designs for marriage, family, and sexuality that were completely relativistic, untied to any absolute, set authority. Once a fixed arbiter is rejected and removed, anything and everything becomes possible. As Dostoyevsky put it, "If God does not exist, everything is permissible."[1]

Sheen, who often quoted Dostoyevsky's prophetic warnings on communism, would have understood that particularly well.[2]

In practice, however, not quite everything was permissible at this point in time, especially for homosexuals in Russia, a country that to this day is not welcoming of homosexual behavior. In the 1930s, well-traveled American "progressives" like millionaire pro-Marxist Corliss Lamont, basking in boatloads of inherited money from his Wall Street father, would sail to Moscow and take satisfaction in the fact that Stalin and the Bolsheviks were rooting out the slightest traces of so-called cultural cancers such as prostitution and "homosexualism."[3] In 1934, the Stalin regime went so far as to make homosexuality a criminal offense.[4] The idea of homosexuals marrying or adopting children into a legal "family" in Stalin's Soviet Union or in America or anywhere in the world in this period was wholly unthinkable.

But that is where secular progressivism needed to enter the historical big picture and begin slowly doing its evolutionary work. Again, progressives believe that things are always in a state of flux. An ongoing and unending and unceasing process of *forward* "change" is the only absolute that progressives really agree on. These changes are societal, cultural, political—whatever it takes to move the always-advancing and ever-morphing *progressive* agenda. The changes are also sexual and, thus, intimately involve human relations and the human family. These changes became even more elastic as modern progressives/liberals heartily embraced not only the sexual revolution but secularism. Unthinkables like "gay marriage" simply needed time to germinate in the progressive petri dish, to grow in their secular evolutionary path.

Still, that kind of really perverse sexual-cultural anarchy was far away, even as a rushing confluence of leftists was coalescing, helping enable a larger takedown of traditional morality, marriage, and the family.

Sticking with my focus here on communist influences, I will highlight a potent Marxist ingredient that was being distilled in the 1920s, 1930s, and 1940s and would intoxicate the 1960s' left and university community, and in turn arguably impact today's runaway sexual ethics more than any previous assortment of Marxist thinkers.

Among the various factions arising from the embers of Marxist-Leninist theory, particularly notable to the realm of sexual-cultural thinking was the Frankfurt School. The Frankfurt School protégés were neo-Marxists, a new kind of twentieth-century communist less interested in the economic/class-redistribution ideas of Marx than a remaking of society through the eradication of traditional norms and institutions. They brought to Marxist theory not a passion for, say, more equitable tax policy or reallocation of private property, but, rather, tenets of psychology, sociology, and even Freudian teaching on sexuality. They would not have surprised Fulton Sheen at all, though they would have certainly alarmed him.

This group, wrote Martin Jay in his history of the Frankfurt School, "focused its energies on what traditional Marxists had relegated to a secondary position, the cultural superstructure of modern society." This meant concentrating on the "emergence and proliferation of mass culture." But to do this, noted Jay, "a gap in the classical Marxist mold of substructure and superstructure had to be filled. The missing link was psychological, and the theory the [Frankfurt School] chose to supply it with was Freud's."[5]

Several of these men pioneered a Freudian Marxism, or "Freudo-Marxism," integrating the extraordinarily influential twentieth-century ideas of Sigmund Freud with the extraordinarily influential nineteenth-century teachings of Karl Marx. It most assuredly was not a match devised in heaven. Marx had conjured up the most noxious ideas of the nineteenth century, whereas Freud had cooked up the most neurotic ideas of the twentieth century; bringing the two together under one madcap communist roof was bound to produce an explosion of disastrous proportions. The Frankfurt School thus concocted a toxic ideological brew that would be devoured by a thirsty 1960s sexual-liberation culture that drank deep from this new extremism, overflowing with prospects for fundamental transformation of the culture, country, and world. Though the Frankfurt School was certainly not issuing joint statements calling for same-sex marriage—again, such would have been considered pure madness in any day beyond our own—its comprehensive push for untethered, unhinged sexual openness with no cultural boundaries or religious restrictions flung wide the door for almost anything down the road.

For the neo-Marxists, orthodox Marxism was old and limiting, too narrow, too restrictive, too wedded to the tight control of the Comintern and its ironclad party discipline that strong-armed national communist parties. This rigidity prevented these more freewheeling neo-Marxists from initiating the rampant transformation they craved. This included trenchant changes in sexuality, marriage, and family. Above all, these Frankfurt leaders were left-wing/atheistic academics and intellectuals who looked to the universities as the home base to instill their ideas.

That in itself was a very communist way of thinking; it was certainly Leninist. Vladimir Lenin often remarked on how controlling education was essential to the communist left's victory. "Give me four years to teach the children," he pleaded in an oft-cited quote, "and the seed I have sown will never be uprooted."[6] Lenin nailed the exact amount of time that his American comrades would need in their universities. The Frankfurt men were ready to sow.

There were many key figures from the Frankfurt School: Georg Lukács, Herbert Marcuse, Wilhelm Reich, Max Horkheimer, Erich Fromm, Theodor Adorno, and others. (Predating the most active period of the Frankfurt School was the Italian Marxist Antonio Gramsci, who was especially influential in adapting Marxism to a cultural perspective, judging that the only surefire way to institute the necessary change was a long and patient march through cultural and elite institutions.) These men and their work lit up the left, the academic world, and (ultimately) our culture in many unappreciated ways. To some degree, even a measure of the angry left's proclivity for nasty name-calling—particularly its freshman infatuation with deriding those who disagree with them as "fascists"—can be linked to work of this school. For instance, Theodor Adorno was the lead author of the very influential 1950 work *The Authoritarian Personality*, which devised an "F-scale" that purported to measure degrees of "fascism." That tag just happened to best apply to conservatives, whom the left has long happily and sloppily dehumanized as "fascists." As Jonah Goldberg wrote in his best-selling book, *Liberal Fascism*, Adorno's work presented "evidence" that "people holding 'conservative' views scored higher on the so-called F-Scale (*F* for 'Fascism') and were hence in dire need of therapy."[7]

I personally learned about Adorno's scale in literally the first course I took in graduate school (it may have been the first day of class), taught by a Cal–Berkeley graduate. I was learning about it in the 1990s. Students in the 1960s were learning about it way back then, equipping themselves with sociological *research* to authoritatively label their conservative opponents with a vicious ideological tag theretofore most associated with Nazis (another epithet they slung at opponents). As Goldberg noted, "whenever the left has met with political defeat, it has cried, 'Fascism!'"[8]

That too often has been the case.

Goldberg added the pivotal partnership of Max Horkheimer with Adorno. Generally, Horkheimer was less an intellectual contributor to the Frankfurt School than its chief manager, fund-raiser, publicist, promoter, and liaison to the Soviet Comintern—though he did his share of writing.[9] Horkheimer would loop the family into his and Adorno's crass research claims. Thus, Goldberg rightly saw a link between Horkheimer's claims and the modern left's visceral denouncing of certain traditional family values as "fascist," or at least as highly objectionable. "The idea that 'family values' are philosophically linked to fascism actually has a long pedigree, going back, again, to the Frankfurt School," wrote Goldberg, pointing to Horkheimer's work in particular.[10]

Ralph de Toledano was particularly appalled by the F-scale smear. He wrote of this line of research: "If an individual had been an unprotesting part of a traditional family or had religious convictions, this was proof positive that whatever his life had been he had an 'authoritarian personality' and was prone to the appeal of fascism." This stood in contrast to the more open-minded and better-minded "revolutionary personality" of the anti-religious left.[11]

The work of Adorno and Horkheimer was just some of countless culturally destructive products penned by the faculty of the Frankfurt School.

So, what was this school? When and where and how did it start?

The school began in 1923–24 as the Institute for Social Research at the University of Frankfurt (also sometimes called Goethe University) in Frankfurt, Germany.[12] Fully revisiting all of that history would be too much for here, but a summation of Lukács, the school's founder;

of Wilhelm Reich, another of its popular theorists; and of Marcuse, its most instrumental Marxist, is worthy of our purposes.

Lukács was one of the original handful who were present at the Marx-Engels Institute in Moscow in 1922, along with Karl Radek, a high-level Bolshevik leader and Lenin representative; Felix Dzerzhinsky, head of the Cheka, later known as the NKVD and KGB; and Willi Münzenberg, the crafty Comintern organizer.[13] The prominent roles of these men in the international Marxist movement cannot be overstated. Probably the least known to modern eyes and ears is Münzenberg, a top German communist known in his day as the "Henry Ford of the Communist International" because of his unmatched organizational and logistical capabilities. It is a sign of Münzenberg's success that he was the first name listed on page 1 of the US Congress's seminal 1961 product, *Guide to Subversive Organizations and Publications*, where he was quoted for his frank admission of seeking "to arouse the interest" of the "apathetic and indifferent . . . who have no ear for Communist propaganda." "These people," conceded Münzenberg, "we wish to attract and arouse through new channels, by means of new ways." He and the Comintern sought out "sympathetic" organizations and individuals who would not join the Communist Party but who "are prepared to follow us part of the way."[14]

Lukács agreed wholeheartedly with that strategy. He had been one of the spearheads of the critical though failed Hungarian communist revolution of Béla Kun after World War I, holding the position of cultural commissar. The Bolsheviks had taken power in Russia in October 1917, had established the Comintern in March 1919, and then started the Marx-Engels Institute toward the end of 1920.[15] It was at the Marx-Engels Institute in Moscow in 1922 that this cadre conceived the Institute for Social Research.[16]

One historian/newsman (he preferred "newsman" to "journalist") who documented the import of this meeting better than anyone is the late Ralph de Toledano (1916–2007), who studied the Frankfurt School and its associated Columbia comrades as well as any single outside observer. His prodigious research and knowledge of the subject will be cited a number of times in this book (as it has been already). That being the case, a few quick biographical words on Toledano:

Ralph de Toledano became a fairly prominent conservative intellectual, one of the original founding editors of *National Review*, along with William F. Buckley Jr. But he had not always been a conservative, or a Republican. He began his political life as a student at Columbia University in the 1930s, where he was a popular editor of the *Jester*, the leading campus humor magazine, and would later be described by the *New York Times* as "one of a brilliant group of students at Columbia" at the time.[17] Included in that group was Thomas Merton, who was a fellow editor with Toledano at the *Jester* and who was initially hoodwinked by the communists, but would firmly break from the atheistic ideology and became a famous Trappist monk and Catholic spiritual writer. Toledano was not taken by Marxism, but was a socialist at Columbia. His anti-communism would increase with what he witnessed at Columbia (as did Merton's) and, worse, with the terrible communist penetration he saw firsthand at the Office of Strategic Services in World War II, where communists and duped leftists would work to undermine the likes of Toledano for being too anti-communist and too anti-Soviet.

A respected commentator who spent decades chronicling the communist and anti-communist causes and intimately knowing the characters and combatants, Toledano worked closely with figures ranging from Whittaker Chambers to Richard Nixon. He authored countless articles and more than twenty books on subjects from Robert F. Kennedy and Barry Goldwater and J. Edgar Hoover to his popular *Spies, Dupes, and Diplomats*. He and Chambers carried on a longtime correspondence, which Toledano shared in his valuable book *Notes from the Underground: The Chambers-Toledano Letters*. In 2006, nearing the end of his long life, Toledano barely published a swan song, *Cry Havoc! The Great American Bring-down and How It Happened*, a riveting, tragic lament at what happened to his country.

In that book, Toledano, more than any writer who lived beyond the period, took great care to detail the deleterious effect of the Frankfurt School. Few newsmen personally knew so many of the perpetrators and victims, and the collateral damage on the eve of the twenty-first century, with the full repercussions still to come. Toledano charted the cultural tornado that the Frankfurt School unraveled upon society, especially through its adherents at American universities, but also in the media, Hollywood, publishing, the theater, the arts, and whatever other cultural conveyor belt was at its disposal.[18] These Freudian-Marxists, he wrote, realized that sex could be a devastating instrument if permitted to run rampant, "and so they advocated the elimination of all sexual restraints along with the destruction of the family, religion, and 'bourgeois' morality. . . . All the guidelines that society had laid down to make sexuality an orderly part of existence were condemned as horrendous capitalist depravity." Their so-called "Critical Theory" would spout everything and anything from "compulsory promiscuity" (Toledano's apt description) to one-parent families, premarital sexual activity, and also homosexuality, "since it struck at the family and child-bearing."[19] Marxist-communist fundamental transformation of society would ultimately come not through economic changes—which were dismally failing to produce their goals and win converts—but through vast cultural-sexual changes directly relating to family and married life.

That was all yet to come.

Toledano began with the 1922 confab at Moscow's Marx-Engels Institute, ordered by Lenin and ultimately "disastrous to Western civilization and culture."[20] He identified Lukács specifically (but not alone) as starting the snowball that would roll over the family in particular.[21]

Born April 13, 1885, Lukács came from polished stock. His mother belonged to one of the wealthiest Jewish families in Hungary, and his father was a self-made millionaire. Like many mansion Marxists who speak for the poor and oppressed masses, he was raised with a silver spoon and hated the world in which he lived. For Lukács, this included a red-hot hatred of gender roles, marriage, and family. "Woman," he sneered, "is the enemy. Healthy love dies in marriage, which is a business transaction. . . . The bourgeois family gives off swamp vapors."[22] It was a cynical Marxist view, for sure—carried into a new and volatile century, with Lukács the ladle.

For Lukács (as well as Münzenberg and others still), the key to undermining Western civilization was not the factory emancipation of the working classes that Marx and Engels fingered, but the culture. "Politics is only the means," he wrote, "culture is the goal." Lukács told Münzenberg, Dzerzhinsky, and Marxist revolutionary Karl Radek that the inability to sell economic Marxism to the world meant that a new means would be needed to bring down capitalism.[23] Class-based economic warfare would take a backseat to an assault on Western civilization. That was where the rupture had to take place. It would be a tall task.

A primary method, wrote Ralph de Toledano, would be to saturate Western culture with a "miasma of unrestrained sex." "The destruction of the West, from which a phoenix-like Marxist utopia would arise," stated Toledano, "was to be achieved by the combination of neo-Marxism, neo-Freudianism, Pavlovian psychology and mass brainwashing, wrapped up in what euphemistically became known as Critical Theory."[24]

The hard fact for these communists was that at the core of Western civilization was a pesky morality derived from the Old and New Testaments, from the traditional family, and from tradition itself, an embedded understanding that freedom was not the license to do anything a person wanted, and the realization that one's passions needed to be occasionally checked. To Lukács, these vital human realities that had served and undergirded Western civilization were repressive obstacles to the new society he and his comrades envisioned. "Of these obstacles," wrote Toledano, "the two greatest were God and the family. . . . The family was not only a receptacle of the continuity in values, but the cement which held society together—and Lukács hotly hated both God and the family."[25]

Lukács would have fully agreed with a later presidential assessment of the family by President Ronald Reagan, albeit with diametrically opposed intentions. Reagan countless times affirmed the vital importance of the family. He extolled the family as "the most basic unity of society," "the most important unit in society," "the most durable of all institutions," "the nucleus of civilization," and "the cornerstone of American society." And children, said Reagan, "belong in a family."[26]

It is in a family that children are not only cared for but, said Reagan, "taught the moral values and traditions that give order and stability to our lives and to society as a whole." It was "more important than ever" that America's families "affirm an older and more lasting set of values."[27] Reagan insisted that it is up to families to "preserve and pass on to each succeeding generation the values we share and cherish."[28] He stated that our "concept of the family" "must withstand the trends of lifestyle and legislation."[29]

Those last sentences merit close inspection: Families preserve and conserve the time-tested values worth preserving. They do this across continuing generations. They persevere against the often unhealthy onslaught of new fads and fashions and legislation.

Lukács would have said that Reagan was unerringly on target; such is indeed what the family has done. It passes on to its children, and its children's children, across generations, those time-tested values: the Old and New Testament, the understanding that freedom is not license, and the realization that one's passions (particularly sexual desires) require boundaries. Families teach these things; they instill faith, morality, virtue. Lukács agreed that families had always done this, and thus was convinced that family was loathsome. He and his Frankfurt-Marxist protégés, from Marcuse to Reich, especially loathed the latent sexual "repression" within this traditional family "construct."

Quite catastrophically, the ideas of these men began to emanate directly from American soil, as they left their Hungarian and German communist parties for the friendly confines of America's most left-wing universities—Columbia foremost among them. Many of these men were Jewish Marxists. Thus, in the 1930s, amid the threats of Hitler's Germany, they and their Institute fled Germany, including their beloved Berlin, which had served as a European Babylon in the interwar years.[30]

They were in desperate search of a home for their unwelcome political pathologies. But would any university accept them? Was there any sort of academic asylum fanatical enough to lay out the red carpet for fugitive freaks of Freudian Marxism? Yes, there was: Columbia University. With Max Horkheimer securing Rockefeller Foundation cash to grease the skids for the relocation, Columbia mavens John Dewey, George Counts, Robert MacIver, and Robert Lynd worked over the university's president, Nicholas Murray Butler, to make it happen.[31]

Pleading the case the hardest was Dewey. He was Columbia's academic celebrity, its pillar, its renowned educator-philosopher, founding father of American public education, who, at this point in his political life, was essentially a "small c" communist, objecting only (as he put it) to Communism "spelt with a capital letter" (meaning he was a communist by philosophy but not a formal Party member). At this point, too, Professor Dewey had fallen head over heels in love with Bolshevik Russia, which he visited, which wined and dined him, and which lavishly incorporated his educational materials—seeing in Dewey's foundational work for American public schools an ideal blueprint for communist-totalitarian Russia's public schools. Dewey was honored and flattered that the Bolsheviks saw his work as perfect for their plans.[32]

Dewey would later turn on Joseph Stalin once the despot started harassing Leon Trotsky, an intellectual guiding light for many of Dewey's "progressive" pals, but the Columbia don never failed to be mesmerized by communists and their fatuous ideas. Communists found that they could easily bring along Dewey to their fads and fashions. Thus, it was no surprise at all that they found in him a fervent ally to relocate the Frankfurt School (formally called the Institute for Social Research) to Columbia.

This was indeed an ideal match, a marriage of two institutions that were truly ideological soul mates. John Dewey lobbied doggedly, and with his intellectual cache among the left, he fairly easily prevailed upon the university's gullible president. President Butler was so won over by his star professor that he vowed to make the Frankfurt School integral to Columbia, even providing a building for the Freudian Reds to set up shop at West 117th Street. The store was soon open for business, with cultural Marxism the Red candy for the college kiddies.[33]

Dewey was beside himself in joyous anticipation of the new horizons ahead. The Frankfurt School could partner with his Columbia Teachers College, which at that point was the standard-bearer and progenitor of teachers colleges around the country, providing probably a majority of the nation's teaching and administrative posts. Likewise thrilling, the Institute for Social Research could do cutting-edge research for Dewey's favorite organization, the National Education Association (of which he was ultimately made honorary president for life), poising the German Marxists for a long-term impact on American education, particularly through politicization and ideological indoctrination.[34]

Back to Lukács and his cadre: Ralph de Toledano said that for Lukács and Münzenberg, John Dewey, cultural Marxism, and the Frankfurt School would become their "Tinkers to Evers to Chance," sending the opposing team to the bench and winning the ball game.[35] They wanted Marxism inculcated in the next generation of children, and then those beyond that—just as the family in the past had educated its children and children's children with a completely contrary set of long-established values. Thus, their primary area of operation would be the educational system to which naïve American parents delivered up their children, and particularly to the teachers' colleges.

It was no coincidence that Columbia, which so excited these European Marxists, housed the nation's top teachers' college, where later '60s radicals such as Weather Underground bomber Bill Ayers would get his doctorate after escaping pursuit by the FBI. It was through higher education that the impact would be most enduring. After their Moscow meetings, Willi Münzenberg said, "We must organize the intellectuals." Marx and Engels had organized the workers in the factories; the neo-Marxists would organize the professors and students in the universities.[36]

"The intellectuals were the key to any hidden assault on Western civilization and culture," explained Ralph de Toledano. "An academic basis for the new endeavor was both essential and mandatory. . . . Class war could engage the attention of fanatics. But only the intellectuals could manipulate the culture . . . systematically destroying the systems and societies which stood in the way of Western collapse and the ultimate victory of neo-Marxism."[37]

In this grand endeavor, Georg Lukács would be one of many players from the Frankfurt-Freudian-Marxism school with sights set on the family. Others included sexual fanatics such as Wilhelm Reich, Otto Gross, William Steckel, A. S. Neill, and the influential leftist psychologist Erich Fromm. Some of them were overboard for even Sigmund Freud's intemperate tastes, with Freud blasting them for being "morally insane" and "complete lunatic[s]."[38]

Where do such men go to be taken seriously? They go to the American academy, where traditionally minded parents have long bathed them with their lifetime savings to "educate" their precious children. And now they were ready to teach and train them.

11

THE WORLD OF WILHELM REICH

THE EFFECT OF MOVING THE FRANKFURT School Reds to America is a stunning story with a wide web too intricate to document here. Sticking with this book's focus on family and marriage, we cannot ignore one of the school's many strange but noteworthy Freudian Marxists: Wilhelm Reich.

Born March 24, 1897, in Austria-Hungary, Reich was the troubled son of secular Jewish parents who did not raise him in the faith, or any faith. They not only refused to nurture religion in the boy—insisting on a purely secular education, a very advanced progressive notion for the day—but also nurtured little else of moral or ethical value. They did not model virtuous behavior.

Wilhelm's father, Leon, was cold, cruel, brooding, jealous, mean, and disinterested in his son. Wilhelm lamented that his father had never treated him with any tenderness. Leon Reich was also neglectful of his wife, who responded to his lack of love with an intense sexual affair that continued behind her husband's back for years. As for little Wilhelm, the affair was no secret to him. It made him feel ashamed, but it also confused, intrigued, and titillated him, so much so that he fantasized about jumping in bed with his mother and her lover and joining them.

Such odd, overbearing sexual inclinations for the boy began very early in his life. He claimed they started as early as four years old, when he tried to have sex with the family's maid, with whom he shared a bed. Reich was extremely candid about these desires in his diary and later autobiographical writings, including his posthumously published *Passion of Youth*. The title was both apt and ironic—and prescient. Not only was Reich never able or interested in controlling his passions, but he believed that doing so was deleterious to his psyche and contrary to his nature as a man. He claimed that by the time he was just eleven, he was already having daily sexual intercourse with another of the family servants. That was not all. He openly admitted to many earlier instances of watching farm animals have sex and engaging in excessive masturbation and borderline sadomasochism and near bestiality. He became hooked on brothels, saying he could "no longer live" without them. To say he was sex-obsessed is insufficient.

Things took a turn for the (further) worse for Wilhelm when he decided to inform his already perpetually angry father of his mother's affair with a younger man, an escapade routinely conducted under the proud senior Reich's roof. Leon was enraged. He proceeded to mercilessly beat the mother, which was nothing new but now was more severe. The mother was so miserable that she killed herself, a dreadful end for which Wilhelm blamed himself.

Leon was now even more unbearable. The despondent father waded into a freezing pond in the hope of picking up pneumonia or something that would kill him, too. It nearly worked; he got quite sick. He died just a few years later from tuberculosis. His death, they believed, was related to his depression and decline over the fate of his wife. For this as well, Wilhelm, by then a yet more tormented and neurotic teenager, took responsibility. In all, Reich could not help but deem this disastrous state of affairs a "catastrophe."[1]

Wilhelm Reich's life was a mess. He was drawn into the awful First World War, where he fought for the losing side as a lieutenant who commanded a group of forty men. He witnessed the war's vast trenches of death. When the war ended, his prospects for life and career were grim. Tragically, the early twentieth century offered two poisonous medicines that he felt might provide a cure and some form of direction: Freudianism and Marxism. These, it seems, Reich picked up from the University of Vienna, where he enrolled once the war had ended.

In 1919 Wilhelm Reich found his first god when he met Sigmund Freud and asked him for a tutorial and list of writings on sexology. Freud obliged. Reich began working as a "physician" for Freud's psychoanalytic clinic in 1922. This new professional direction did not help his personal life—quite the contrary. For Reich, there would be many women, several muddled affairs, more ruined lives, plenty of untidy premarital sex, failed marriages, plus abortions, suicides, death, and general assorted debauchery and misery.

Speaking of misery, it was the 1920s in elite Europe, which meant that the Soviet Comintern was in full bloom and that intellectuals in the academy and elsewhere were filling their pipes with smoky dreams of Marxist utopia. To that end, Wilhelm Reich would encounter his second god when he dug into the writings of Marx and Engels. He joined the Communist Party in Austria in 1928 and visited the USSR the next year, almost the same time as the visit by his future American colleague, John Dewey, who sojourned to Moscow with a literal boatload of admiring American "progressive" educators soaking in the Bolshevik experiment.[2] There, Reich lectured and was received enthusiastically. He visited Soviet schools and day nurseries, and received the customary Potemkin village treatment intended to woo Westerners. To his communist brethren in the Motherland, Reich trumpeted the virtues of psychoanalysis and Freud as good things that good Leninists and Stalinists and even Trotskyites (he corresponded with Trotsky) should eagerly adopt.

By this time Wilhelm Reich was well on his way in search of a unifying theory of Freudianism and Marxism. He hoped that the theory could become therapy, a grand cure for individuals, for freedom, for cultures, for societies, for states, and for the world. It was no small vision for this budding Freudian-Marxist-fusionist-revolutionist.

Reich immediately began crafting a report on his Soviet visit, which ultimately would become his revolutionary sexual manifesto, *The Sexual Revolution*. It was destined for a lasting impact. Reich was impressed by what the Kremlin was doing, but he underscored some shortcomings, particularly in areas of sexuality and the family. As noted by the authoritative *Encyclopedia of Marxism*, Reich was pleased with the undermining of patriarchal authority he observed in Soviet collective farms but warned that the banning of homosexuality in Russia and any restrictions on abortion would foretell "the demise of the Revolution." For Reich, full communist revolution required full sexual license, including homosexual sex. His experience in Bolshevik Russia reaffirmed his conviction that serious "social change" would need to transpire before Marxist-psychoanalysis could rule the day.[3]

In 1930 Wilhelm Reich moved to Berlin with his wife and two children. It was back to Babylon, a place to imbibe all sorts of wanton behavior. His personal behavior reflected his professional views; like Marx and Engels, he practiced what he preached. He had never been sexually chaste, and sadly, he inherited some of his father's authoritarianism. He could be quite authoritarian in his Marxism. He demanded that his wife consent to his desire to place their two children in a Marxist commune, or he would divorce her.[4] She submitted, but she could only endure so much. Their marriage would last only a few more years, a victim of Reich's maniacal views.

In Berlin, Reich established the Association for Proletarian Sexual Politics, which reached a striking membership of forty thousand in left-wing Europe. He also found a more suitable marriage with ideological bedfellows at the Frankfurt School. He settled in with these kindred spirits, working diligently (especially with Erich Fromm) on a synthesis of Marxism and psychoanalysis, which included full-scale sexual experimentation, few to no holds barred.

Ralph de Toledano called Reich the Institute for Social Research's "point man" in its first onslaughts on the family as the sustaining unity in society, particularly through sexual immorality, misguided sex education, and radical feminism. Toledano went so far as to argue that radical feminism was a "direct product" of the Frankfurt School, with Reich providing the initial thrusts.[5] One could debate that to the letter, but Reich was no doubt an influence.

Despite such growing and eventual impact, Reich had major problems with the Communist Party, which (under fidelity to Moscow) had a more orthodox approach to traditional class-based Marxism. Various conflicts ultimately earned his expulsion from the Party in March 1933. Expulsion was not unusual for any Marxist, least of all one as weird as Wilhelm Reich. The Party was always paranoid and outright fascistic in its unyielding rigidity to Moscow discipline. Communist parties were notorious for angrily expelling members suddenly deemed apostates. Reich remained a communist, of course, but an anti-Soviet one.

Reich's banishment from the Communist Party could not and would not terminate his conviction to fuse Marxism, Freudianism, and his own burgeoning ideas of sexual politics and sexual revolution. Quite the contrary, Reich would lead that charge and never relent. Indeed, it is critical to know that Reich is credited with coining the term "sexual revolution." As noted by one Reich scholar, Christopher Turner, as early as the 1930s Reich had started using the term to express his Marxist-based conviction that (in Turner's words) "a true political revolution would only be possible once sexual repression was overthrown, the one obstacle Reich felt had scuppered the efforts of the Bolsheviks." Reich insisted—not incorrectly albeit prophetically early—that the sexual revolution was under way and that "no power in the world" would stop it.[6]

In an insightful observation, Reich believed that sexuality itself would change, becoming even more licentious. "The truth of the matter is that sexuality changes in the course of the revolution," stated Reich.[7] The revolution and the sexual permissiveness would feed off and fuel one another, a kind of cultural-political symbiosis.

For Reich, like so many other communist theorists, his ideal world required the rejection of a natural moral law. In *The Sexual Revolution*, he argued that the pleasure life—which for him was the "free love" life—was incompatible with the moral life; it was, he said, "antithetical to nature."[8] He spurned the notion of any divine law or authority, as well as divinely ordained conscience, governing sexual behavior among men and women.

Every utopian has his key to utopia. For traditional communists, the key lay in economics, liberating the workers from their factory bosses. For the New Left Marxists, it would lay more generally in culture. For Reich in particular, it would lay within the culture's revamped perceptions of sexuality. This meant an overhauling of cultural perceptions of the family. As Donald De Marco and Ben Wiker note, "Reich saw the family, with its inevitable patriarchal authority, as the chief source of repression. Therefore, the family had to be dismantled."[9]

These same authors noted that Reich rejected the parental authority of both father and mother. His rejection of the father, they wrote, lent him a certain stature "as a feminist." They quoted Reich stating that his heroines were "courtesans who rebel against the yoke of compulsive marriage and insist on their right to sexual self-determination." Moreover, Reich insisted that the children of marriage must be freed from the sway of "parental ideas." This included (in Reich's words) "defending children's and teenagers' right to natural love." De Marco and Wiker asserted that, in rejecting the authority of both parents in teaching their children sexual morality, Reich allied himself with a broad spectrum of modern secular sex educators.[10]

All of this was, Reich believed, a natural extension and next step in communism. It was, in short, the next step in the dialectic. In that strict Hegelian sense, Wilhelm Reich was showing himself a good communist.

Reich was content to sow the seeds for his utopia on the soil of European universities. But that would soon forcibly change.

Reich fled Germany at the height of Hitlerism. This came almost belatedly, in late 1938, after Hitler had made great headway across Europe. Reich's children and ex-wife had already fled. Reich seems to have been persuaded to come to the United States by a Columbia University comrade visiting and studying in Europe—Theodore P. Wolfe, a professor of psychiatry. Wolfe not only offered to settle Reich and arrange a visa, with the help of Franklin Roosevelt's heavily communist-penetrated State Department, but also assisted in cobbling together an offer for Reich to teach a course on "character formation" at the New School in New York, better known as the New School for Social Research, founded in 1919 (the same year as the Comintern) by "progressive" educators, most notably, John Dewey and several other Columbia professors. Wilhelm Reich was on his way to America to spawn his ideas in the home of the free and the brave.

Reich thus settled in the United States, more free to publish his ideas and nurse them to the freshmen and sophomores that tradition-minded American parents were feeding into the higher education machine.

To that end, one of Reich's signature works was his book *The Function of the Orgasm*, which he first began releasing (in segments) in the 1940s. He would publish it mainly through his Orgone Institute Press. A full translation was issued by Farrar, Straus, and Giroux in 1973.[11] The book is plainly difficult to read and understand, but certain passages clearly convey his Marxist/Freudian-rooted thoughts on sexuality and family and marriage. Some of them are also notably Frankfurt-like (i.e., Adorno and Horkheimer) in their disparagement of authority and "the authoritarian family."

On page 8 of *The Function of the Orgasm*, Reich wrote: "The structuring of masses of people to be blindly obedient to authority is brought about not by natural parental love, but by the authoritarian family. The suppression of the sexuality of small children and adolescents is the chief means of producing this obedience." Reich added: "The unity and congruity of culture and nature, work and love, morality and sexuality, longed for from time immemorial, will remain a dream as long as man continues to condemn the biological demand for natural (orgastic) sexual gratification. . . . The destruction of life by means of coercive education and war will prevail." Only "genuine democracy and freedom" could liberate these repressed urges.

On page 202 Reich addressed the "Problem of Marriage," as he perceived it: "Marriage is neither a love affair pure and simple, as one group of people contends, nor is it a purely economic institution, as another group contends. It is a form which was imposed upon sexual needs through socio-economic processes." In a linking of his sexual, cultural, and economic Marxism, he continued: "Marriages fall to pieces as a result of the ever deepening discrepancy between sexual needs and economic conditions. The sexual needs can be gratified with one and the same partner for a limited time only. On the other hand, the economic tie, moralistic demand, and human habit foster the permanency of the relationship. This results in the wretchedness of marriage." Reich then condemned the idea of sexual purity before marriage: "Premarital abstinence is supposed to prepare a person for marriage. But this very abstinence creates sexual disturbances and thereby undermines marriage. Sexual fulfillment can provide the basis for a happy marriage. But this same fulfillment is at variance with every aspect of the moralistic demand for lifelong monogamy."

The '60s cultural Marxists of the New Left would pick up this sentiment with abandon, seeking to (as they put it) "smash monogamy."

Wilhelm Reich was leaving his footprint in America and its campus classrooms. But he was also seeking to occupy a place in American bedrooms. His hatching of his ideas in the United States would eventually, ironically, lead to his criminal pursuit by (of all things) the US Food and Drug Administration. Reich had established something called the Orgone Institute, which extolled the liberating power of the orgasm. This came replete with an innovative "product" that Reich called the "orgone." The device was "manufactured" and shipped as interstate commerce throughout the country in large empty boxes for consumers to sit in for stimulation. The idea seems to have been picked up by Woody Allen in his 1973 comedy, *Sleeper*, where Allen (whose politics and sexuality were likewise skewed far to the left) had his characters comically enjoy a futuristic sex chamber called "the Orgasmatron."[12]

Woody Allen might have found this funny, but the FDA did not, and Reich was prosecuted for fraud and sent to federal prison in Lewisburg, Pennsylvania, an ignominious end to an ignominious career, if not life. (Had Reich ended up in Lewisburg a decade earlier, he might have shared a cell with Alger Hiss.)

Overall, how influential was Wilhelm Reich? The answer is complex, one prone to understatement and overstatement. It depends on where one seeks to measure his impact.

Harvey Klehr, the excellent scholar of American communism, argued that "most socialists looked askance at William Reich, who tried to combine socialism with sexual liberation. His sex-pol movement made very little headway in the US." Klehr added: "In the US, there was great hostility between the German-born socialists of the Socialist Labor Party and the American radicals like Victoria Woodhull more identified with sexual freedom or the utopian communities like Oneida which sought to uproot the family."[13]

No doubt, the sexual beliefs of the likes of Reich and friends were radical, particularly in their given time; they were firmly out of the mainstream of American life. Klehr is correct. And yet, at the same time, Reich and sympathetic cohorts were always seeking to move the ball forward, and eventually, in the long run, slowly but surely did just that, with their sexual radicalism (and especially their promotion of promiscuity) widely infecting the mainstream. Reich affected enough people in the right places.

What Wilhelm Reich really needed was the 1960s and the New Left university community that comrades of his, such as Herbert Marcuse, were massaging with Marxist messages derived from similar cultural (and antifamily) roots. And with that, Reich's broader ideas (if not the weirdest of them) found a certain resonance.

And thus, Reich, remarkably, would be called no less than the "Father of the Sexual Revolution" by the *New Yorker*, among other sources.[14] Donald De Marco and Ben Wiker, two orthodox Roman Catholics, agree with the *New Yorker* on that point, stating that no man "did more than anyone else" to warrant that title. They argue that Reich to this day "continues to maintain considerable influence on modernity," despite his unscientific claims and nihilist tendencies. They note that his influence is "particularly evident" among radical feminists, left-wing college students and professors, secular sex educators, and "enemies of the family."[15] That is indisputable. Enemies of the family can identify with Wilhelm Reich.

Time magazine in 1964 stated that Reich "may have been a prophet."[16] In certain respects, he may have. He left an indelible mark on the culture that should not be dismissed.

As for being dubbed the Father of the Sexual Revolution, such was no small feat. It is an epitaph that surely would have pleased Reich.[17]

For our purposes here, it must be remembered that Wilhelm Reich represents a major attempt at a full fusion of Marxist revolution and sexual-Freudian practice. This would provide a notable spark to help revolutionize the culture and to try to begin changing marriage and the family in America and the wider West.

12

HERBERT MARCUSE'S NEW LEFT

IF WILHELM REICH FATHERED THE SEXUAL revolution, then Herbert Marcuse fathered its bastard son, the '60s Marxist flower child. Marcuse has rightly been called the Father of the New Left due to his huge popularity and influence among the '60s student radicals. He has also been called the leader of the New Left's "academic brain trust."[1]

"[Marcuse] became the guru and inspiration of the New Left in its war on education, religion, and the family in the 1960s, and its call for violence against all authority," wrote Ralph de Toledano. "His leadership role in imposing Critical Theory on educational institutions such as Harvard, Yale, Brandeis, and the University of California [as well as Columbia] became one of the Frankfurt School's most awesome successes."[2]

Marcuse (mainly pronounced "Mar-koo-zeh" but also "Marquse"[3]) was born in Berlin in July 1898 to Carl Marcuse and Gertrud Kreslawsky. Like Wilhelm Reich, he fought for the losing side in World War I, and then emerged to pursue graduate work. In 1922 he completed his doctoral work at the University of Freiburg. In 1924 he married Sophie Wertheim, his first of three marriages. In 1933 Marcuse joined the Institute for Social Research, i.e., the Frankfurt School, but, like other Jews, was soon forced to flee Germany as Hitler took power. He first fled to Geneva with the Frankfurt comrades and then came to the United States, compliments of the Rockefeller Foundation and Columbia gang.

During World War II, Marcuse served the United States via the most heavily communist-penetrated of federal agencies: the Office of War Information (OWI). Communist infiltration of OWI was a major problem that had serious repercussions in countries that would fall to Stalin's domination after the war, particularly Poland. OWI's stunning, quiet success in advancing the Moscow line is only now beginning to receive adequate attention.[4] Like many OWI Marxists, Marcuse then slid to another surprisingly penetrated US entity, the Office of Strategic Services, precursor to the CIA. From there, like many more communists, Marcuse next took employment at the US State Department, just as the Alger Hiss revelations were exploding.

Not surprisingly, Marcuse's name has appeared in recent literature relating to declassified wartime KGB documents. He was not, to my knowledge, a spy for Moscow, though he probably fell within the often equally dangerous sphere of "agents of influence" and pro-Soviet communists who advanced the Kremlin line on extraordinarily important matters like the postwar division of Europe. Many of these figures did their damnedest to get countries like Poland, Czechoslovakia, and Hungary behind the Iron Curtain. In an amazingly stupid security breach, Marcuse was assigned to the Central European Section of OSS, which could not have been a worse positioning for the cause of the United States and for the cause of freedom of hundreds of millions of Europeans who would fall under the Soviet jackboot. Marcuse's section sought to place all of postwar Germany within the communist camp.[5]

Much more should be said about this elsewhere (again, the focus here is marriage and family), but it is important to know that a treacherously wide swath of Frankfurt School comrades and their associates were agents of influence or (in other cases) outright spies during the war and crucial years immediately thereafter, many of them working directly for the US government. Probably the worst were Richard Sorge and Franz

Neumann. Sorge recruited Hede Massing from the Frankfurt School into the Soviet espionage apparatus. She would become a prominent figure who would later recant and testify against Alger Hiss.[6]

The Hiss–Chambers case and other high-profile investigations prompted many unrelenting and unremitting Marxists like Marcuse to leave the federal government for a more hospitable home: American universities. Predictably, there to first roll out the red carpet was Columbia University, where Marcuse began to really spread his wings and lay the foundation for his version of Marxist revolution. Columbia was followed by stints at Harvard, Brandeis, and the University of California–San Diego.

As the leading voice and face from the Frankfurt School, the German-born Marxist produced what some have called an "eroticized Marx," most notably in his 1955 work, *Eros and Civilization: A Philosophical Inquiry into Freud*. The book came just in time to be digested among faculty intellectuals and regurgitated for consumption by students arriving on campuses in the tumultuous '60s. Funded in part by a grant from the Rockefeller Foundation, it became must-reading in many college classrooms. Ralph de Toledano dubbed it "the Bible of the New Left movement," inspiring Marxist rabble-rouser Angela Davis, hippie leader Abbie Hoffman, the Black Panthers, Students for a Democratic Society (SDS), and (to a degree) even the Weathermen (whose influence we will discuss in chapter 14).

One can expend hours reading through *Eros and Civilization* and come up empty-handed, painfully confused and frustrated, and lesser for the experience, longing for something of takeaway value or mere concrete comprehension. Marcuse's prose is dense and impenetrable, even to someone who has studied Freudian theory. Take this example on "the father":

> The rebellion against the father is rebellion against biologically justi-
> fied authority; his assassination destroys the order which has preserved
> the life of the group. . . . The patriarch, father and tyrant in one, unites
> sex and order, pleasure and reality; he evokes love and hatred; he
> guarantees the biological and sociological basis on which the history

of mankind depends. The annihilation of his person threatens to annihilate lasting group life itself and to restore the prehistoric and subhistoric destructive force of the pleasure principle. But the sons want the same thing as the father: they want lasting satisfaction of their needs. They can attain this objective only by repeating, in a new form, the order of domination which had controlled pleasure and thereby preserved the group. The father survives as the god in whose adoration the sinners repent so that they can continue to sin, while the new fathers secure those suppressions of pleasure which are necessary for preserving their rule and their organization of the group.[7]

Marcuse's work continues like this in page after page. The essential argument that he made (in a Freudian sense) is that societal and psychological structures are based on models of embedded repression, and that we can be liberated from these repressive restraints by greater measures of sexual freedom. As he wrote on page 55 of *Eros and Civilization*: "The quest for the origin of repression leads back to the origin of instinctual repression, which occurs during early childhood. The superego is the heir of the Oedipus complex, and the repressive organization of sexuality is chiefly directed against its pregenital and perverse manifestations." Marcuse then held forth on the "trauma of birth," the "death instinct—the impulse to return to the Nirvana of the womb," the fact that "protracted dependence of the human infant, the Oedipus situation, and pregenital sexuality all belong to the *genus* man," and other ruminations. These meanderings occur in the first paragraph of chapter 3, "The Origin of Repressive Civilization."

Many readers of this book will laugh off these writings as pseudo-intellectual nonsense. Nonetheless, the students of the '60s spent hours wooed and wowed by this material. It became integral to their cultural-political worldview.

And the German Marxist was just warming up.

In 1964, perfect timing to provide the shock to the wave that became the radical '60s, Marcuse published his acerbic critique of capitalist society in his best-selling *One-Dimensional Man*. The book sold more than three hundred thousand copies, a best seller by any standard, but especially by academic standards. It was translated into sixteen different languages. As one writer on the left remembers, "the phenomenon of Herbert Marcuse was born." Only four years later, as young Marxist Mark Rudd and friends were readying to shut down Columbia University, which, for them was not radical enough, the *New York Times* called Marcuse "the foremost literary symbol of the New Left." The old man became the flower children's celebrity, their "unlikely media star," profiled in publications ranging from radical-left periodicals to (appropriately) *Psychology Today* and *Playboy*.[8]

Marcuse is often said to have been critical of Wilhelm Reich, which he was, but the differences were more akin to two friendly Baptist preachers dissenting in their exegetical interpretation of a certain passage of Scripture rather than taking issue with the entirety of the New Testament. For both Marcuse and Reich, the covenant had been established long ago, with the gospel proclaimed through Marx and Engels. The two apostles, like communist Saints Peter and Paul, simply needed to hash out their interpretations, their applications, and their extensions of the Freudian-Marxist Pentecost. They quibbled over next steps, but they agreed on their messiah.

Both comrades-in-arms battled the "repression" represented by traditional notions of morality, especially *cumbersome* sexual restraints. They felt that erotic desires needed to be unleashed rather than inhibited. Both men saw religion as repressive, though Marcuse went further, arguing that modern Judeo-Christian society had become "totalitarian" in its suppression of man's "natural" sexual instincts. Of course, therein is a terrific paradox. Marcuse was, bear in mind, a Marxist, a communist, an inherently totalitarian ideology; he became a communist under Stalin, the master totalitarian. And yet, Marcuse attempted to turn the tables and argue that modern Western/American capitalist society and Judeo-Christian-rooted culture were themselves stifling forms of totalitarianism. He advanced this belief at the height of the Cold War and from American soil, at a time when US policymakers were rightly making the case against the USSR, the true home of totalitarianism.

It was a ludicrous charge, but unpacking it is revealing of Marcuse's radicalism. Much has been written on the term "totalitarianism" and what it really means, from the writings of Hannah Arendt and Richard Pipes to those of Zbigniew Brzezinski and Robert Conquest, with all of them understanding that few societies so embodied the complete meaning of the term quite like the USSR. The word can, however, be boiled down to a three-word definition: totalitarians seek to *transform human nature*. That was precisely what the twentieth century's most drastic totalitarian dictators aimed to do, from Moscow to Peking to Phnom Penh to Havana. But the likes of Marcuse (and Wilhelm Reich) had a fundamentally different conception of human nature. They believed that human nature in American and Western society had been warped by its traditions and faiths and capitalist system. For them, America and the West had human nature wrong.

Marcuse's New Left radicals, especially the anti-Americans in the academic asylums, loved this stuff. In reference to his accusation of American/Western "totalitarianism," one of Marcuse's students wrote with impish satisfaction on the fiftieth anniversary of *One-Dimensional Man*: "Marcuse is hurling back at the 'Free World' its own epithet for the Soviet enemy." The professor deliciously "describing capitalist societies as totalitarian" was "an especially pointed barb."[9]

To be sure, it was a barb based on intellectual buffoonery, on addled writings often nearly impenetrable, and utterly way too lengthy. Nonetheless, the New Left flower children really "dug" this stuff. Here in Marcuse, they hoped, was a god that would not fail.

This same student of Marcuse opened his modern-day tribute with this: "When Herbert Marcuse's *One-Dimensional Man* appeared fifty years ago, it was a revelation. To many of us who were becoming the New Left, Marcuse reflected and explained our own feeling of suffocation, our alienation from an increasingly totalitarian universe that trumpeted its freedom at every moment. We had grown up in it."

They did not like the culture in which they had grown up, the "flat, gray American society" that raised them; their "world of conformity." When Marcuse boldly described their America in terms more properly directed at the Soviet Union, railing against the culture as totalitarian, the New Left was all ears. They believed that his "unsettling blend of Hegel, Marx, and Freud, with his placement of the utopian beside the grimly realistic . . . made sense." He "so darkly captured" his students' "alienation," and yet also thereby "inspired, encouraged, and outraged" them.[10]

Marcuse blasted capitalism, technology, culture, the West. But like so many of his far-left forebears, what the Ivy League professor was cogitating was not all that new. He was simply coming up with his own new system of new ideas and new absolutes, based entirely on his own new perspective—even as Hegel and Marx and Freud and other old ideological-moral relativists offered the same old springboard.

Marcuse's words were extreme, in keeping with his thoughts. In addition to hurling charges of "totalitarianism" where they did not belong, Marcuse argued that traditional morality was "sadistic" in its perversion of human nature. Here, too, he inverted the terms, as he so often did. What were sadistic and perverted were not the new forms of unleashed sexual activity he felt should be uncorked, but the old restraints that twisted our better nature. As noted by Professor Kevin Slack:

> Marcuse heralded a new society to accompany his philosophic teaching. Historically, repression was needed because man faced necessity; political regimes, including the modern capitalist society, had been constructed upon moral teachings that erected a severe conscience: the self-denial required for industrial production. But now these virtues, which had been inculcated to solve the economic problem, were no longer necessary; indeed, he claimed that they intensified human aggression and thereby posed a threat to society. Marcuse sought a progressive revolution to end what he called "surplus repression."[11]

For Marcuse, and the rest of the Frankfurt School, the next step in the battle was to be waged at the cultural level, which included the sexual stage. Sexual activity would be liberated at the expense of the capitalist work ethic. As Slack noted, "The workday would be dramatically shortened, and individuals would choose their work, viewing it more as play. Modern man would accept a lower standard of living in return for the pleasures of instinctual gratification. He would fully detach sex from monogamy and reproduction and completely accept what he formerly viewed as sexual perversion."

This would constitute the new "progressive society," with the human body undressed to new vistas of pleasure and desire.

Marcuse advocated what he called "polymorphous sexuality." This term, a psychoanalytic concept also known as "polymorphous perversity," allowed for sexual gratification outside the conventional channels of accepted sexual behavior—really almost any means that allowed for gratification, including stimulation from or intercourse with the same sex.

Freud applied this to the "infantile" stage of development of human development, which went up to age five. He said that a child at this stage is "polymorphously perverse" and demonstrates receptivity to almost any kind of sexual pleasure and behavior without any restraint. In *Eros and Civilization*, Marcuse picked up this notion, mixed within his Marxist framework and cultural adaptation, and applied it wider and later into life and adult sexuality. Culture had introduced restraints on such behavior, which Marcuse wanted to eliminate.[12]

This no doubt included sex that was nonreproductive and nonheterosexual, and that sought to derive erotic pleasure from any part (or portal) of the body. An instructive explanation comes from the online entry on Marcuse in *glbtq: An Encyclopedia of Gay, Lesbian, Bisexual, Transgender, and Queer Culture*, which merits quotation at length and without interruption:

> During the early 1950s Marcuse returned to this line of thought in *Eros and Civilization*. In it he offered a dramatic re-interpretation of Freud's theory of repression and criticized Freud's stress on the genital organization of sexuality and on heterosexual intercourse. According to Freud, adult sexual development is a progression from oral and anal eroticism in infancy to the final adult stage of genital sexuality. In response, Marcuse proposed sexual liberation through the cultivation of a "polymorphous perverse" sexuality (which includes oral, anal, and genital eroticism) that eschews a narrow focus on genital heterosexual intercourse.[13]

Marcuse believed that sexual liberation was achieved by exploring new permutations of sexual desires, sexual activities, and gender roles—what Freud called "perverse" sexual desires, that is, all non-reproductive forms of sexual behavior, of which kissing, oral sex, and anal sex are familiar examples.

Marcuse was himself heterosexual, but he identified the homosexual as the radical standard bearer of sex for the sake of pleasure, a form of radical hedonism that repudiates those forms of repressive sexuality organized around genital heterosexuality and biological reproduction. . . .

Marcuse, like other leading theorists of sexuality, such as Freud and Wilhelm Reich, argued that homosexuality was a form of sexuality of which everyone was capable—that in fact, everyone was fundamentally bisexual.[14]

Herbert Marcuse represents a significant step in the extension of Marxism into the broader culture and sexual realm. His writings were a watershed. This Father of the New Left was so influential in the sexualization of Marxism and in "deconstructing" traditional understandings of marriage and family that he is today highlighted for his "enormous influence" on the *glbtq* encyclopedia's website: "Marcuse had an enormous influence on theories of sexual liberation, particularly in the early post-Stonewall gay movement and on the left. Many young people in the 1960s adopted Marcuse-like sexual politics as the basis for the counter-culture's radical transformation of values."[15]

The entry on Marcuse in *glbtq* concludes with some added crucial information:

Dennis Altman's *Homosexual: Oppression and Liberation* (1971), one of the earliest theoretical discussions of gay liberation and sexual politics, reflected the same assumption and relied extensively on Marcuse's work. . . .

Like Marcuse, Altman also emphasized "polymorphous perversity," the undifferentiated ability to take pleasure from all parts of the body. "Anatomy," Altman noted, "has forced the homosexual to explore the realities of polymorphous eroticism." Thus, homosexual sex represented an expression of pleasure and love "free of any utilitarian ends."

The Red Butterfly Collective, a Marxist faction of the Gay Liberation Front, also echoed Marcuse. The group stressed the importance of a democratic socialist perspective. "Human liberation," it noted in its comment on Carl Wittman's path-breaking *Gay Manifesto* (1969), "in all its forms, including Gay Liberation, requires effective self determination, i.e. democracy, in all spheres of social life affecting the lives of people as a whole."

Extremely revealing is the fact that the Red Butterfly Collective not only echoed Marcuse but adopted as its motto the final line from the "Political Preface" of the 1966 edition of *Eros and Civilization*: "Today the fight for life, the fight for Eros is the *political* fight."

Needless to say, the *glbtq* website strongly advocates same-sex marriage. Modern "GLBTQ" individuals see Marcuse as no less than a pioneer to their movement, to whom they are deeply grateful. (A full reading of that bio is very illuminating.)

As we can see here, it is difficult to overstate Marcuse's influence among Marxists when it came to culture and sexuality.

One of Marcuse's former students, writing in the left-leaning *Boston Review*, sees in today's culture a myriad of manifestations linked to a "Marcusean analysis": more diversity, more "tolerance," more multiculturalism, more feminism, and a culture in which "same-sex marriage rites become common," when "the watchword of our times is no longer 'conformity' but 'individual freedom.'" Sure, Marcuse might not have anticipated precisely these things at this time, but we can see them as extensions of the "liberation" he had in mind. The appreciative *Boston Review* writer is generous in the areas he credits to Marcuse: "Marcusean analysis is immensely useful in understanding the profusion of tattoos and pornography, the Internet and smart phones, coffee houses and art fairs, T-shirts and jeans, oral sex and divorce . . . [a] freer, more inclusive, more interesting and diverse, and humanly and socially richer than any of us would have imagined upon closing the pages of *One-Dimensional Man.*"[16]

That is a mouthful, or a mindful. And there are many people, on the left and the right, who would agree with this. One colleague of mine, a leading German scholar of the laissez-faire Austrian School of Economics, who had to read *One-Dimensional Man* from cover to cover, told me recently, "It's amazing how so much of what Marcuse wrote about has come to fruition today." My colleague meant that in a negative way.

As to this book's focus, the effect of all of this on marriage and family was significant. At the core of the family is the committed husband and wife, whose marital commitment and intercourse start and perpetuate the family. And their respect for one another and their bond and what they reproduce is the glue that keeps the marriage and the family together. In that sense, Marcuse's student is right to emphasize pornography, divorce, and same-sex marriage, which militate against the husband-wife bond.

Finally, we cannot leave out maybe Marcuse's most culturally pervasive and pernicious legacy on these hot-button issues and Culture War debates today. To the university students of the 1960s, Marcuse heralded what he called "liberating tolerance," or "repressive tolerance." The Frankfurt School neo-Marxist urged "intolerance against movements from the Right, and toleration of movements from the Left."[17]

In short, this was a prescription for the *selective tolerance* we see incessantly from the political left today, which trumpets "tolerance" loudly and proudly, but, in truth, only tolerates ideas with which it agrees. This, of course, is not genuine tolerance. It takes no great effort to tolerate only things you like. What today's liberals/progressives really mean when they speak of "tolerance" is a highly selective tolerance. That is precisely what Marcuse supported. He urged a withdrawal of toleration of speech for groups that opposed the left and its goals. That phony tolerance also translates into the left's phony claims of "diversity" and "multiculturalism," which only extend to certain approved categories of race, gender, and sexual orientation, and not to (say) undesired religious or conservative organizations. The ultimate stage for this insanity is the modern university, where all of these awful Marcusean-progressive-liberal-leftist contradictions are on display at every moment. These closed-minded and (ironically) *in*tolerant tactics have been a tremendous asset for the culture changers, especially those who steamroll and silence the "intolerants" who dare to disagree with them on issues like same-sex marriage.

And so, the Frankfurt School, launched by Lukács and friends at the Marx-Engels Institute in Moscow and coming to full fruition under the likes of Marcuse and others at American educational institutions, would be one of numerous academic social laboratories from which a long-term project of sexual-cultural change and indoctrination could begin. It would not take as long as some imagined. Really, it would take only a generation or so. By the 1960s, it was working magic, as wide-eyed, would-be radicals and revolutionary cultural communists like Bill Ayers and Kate Millett and Mark Rudd and so many, many more began marching through Columbia University's front door. Many walked in as innocent, impressionable freshmen and exited as fist-in-the-air, full-fledged revolutionary communists, exploding upon the landscape and ready to burn it up.

Through such disciples, Georg Lukács, who had hoped and boasted that the "abolition of culture" was just ahead, might finally fulfill his grand Marxist dream.[18]

13

THE '60S AND THE NEW LEFT
MARXIST FEMINISTS

IT WAS THIS RISE OF THE '60s New Left that began to dramatically attack the very foundations of marriage and family life.

David Horowitz was a leader among the New Left, yet always uneasy about these sexual-culture blow-ups. As editor of the radical publication *Ramparts*, he was one of the most prominent rising communists in the country. As noted earlier, the communists that Horowitz had observed around his Marxist parents in New York as a child were "very middle class," "proper," and even "quite bourgeois" in their sexual attitudes and practices. This would change, said Horowitz, with the 1960s.

"The phenomena that you're seeking to explain," Horowitz told me, referring to the left's long-term assault on marriage and family, "came when the Marxist working class model failed and the New Left started applying Marxist categories to gender. This started at the very end of the Sixties and was a phenomenon of the Seventies."[1]

Horowitz notes that the new neo-communist radicals added new dimensions of oppression to the Marxist model, moving beyond class and economics to areas like racism and "sexism."[2] Today one might add "homophobia" to the New Left's new list, or those opposing "marriage rights" and "abortion rights." The things the left is against are, like progressivism itself, always evolving. But staying with the '60s for now, "sexism" and women's issues were a major thrust for the New Left.

Leading that charge on the women's front—aptly named "the women's *movement*"—were feminists such as Betty Friedan and Kate Millett, early faces of the National Organization for Women (NOW), who, unbeknownst to many of those who elevated them to the status of paragons of women's rights, were not mere feminists but Marxist feminists. (Another influential Marxist feminist from the period was Gerda Lerner, the University of Wisconsin professor who wrote *The Creation of Patriarchy*, and who started the Seminar on Women at Columbia University, where she went to graduate school.) Their advocacy of *equality* for women was not separate from their advocacy of a Marxist view of equality.

Betty Friedan, born Bettye Naomi Goldstein on February 4, 1921, was raised in Peoria, Illinois, which just happened to be the home diocese of a dynamic young priest named Fulton Sheen. Goldstein, however, would have had little patience for Sheen homilies against Marxism, which she would have dismissed as diatribes. For the young daughter of Harry and Miriam (Horwitz) Goldstein, whose families hailed from Russia and Hungary, the faith was Marxism-Leninism.

Bettye Goldstein always had been on the far left, but a particularly strong wind blew her further still when she enrolled at Smith College in the late 1930s, where she came under the special influence of Dorothy Wolff Douglas.

Dorothy herself had solid far-left bona fides. In 1915 Dorothy Wolff had married Paul H. Douglas. Whereas he was a Quaker and she was Jewish, there was much more that drew them together. Both had earned doctorates from Columbia University en route to becoming college professors. Both, too, seemed to be enamored with Bolshevik Russia, or at least felt a tug in that direction.

Paul Douglas expressed his ardor for the Soviet experiment by making a pilgrimage to Moscow, having been literally targeted by the Comintern. In a December 1920 letter, he was one among seventy-eight

American professors identified for their potential usefulness.[3] Seven years later, in July 1927, Douglas and comrades sojourned to the Motherland aboard the aptly titled SS *President Roosevelt*, named for the first progressive president, Teddy Roosevelt, and which really should have been called the SS *Useful Idiot*. They boarded with a motley crew, a mix of progressives, of varying sorts of liberals, and of communists—most to all of whom were *closet* communists. Especially well represented were intellectuals from Columbia, including Dr. George Counts, the pal of John Dewey, who also helped make Bella Dodd a communist and helped bring the Frankfurt School to New York. Douglas and friends met directly with Joseph Stalin in a marathon but chummy get-together that listed six hours.[4]

To his credit, Paul Douglas, who would eventually become a Democratic senator, came to reject his naïveté toward Bolshevism. He remained a liberal, but an anticommunist one.[5] He also had another separation—from his wife, Dorothy, and their four children. But Dorothy's political passions did not die, and her views of womanhood became even more strident.

Dorothy remained an unflagging leftist feminist and took a position teaching economics at Smith College. If she was not an actual member of Communist Party USA (evidence to that effect was presented by the House Committee on Un-American Activities), she was at the least highly like-minded. There at Smith, Dorothy would mentor a young Bettye Goldstein, who arrived at campus in 1938. (She dropped the final *E* in her name while in college. She thought it was pretentious.)

Dorothy's influence on Betty is revealed in the fascinating biographical work on Betty Friedan by Daniel Horowitz, a sympathetic Smith College professor—and also a commendably honest liberal and incisive historian.[6] In his *Betty Friedan and the Making of "The Feminine Mystique,"* Horowitz carefully documented Friedan's ideological path, showing meticulously how closely it adhered to the communist line.[7]

David Horowitz (no relation to Daniel), who also has written on Friedan, stated that Friedan was, in reality, closer to the role of "Stalinist Marxist" than the "suburban housewife" legend she later invented for herself.[8] In an important January 1999 piece for the leftist publication *Salon*, Horowitz asserted that not only was Friedan a Stalinist and committed Party activist but diligently concealed and lied about that unseemly past throughout her life, with a hagiographic liberal media counted on as predictably reliable dupes to the cover-up.[9]

Friedan's Marxism was cloaked in feminism to make it palatable to the normal middle-class American—*to play in Peoria*, if you will. She early on mastered the communist tactic of duping the innocent masses, from easily suckered liberals/progressives—to whom she claimed she was merely one of them, and that anyone suggesting she was a communist was a fanged, horned Neanderthal McCarthyite—to the politically naïve and unsophisticated mainstream, to whom she presented herself as just another housewife looking for a little equality for the gentler gender. To this huge group of hoodwinked masses, Ms. Friedan would find an enormous market to open their minds and wallets to her ideas and books.

She emerged thunderously on the national stage with her seminal 1963 book, *The Feminine Mystique*, a gigantic best seller that sold millions of copies. The book contained many outrages, including Friedan's assertion that the suburban homesteads of American housewives were akin to "comfortable concentration camps." Like many on the left, she had a juvenile fondness for brutal Nazi metaphors to denigrate what she didn't like, and she used them repeatedly in her magnum opus, outraging many Jewish observers (especially given that Friedan herself was Jewish), and prompting her to later recant the hysterical imagery.[10]

Not all radical feminists, however, objected to her hyperbolic caricatures of the horrors of being a housewife. All was forgiven three years later, in 1966, when Friedan was a natural as founder and first president of NOW. She wrote the mission statement for NOW, which she coauthored with Pauli Murray, the first black, female Episcopal priest, who was bisexual, if not actually homosexual.[11] Married for a short period and then divorced, Reverend Murray candidly admitted to struggling with sexual and gender-identity issues.

Friedan's work was affected by her communist worldview and instruction. The examples are obvious and legion. To cite just one telling example that Daniel Horowitz found in his research of Friedan's papers, sometime in 1959, while compiling her feminist opus, Friedan scribbled into her notes lines from Engels's classic 1884 treatise, *The Origin of the Family, Private Property, and the State,* and from Marx and Engels's *Selected Works.* These included trenchant verses on "the emancipation of women" and the preeminence of their industrial production over "domestic duties," the latter of which should "require their attention only to a minor degree."[12]

Ralph de Toledano (as well as Daniel Horowitz, but less so[13]) detailed where Friedan was influenced not only by orthodox Marxists such as Engels and Marx, or by Dorothy Wolff Douglas, but also by the cultural Marxists of the Frankfurt School, and namely, Kurt Lewin, the aforementioned colleague and coauthor of Margaret Mead.

Toledano's assessment is no softball treatment. He argued that what Lewin offered to Betty helped satiate the "towering rages" and "anti-male obsessions she had been developing since childhood." Toledano's characterization of "what she [Betty] got from Kurt Lewin" is pretty tough. He claimed that what appealed to Betty was less socialist-Marxist economics than "penis envy," the "rooting out of penises," the "humiliation of the male," the "victory of matriarchy," and the advancement of "women's liberation" and "women's rights" as a "potent tool" to destroy elements of the "bourgeois" society "which stood between Greenwich Village rebellion and the Frankfurt School heaven." In all, this would allow a "Critical Theorist takeover."[14]

Readers can dissect those audacious assertions, but one overarching point from Toledano is not debatable: Betty's views on sexuality and feminism, for which she is famous and had a major impact, were influenced by Marxism, including the cultural Marxists of the Frankfurt School.

In 1969 Betty would divorce Carl Friedan, her husband of twenty-two years, accusing him of physical abuse, which he vehemently denied. He claimed that she was mentally disturbed. He also disputed her successful media portrayal of herself as a victimized housewife manacled to her suburban kitchen oven. To the contrary, he claimed that his wife spent much of her time outside the home, propagandizing and agitating.[15]

In 1973, four years after her divorce, Betty joined a group of fellow self-styled "progressives" in signing the *Humanist Manifesto*. But that year held something much greater in store for Betty and her feminist sisters at war with patriarchy and at the vanguard of the women's front: *Roe v. Wade*. Their wildest dreams for legalized abortion had come true.

Friedan would also help found what became the National Abortion Rights Action League (NARAL), the true sister organization to NOW. For these fanatics of feminism, "abortion rights" became almost sacramental to their ideology. Few issues were so sacred to so many feminists. And, of course, abortion would devastate—and, in some cases, literally eliminate—American families. It would snuff out tens of millions of unborn lives, just as it had in Russia, where Friedan's ideological forebears had legalized the procedure fifty years before the United States. Yes, an American Bolshevik, Betty Friedan, helped make that possible. Since then, abortion in America has robbed the lives of more than 50 million unborn babies.

And all along, Ms. Friedan never dared to divulge to those admiring and marvelously duped American housewives the debt she owed to Karl Marx and his disciples for her brand of feminism—a communist's feminism.

***

When it comes to communist feminists, one must acknowledge Kate Millett.

Millett was thirteen years Freidan's junior, and was likewise launched via authorship of a highly touted feminist screed, *Sexual Politics*.[16] The book had been Kate's dissertation at (yet again) Columbia University, and it became a cultural juggernaut when published in 1969, the height of '60s mayhem and three years after Betty Friedan became the first president of NOW. Millett decried the vile "patriarchy" of the monogamous nuclear family and the so-called *heterosexism* of popular leftist novelists such as Norman Mailer.

Take this example from page 33 of *Sexual Politics*, which is an extension of Millett's broader argument that the family is the foundational unit of a stifling patriarchy: "Traditionally, patriarchy granted the father nearly total ownership over wife or wives and children, including the powers of physical abuse and often even those of murder and sale. Classically, as head of the family the father is both begetter and owner in a system in which kinship is property." In the footnote to this passage, Millett said of the father: "Marital as well as consanguine relation to the head of the family made one his property." Millett drew many comparisons between family/patriarchy and slavery.

Sexual Politics is riddled with quotables concerning the alleged inherent violence of patriarchy and how men are, by their nature, vile and violent creatures. Millett did not spend too much time on homosexuality in her book, beyond seemingly mentioning it as a feature of "men's house cultures." She did, however, state some notable things under the umbrella of a wider sexual revolution. On page 62, she wrote: "A sexual revolution would require, perhaps first of all, an end of traditional sexual inhibitions and taboos, particularly those that most threaten patriarchal monogamous marriage: homosexuality, 'illegitimacy,' adolescent, pre- and extra-marital sexuality. The negative aura with which sexual activity has generally been surrounded would necessarily be eliminated, together with the double standard and prostitution." She concluded: "The goal of revolution would be a permissive single standard of sexual freedom, and one uncorrupted by the crass and exploitative economic bases of traditional sexual alliances."

As a committed Marxist feminist, Millett picked up the torch ignited by the Frankfurt–Friedan rebels. She was now running with that torch, from the streets of Columbia to the suburbs of every male-dominated household in the heartland.

A flash point of Millett's mind-set at the time is provided by her younger sister, Mallory. Mallory suffered her own inner turmoil at the hands of the university system before eventually pulling herself out, rediscovering her faith, remarrying in a long and loving relationship, and even becoming a successful CFO for several corporations. She vividly recalls an exchange during her junior year in high school. The nuns at her parochial school asked her and her classmates about their plans after graduation. When Mallory explained that she would attend a university, the nuns were disappointed. She asked her favorite nun why. "That means you'll leave four years later a communist and an atheist!" said the nun. Mallory and the other girls giggled. "How ridiculously unsophisticated these nuns are," they scoffed. And yet, conceded Mallory, "I went to the university and four years later walked out a communist and an atheist, just as my sister Katie had six years before me."[17]

A stint after college in Southeast Asia, where Mallory had been married to an American executive, was a quick wake-up call to just how special the America of her youth had been. Maybe the United States was not so awful after all. She soon lost her coed fascination with Marxism, but her older sister did not.

No, Katie was hard-core, with no looking back. She drank deep from the Marxist chalice, and the intoxication never left her. Katie implored Mallory, who was now a divorced, single mom, to stay with her. "Come to New York," she urged. "We're making revolution!" She and some of the other girls were fired up for the new National Organization for Women. To borrow from Lenin, who recalled his own moment of liberation when he removed the cross pendant from his neck and "tossed it in the rubbish bin," Kate now excoriated her Irish-Catholic upbringing in St. Paul, Minnesota, which she angrily dispatched to the dustbin of history.[18]

And so, Mallory went to Kate's gathering in New York, thus becoming an eyewitness not only to how radical the left had become, but to where things were headed thanks to the culture rot bequeathed by the maggot of Marxist ideology. Mallory remembers:

> I stayed with Kate and her lovable Japanese husband, Fumio, in a dilapidated loft on The Bowery as she finished her first book, a PhD thesis for Columbia University, "Sexual Politics."
>
> It was 1969. Kate invited me to join her for a gathering at the home of her friend, Lila Karp. They called the assemblage a "consciousness-raising-group," a typical communist exercise, something practiced in Maoist China. We gathered at a large table as the chairperson opened the meeting with a back-and-forth recitation,

like a Litany, a type of prayer done in Catholic Church. But now it was Marxism, the Church of the Left, mimicking religious practice:

"Why are we here today?" she asked.

"To make revolution," they answered.

"What kind of revolution?" she replied.

"The Cultural Revolution," they chanted.

"And how do we make Cultural Revolution?" she demanded.

"By destroying the American family!" they answered.

"How do we destroy the family?" she came back.

"By destroying the American Patriarch," they cried exuberantly.

"And how do we destroy the American Patriarch?" she replied.

"By taking away his power!"

"How do we do that?"

"By destroying monogamy!" they shouted.

"How can we destroy monogamy?". . . .

"By promoting promiscuity, eroticism, prostitution and homosexuality!" they resounded.[19]

Mallory says that the comradely sisters then proceeded with a sustained discussion on how to advance these goals via their National Organization for Women. "It was clear they desired nothing less than the utter deconstruction of Western society," she said. How would they do this? They explained that their goal—a very Frankfurt-like goal—was to "invade every American institution. Every one must be permeated with 'The Revolution.'" This included the judiciary, the legislatures, the executive branches, media, and education: universities, high schools, K-12s, school boards, even the library system.

Why would any American want Chairman Mao's ghastly Cultural

Revolution, or any form of Asian communism? Because she had lived in Asia, Mallory had not witnessed the bewildering surge of Mao portraits and slogans and *Little Red Book*s all over American campuses since she had left for a Third World hellhole. She had not glimpsed the numerous hippie "communes" that had popped up everywhere in imitation of Mao's Sinification of Marxism. When she had gratefully returned to America, she fell to the ground covering it with kisses, "blubbering with ecstasy" at being home. She was faced with baffling questions that had confounded her, but would not have surprised those nuns from her high school. She asked of these New Left university women:

> How could twelve American women who were the most respectable types imaginable—clean and privileged graduates of esteemed institutions: Columbia, Radcliffe, Smith, Wellesley, Vassar; the uncle of one was Secretary of War under Franklin Roosevelt—plot such a thing? Most had advanced degrees and appeared cogent, bright, reasonable and good. How did these people rationally believe they could succeed with such vicious grandiosity? And why?[20]

Well, that agonizing mystery is indeed an ongoing frustration. How could anyone, let alone "smart" people, fall for such silly ideas? A cursory reading of Kate Millett's *Sexual Politics* immediately strikes one with its inanity, its unsoundness, and its obvious lack of grounding in anything durable. With apologies for my harsh appraisal, Millett's unintelligible forms of university-speak should not be viewed by readers as hard to understand because of their mental inferiority or because the words represent some higher form of superior intellectualism beyond their grasp. The ideas are simply bad ones, very poorly articulated with no concrete foundation. When Nixon bad-boy Spiro Agnew referred to "nattering nabobs" and an "effete corps of impudent snobs who characterize themselves as intellectuals," he was probably referring to the likes of Millett and Marcuse. And yet, for whatever reason, a significant segment of young people in our universities have been supple prey for this fatuous nonsense for decades, just as the Frankfurt School cadre imagined they would. Such supercilious indoctrination has somehow managed to have a lasting ripple effect through today, including on once-hallowed institutions such as marriage and family.

To that end, the university miseducation that Kate Millett and her comrades received at a deceased John Dewey's Columbia University and other colleges would, over the years, become fodder for indoctrinating many more Kate Milletts, with further destruction wreaked upon marriage and the family.

Here again, Kate's sister Mallory adds unique, firsthand testimony to the cultural wreckage that came careening down the track:

> I continued with my new life in New York while my sister became famous publishing her books, featured on the cover of "Time Magazine." "Time" called her "the Karl Marx of the Women's Movement." This was because her book laid out a course in Marxism 101 for women. Her thesis: The family is a den of slavery with the man as the Bourgeoisie and the woman and children as the Proletariat. The only hope for women's "liberation" . . . was this new "Women's Movement." Her books captivated the academic classes and soon "Women's Studies" courses were installed in colleges in a steady wave across the nation with Kate Millett books as required reading.[21]

And what effect did the works and thinking of the likes of Kate Millett have on some mothers and their notions of motherhood, of being a wife, of marriage, of family life? Mallory has absorbed her share of arrows from women betrayed by this Marxist matron, whom *Time* featured on its cover (August 31, 1970) as "the Mao Tse-Tung of Women's Liberation." Mallory adds:

> I've known women who fell for this creed in their youth who now, in their fifties and sixties, cry themselves to sleep decades of countless nights grieving for the children they'll never have and the ones they coldly murdered because they were protecting the empty loveless futures they now live with no way of going back. "Where are my children? Where are my grandchildren?" they cry to me.
>
> "Your sister's books destroyed my sister's life!" I've heard numerous times. "She was happily married with four kids and after she read

those books, walked out on a bewildered man and didn't look back." The man fell into despairing rack and ruin. The children were stunted, set off their tracks, deeply harmed; the family profoundly dislocated and there was "no putting Humpty-Dumpty together again."[22]

Like many Marxists, Kate Millett incorporated her ideas on marriage and sexuality into her personal practices. Though she married, she practiced lesbianism, becoming bisexual. She had started that lifestyle at Columbia while writing *Sexual Politics*. This would, predictably, end her marriage to her husband, who apparently found the trashing of these norms unnatural to the health of their marriage. Like Betty Friedan, however, her career health outlived her marriage health, and the college culture continued to drink up her writings.

Again, why do people in our universities fall so easily for this vapid claptrap so contrary to their human nature? Their impressionable youth alone is not a sufficient explanation. For whatever reasons, they do. They did in the past and they do still.

Kate Millett: Marxist, feminist, advocate for gay rights, for new sexuality, for new spousal relationships, and on and on. She channeled all of her revolutionary nostrums into a campaign to take down traditional marriage and family, the backbone of American culture from the nation's inception. Today, the bio for the eighty-year-old Millett at glbtq.com describes her as a "groundbreaking" "bisexual feminist literary and social critic."[23]

She was precisely that. And she did not stand alone. She stood on the shoulders of a long line of previous Marxists.

14

SMASHING MONOGAMY: THE WEATHERMEN'S SEXUAL REVOLUTIONARIES

WHO WERE THE ACCOMPLICES TO THE likes of Kate Millett in this take-down of traditions? The list is vast. Where to begin? Where to end? It is impossible, but a few highlights and lowlights deserve attention.

Joining Kate Millett at Columbia was a male comrade, Mark Rudd, the campus leader of Students for a Democratic Society (SDS) who, along with Bill Ayers and Bernardine Dohrn, would create a splinter group called the Weathermen, which was so literally terroristic that it went underground to escape a nationwide FBI manhunt and charges of bank robbery, murder, and all-around domestic terrorism. The Weathermen became the Weather Underground, a violent organization of bomb makers and bomb planters who plotted political murders as part of an insidious plan to overthrow the government of the United States. Their goal was a coup d'état of the existing political-cultural order according to a Marxist design.

For these individuals, it was absolute political-moral mayhem. In Rudd's words, "the message" of him, Ayers, Dohrn, and friends was "we sh-t on all your conventional values. [. . .] There were no limits to our politics of transgression."[1] Sex was foremost among the transgressions.

The young communist change agents had it as often as they could, with no regard to marriage, monogamy, feelings, or disease. They were uncontrollable. It was Sodom and Gomorrah at the late Professor Dewey's Columbia.

Herbert Marcuse must have taken a measure of pride in these ideological grandchildren. In their SDS days, the Weathermen had read so much Marcuse that Ralph de Toledano described the Frankfurt grandfather as their "intellectual inspiration."[2] By the 1970s, the Weather Underground was reading Frantz Fanon, who, ironically, would also be read by a future Columbia student named Barack Obama.[3]

A central figure in the SDS-Weathermen drama was Mark Rudd. His account of those days is stunning, revolting, and telling.

Born June 2, 1947, in Irvington, New Jersey, Rudd was the son of working-class parents from the suburbs. His shockingly candid memoirs, *Underground: My Life with SDS and the Weathermen*, provide no indication of much of a religious upbringing or underpinning, other than the pro forma rites of passage, such as the expected bar mitzvah at the proper age. He read Freud in high school, and also took in some Marx, plus lots of sex, but apparently not much God. In fact, a striking element through Rudd's riveting memoirs is an unacknowledged but obvious lacking of and longing for God, especially as he expressed certain regrets later in life. All along, he looked not to a church, a confessional, a synagogue, but to psychiatry and psychiatrists, to sex and Freud, to communist revolution and Marcuse and Marx.[4]

A common thread throughout Rudd's memoirs was sexual and communist revolution. Utterly liberating to him as much as to any woman was the advent of the pill in the '60s, which he described as "perfect," as ridding him of his fear of getting a girl pregnant, "the dark side of my adolescent dream." This allowed Rudd (and his male friends) to go wild, especially in the pursuit of what he called "gentile girls . . . the forbidden object of desire for me." But perhaps most formative to Rudd's thriving sexual politics was not sharing a romp with a gentile girl but his high school senior-year hookup with a girl named Liliana, whom he described as "the school intellectual."

Rudd does not offer much detail on Liliana, including her last name, but the information he does provide is quite revealing. She was the daughter of German-born Jewish immigrants who were Freudian-Marxists who had fled Hitler in the 1930s. Rudd does not say so, but Liliana's parents very well sound as if they could have been literal Frankfurt schoolers, if not faculty. They probably were not faculty, but they fit the school's ideological template flawlessly. Certainly, they possessed the Frankfurters' cultural Marxist views of sexuality. "Her parents were Freudians and Marxists," wrote Rudd of Liliana, "and so, opposing all forms of repression, they condoned teenage sexuality. In practice this meant we'd walk to her house every day after school and jump into bed until her folks came home from work. What an arrangement."[5]

What an arrangement, indeed. And for Rudd, his introduction to this kind of sexual-cultural Marxism was about to go into warp speed, as he left his high school for the worst political-ideological zoo in America: Columbia University. There, Rudd would become one of the leading revolutionaries in a disintegrating country. As head of the Columbia chapter of SDS, he and his comrades "occupied" and shut down the university in April 1968, a flying circus, educational eruption, and much-deserved cultural-political cesspool made possible by John Dewey and his "progressive" pals turning on the spigot.

There, Rudd and friends imbibed in hour after hour of arguments over Marxism. He formed Marxist alliances not only with Columbia students but with young Reds from other campuses who were part of the SDS orbit that morphed into the Weathermen. These included Bernardine Dohrn, Bill Ayers, John Jacobs, Jeff Jones, Michael Klonsky, and (among many others) David Gilbert and Kathy Boudin, the latter two of whom would ultimately do long-term jail time for robbery and murder. All were hard-core communists, most of them Maoists and devotees of Che and Fidel, but also a Stalinist or two.

The youthful apparatchiks were especially taken by Che, whom Rudd described as their "revolutionary martyr and saint." Che was their Jesus Christ: "Like a Christian seeking to emulate the life of Christ," wrote Rudd, "I passionately wanted to be a revolutionary like Che, no matter what the cost." When Rudd's best friend, John Jacobs, died a few years after their failed revolution, they scattered his atheistic ashes at the tomb of their beloved Che in Cuba.[6]

As noted, some of these communists (i.e., Michael Klonsky) even had a kind word or two for Stalin, whereas others fell into near-Stalinist tactics. (Rudd recalls a meeting in 1969 when Klonsky "several times" said that "Stalin is the cutting edge.") Rudd found himself using the word "Stalinism" a lot to describe the evolution of the thinking of his comrades by the mid-1970s, especially the criminal work of Dohrn and Ayers, which he said had "degenerated into mindless Stalinism, cruelty, and betrayal."[7]

This was Dohrn's mind set especially. Born Bernardine Ohrnstein in Milwaukee in January 1942, Dohrn was a fanatic. Like a dour KGB colonel, she would purge you if you did not fit her ideal of the communist revolution. She excommunicated from their circle John Jacobs, whom Rudd described as akin to "a victim of one of Stalin's purges." As for Jacobs, he nervously joked that "at least they're not going to liquidate me."[8]

Well, maybe not. But the ruminations of Dohrn and Ayers grew so violent that the likes of Rudd would need to flee them—but not quite yet. That would come several years later.

A symbol of what was to come occurred in Flint, Michigan, the day after Christmas of 1969. There, the SDS-Weathermen cadre held their so-called War Council, which they laughingly described as a giant, collective "wargasm," an appropriate term given their seamless confluence of sex and violence.

It was like a radical revival meeting, with the Right Reverend Dohrn preaching the revolutionary gospel to the disciples who were ready to ignite the world ablaze with tongues and weapons of fire. Miss Dohrn mounted the pulpit and enriched the faithful with her unique thoughts on the vicious Tate–LaBianca murders executed by the satanic Charles Manson "family." Their demonic homicide was gruesome, most saliently in the mutilation of pregnant actress Sharon Tate by the swastika-tattooed Manson brood. The crime done by the Manson clan is too grotesque to describe here, particularly the ripping open of Tate's belly, but it was not to Bernardine Dohrn. The future professor of child education at Northwestern University saw a kind of deliciousness in the gory actions of these Manson "revolutionaries." To the assembled, Dohrn thrilled at what had been done to Tate in particular: "Dig it! First they killed those pigs. Then they ate dinner in the same room with them. Then they even shoved a fork into the victim's stomach! Wild!"[9]

They dug it, all right. The brethren celebrated the image of the slaughter of the Tate child. The faithful, from Bernadine's sweetheart, Bill Ayers, to everyone else in the hall, knew that Bernardine was serious.[10] As Rudd reported, the assembled "instantly adopted as Weather's salute four fingers held up in the air, invoking the fork left in Sharon Tate's belly."[11]

As the night wore on, the '60s radicals danced and devoured one another, breaking into spontaneous, animalistic acts of intercourse right there on the dance floor. One of the witnesses was a brave FBI informant named Larry Grathwohl, who observed horrible things from this group of comrades he had penetrated more deeply than anyone. Grathwohl vividly recalled a discussion between the bomb-plotting Bill Ayers and Columbia cronies on how their revolution would logically necessitate the killing of upwards of 25 million Americans rounded into concentration camps for indoctrination or elimination. Ayers and friends would be the new commissars who from their "central committee" perch would rule the new communist America.[12]

At this evening in Flint, the mass "wargasm," Grathwohl was sickened by the spectacle of the peace-evoking flower children responding to Rev. Dohrn's four-finger salute with a novel four-finger dance routine. They gleefully danced with their fingers in the form of the four-finger salute, moving their arms up and down and back and forth, chortling joyfully.[13]

Bernardine Dohrn was her own brand of woman. Her version of femininity was not a turnoff to the Weather Underground dudes. She dated Jeff Jones before Bill Ayers. The guys were attracted to the militant maiden. In fact, everyone in the group seemed attracted to one another.

They and their wider movement were all about easy intercourse.

Mark Rudd talks about one of the forays that "fourteen or so of us" took in a long "van" ride from Chicago to Detroit. All of them, he said, "except perhaps for the driver, writhed naked on the floor of the van while hurtling down the interstate, legs, arms, torsos, genitals interlocked with no particular identity attached."

This was as physically unhealthy as it was morally unhealthy. The New Left comrades were plagued by chronic sexually transmitted disease. Rudd recorded: "Gonorrhea, pelvic inflammatory disease, crab lice, and a nonspecific genital infection we called 'Weather crud' were epidemic among us." Rudd remembers one moment when "making love" to an old sex partner from Columbia; he looked into her face and saw a "crab" lodged in her eyebrow. "I could not go on," he said.[14]

Alas, there was one obstacle the revolutionaries could not chalk up to mere cultural inhibitions. Reality offered the occasional biological-medical barrier that was undeniable even to the most thoroughly brain-washed cultural Marxist. And of course, when STDs were not a concern, pregnancy was, even with the glory of the pill, which was not perfect in preventing conception. When an unwanted baby was produced amid this debauchery, it was simply destroyed by an abortion doctor in Betty Friedan's new "pro-choice" America, likely at one of Margaret Sanger's Planned Parenthood clinics.[15]

Rudd explained all of this as part of an ongoing effort at "extreme sexual experimentation" that included "group sex, homosexuality, casual sexual hook-ups." In cultural Marxist fashion, it was all intended "to break out of the repression of the past into the revolutionary future." It was all key, he said, to "smashing monogamy."

In fact, said Rudd, there was an official "anti-monogamy line" among the SDS-Weathermen officers. It included a refusal of fidelity among unmarried boyfriends and girlfriends, who were ordered to be separated as they traveled to different "collectives" in different cities, where they were expected to take on new sexual mates.[16] (This was actually similar to a Soviet practice, though married Soviet officials were often told to divorce and take on new spouses in new cities; the

Bolsheviks at least preferred some semblance of marriageable respectability, probably for the sake of appearances and acceptance in noncommunist cultures.)

But even then, Rudd admitted, "our sexual ideology quickly proved to be disastrous." He said that "smashing monogamy drove many good people out of the collectives." Many found these forced arrangements unnatural and undesirable. They fell in love and did not want other partners. According to Rudd, the situation became "inherently unstable."[17]

As for homosexuality, that was encouraged, too, but with very little success among the men. "In a revolutionary collective," explained Rudd, "there should be no [sexual] barriers between people."[18] In practice, this meant that mainly women slept with women. Rudd and the boys occasionally tried to engage in a little male-to-male sex, but, for reasons he attributed not to biology but to repressive culture, largely were not aroused by the naked private parts of other men. Nonetheless, they tried—in Marcusean–Wilhelmian fashion—to break down those barriers, those "hang-ups." Rudd detailed moments when he considered giving a few strokes to his buddy while they partook of the same woman, but this just did not appeal to him the way fondling women did. "My own internal taboo never let me do more than fondle JJ's [his best friend, John Jacobs] penis during a threesome with a Weatherwoman one night," said Rudd.

Note the logic in Rudd's thinking, disordered as it was by his unnatural political ideology: It assumed that, were it not for a miserably repressive/homophobic culture, Rudd and his buddy would not be retarded by oppressive "inhibitions" and would be going at each other like two virgin newlyweds on their honeymoon. Rudd would be devouring men precisely in line with his self-admitted unquenchable thirst for women. *What a tragedy this repressive culture is! It's all the fault of the culture. It's isn't biology or theology, natural law or biblical law, but culture alone—a fascist, oppressive culture.*

What about the "crab" in the eyebrow that made Rudd stop giving sex to the girl? Was that also mere internal "taboo?" Of course, it wasn't. But Rudd's demented political ideology did not force him into a demented cultural excuse for being turned off by a genital insect protruding from a woman's eyebrow. That warped ideology did, however, browbeat him into a weird sense of guilt for not being sexually turned on by his best friend of the same gender.

Only a leftist so saturated with so perverse an ideology could be indoctrinated into such imbecility. Rudd's ideology had destroyed his capacity for normal thought and basic biological instinct. It compelled him to deny his very design and war against his own nature. The fact that he had always had an insatiable desire for women but no interest whatsoever in men was a curiosity he chalked up to mere societal-cultural constructs. If ever there was a poster boy for the twisted erotic Marxism of Herbert Marcuse and Wilhelm Reich, this was it.

But while homosexuality was too hard for Rudd and his buddies to embrace, sex with virtually any woman, married or unmarried, was eminently attractive. And thus, smashing monogamy there went ahead unhindered.

Rudd recounted him and his best friend, JJ, doubling up with a happily married young woman named Barbara, who, along with her husband, Carl, had naïvely opened their New York home to the two Weathermen to stay for a time and share their roof and radical worldview. Of course, this had some major marital implications in store for Barbara and Carl.

When Carl left the house for work, JJ seduced Barbara first. Mark found them in bed together. In classic Weathermen style, Mark was the next man up. Mark then took Carl's wife, with JJ lying asleep next to her. Mark felt "an intense excitement" at the thought of his and JJ's fluids mixing together inside a shared woman.[19]

In a Marx-Engels frame of mind, Rudd saw himself as liberating this poor, wretched housewife, even though he conceded that she and her husband were "decent, gentle" people who showed him an appealing form of domesticity that he was privately longing for. Rudd and JJ showed their appreciation to Carl by taking turns having sex with his wife. It was, of course, a form of acceptable political sex. For Rudd, sex was often "a kind of political event, an encounter with the revolution in bed." Barbara was about to be the next revolutionary partner. "I was Barbara's liberator," Rudd asserted, "bringing her freedom from her life of quiet desperation. My penis was a magic wand of liberation."[20]

That night, a liberated Barbara spilled the beans to a crushed Carl, and a heated, loud argument ensued. Rudd intervened. He and Carl exchanged words. JJ split immediately for Philadelphia. Rudd stayed in the wrecked home another week, bedding Barbara once more. Barbara muttered some sappy, sad Freudian–Marxist psychobabble to Rudd, claiming she "liked her new self" and "felt free of the old oppressed person." She was free of the bonds of patriarchy. She was also soon free of Rudd, too, who flew the coop, heading for California.

Now, Barbara was so free that she was fully alone. No more lovers, no more revolutionary partners, and no doubt a dose of "Weather crud" to give Carl, who was so distraught that he was likely her soon-to-be former husband.

The Weathermen neo-Marxists had succeeded in blowing up yet another marriage, sacrificed at the atheistic altar of their obscene politics, another casualty of cultural Marxism. "The slash-and-burn, scorched-earth policy of the Weathermen had left destruction in its wake yet again," Rudd affirmed. "I never saw Carl or Barbara again."[21]

For the New Left, this ideological-sexual experimentation was part and parcel of the new revolution, with no institutional stone left unturned. I have here thus far focused on Mark Rudd's account, but the activities of any number of these '60s comrades would be shocking.

A pal of Rudd at Columbia was another kid from New Jersey, Michael Lerner, who later became editor of the Jewish spiritual magazine *Tikkun*. Later still, in the 1990s, Lerner became the celebrated "Politics of Meaning" guru to First Lady Hillary Rodham Clinton. Lerner married his '60s sweetheart, but their vows were hardly conventional. He and his New Left bride, whose father had been a conservative military man, exchanged wedding rings hammered from the debris of a downed US aircraft in Vietnam. The proud bride had gotten them from North Vietnam. The metal from the downed fuselage was to be an eternal symbol of their love. Their wedding cake was inscribed with the Weatherman slogan, "Smash monogamy." The marriage lasted less than a year, smashed by their sexual politics.[22]

Michael Lerner had been a graduate assistant to Herbert Marcuse. More than that, he stayed in Marcuse's home and became friends with him. Lerner called Marcuse "an inspiration," especially in the "struggle for inclusion."[23] Today, Lerner is chair of the Network of Spiritual Progressives and a signatory to the Beyond Marriage campaign. He is another product of the Frankfurt School Marxists.

Such wedding rings worn by the likes of Lerner were a badge of honor to certain faithful at the late John Dewey's beloved Columbia.[24] Mark Rudd also owned one that he wore with pride. He couldn't wait to put it around his finger. "I wore mine proudly for years afterward," he said.[25]

The 1960s were a huge boost to the destruction of traditional marriage in the West. In radical circles in the '60s (and into the '70s), "smashing monogamy" was the buzzword; it was all the rage.

That brings us back to the inner orbit of the Weathermen.

An enlightening read is the late Larry Grathwohl's telltale *Bringing Down America: An FBI Informer with the Weathermen*. As noted, Grathwohl, who died in July 2013, had infiltrated the Weathermen in the 1970s. Day after day for month upon month, this Vietnam vet and war hero had to buddy around with Mark Rudd and Bill Ayers and Bernadine Dohrn and crew. His horrible task meant doing what they did, living as they lived. A thread throughout Grathwohl's account is how the Weathermen were dedicated to abolishing monogamous marriage, which they viewed as a repressive remnant of both male and white supremacy.

Grathwohl's account of the tawdry details (which he also shared with me in conversation) matches those of Rudd. Particularly poignant was his account of a struggling mother in the Weather Underground, a woman named "Melody," and her four-year-old daughter, "Debby." It says much about the Weathermen's views on family—and particularly motherhood.

To say that the women in the Weathermen collective were militant feminists is inadequate. They were bomb-laying feminists, in both a literal and figurative sense. When they were not literally inserting and exploding bombs in toilets of women's restrooms at targeted offices, or helping to build bombs—one of the Weatherwomen, Diana Oughton, was killed in a premature detonation at a town house in Greenwich Village—they were laying figurative bombs at the feet of motherhood.

Grathwohl recalls the heart-wrenching story of lonely Debby, a "frail, pensive child" who played by herself each day in the courtyard of the collective while the adults planned war against America. It was a dismal existence, but the daughter and mother loved each other and gave each other affection.

All of a sudden, one day, one of the ferocious women of the pack began berating Melody and insisting that her precious girl be separated from the mother in a children's commune. It was the Kollontai ideal. The mother cried and protested; the little girl was causing no one any trouble. The militants bore down, descending upon the mom and child, who were frightened, scared, confused, as they clutched each other. Grathwohl was appalled at "how cruel the process was."[26]

Debby was pulled from her mother and dispatched to the children's collective, with Melody forced to accept the fiat of the female despots. It was a scene done countless millions of times in places like Red China and Pol Pot's Cambodia. Now it was being done in America by John Dewey's educational grandchildren.

Grathwohl explained how all of this was symptomatic of the women comrades being more independent, being fully liberated, and, most of all, not needing men, including for sex. "Some of [the women] said that men were unnecessary for sex," stated Grathwohl. "Any man who believed in women's liberation had to agree with this. A liberated man would refuse to accept women as sex objects and could enjoy sex with other men."[27]

This was the new family for the communist revolutionaries. New family, new views of marriage, new views of sex.

Yet again, these Marxist disciples had no intent of waiting for "sublation" or "transcendence" of marriage and family. They were taking it down here and now on behalf of the revolution. It was abolition time.

Finally, no analysis of the Weathermen would be complete without a few words on the manifesto of the Weather Underground, the group's crowning opus, *Prairie Fire: The Politics of Revolutionary Anti-Imperialism*. Published in 1974 as the official "political statement of the Weather Underground," it was signed by the four leading members: Bill Ayers, Bernardine Dohrn, Jeff Jones, and Celia Sojourn, with Ayers and Dohrn the chief writers.

"We are a guerrilla organization," the authors declared. "We are communist women and men, underground in the United States," seeking to "give coherence and direction to the fight, seize power and build the new society." "We have only begun," they vowed. "The only possibilities are victory or death." "Our intention," they wrote of their "revolutionary program," was "to disrupt the empire" of "US imperialism," "to incapacitate it." The manifesto pledged: "The only path to the final defeat of imperialism and the building of socialism is revolutionary war." That "war," the authors promised, "will be complicated and protracted. It includes mass struggle and clandestine struggle, peaceful and violent. . . . Without armed struggle there can be no victory."

It was a violent work that looked to take down not only the country but also many of its traditions related to sexuality and the family. Pages 126–31 of the manifesto focused on women, the women's movement, women's "subjugation," "tasks for revolutionary women," "breaking the chains" that bound women, the home, the family, marriage, sexuality, and the "culture of sexism." Kollontai-like, it pushed the need for an "uprising of women" and a "revolutionary feminism" to advance "the collective interests of women."

Perhaps most interesting, in a culturally revolutionary statement for its time, was the section of the manifesto on "Women liking women" (page 129), which challenged—especially via an "affirmation" of "lesbianism"—the "dominant culture's treatment of homosexuals" (i.e., mistreatment) for not conforming to standard sexual roles and morality. *Prairie Fire* linked discrimination against gay people with "sexist ideology which subjugates women."

To be fair, much of what the manifesto said about unfair treatment of gays and women, and especially of the sexual objectification of women, was merited. Nonetheless, the Weather Underground, like its leftist friends in the years ahead, had in mind much more than just reversing discrimination. Ayers and Dohrn and friends were conceiving an entirely new paradigm for a Red family that would set the new standard for American family life.

15

THE RED FAMILY

TWO OTHER ACCOUNTS FROM THIS '60s period are especially valuable: the fascinating stories of Ron Radosh and David Horowitz, both former communists who would record their experiences in probably the two best memoirs of the period. Those accounts will also bring us back to the Weathermen.

Ron Radosh spent much time with the New Left. He was a communist, with a steady diet of Marxism-Leninism in a Red-diaper-baby upbringing. Radosh tells his story in his riveting memoir, *Commies: A Journey Through the Old Left, the New Left and the Leftover Left*, highly recommended as one of the most illuminating political-biographical accounts of the period. Radosh, who, like David Horowitz, is today a conservative, was always far more sensible than Mark Rudd, which means that his memoirs lack the incessant flow of depravity that makes one feel like taking a bath after reading Rudd's remarkably honest account.

But Radosh, too, is fully candid. Certain aspects of what he recorded about the New Left and the revolutionary culture at the time are especially relevant to this book.

Radosh was raised in a thoroughly (ethnic) Jewish culture that included (as he put it) "a complete rejection of anything to do with religion." Other than attending an occasional bar mitzvah, he said he never set foot in a synagogue and learned nothing of the Jewish faith. For him and many of his friends in New York's Upper West Side, the faith became Marxism-Leninism. As an adolescent, Radosh attended "Commie Camp" in the summertimes. Many of these were held in the Catskills, where the New York faithful sent their children. These spectacles were a sort of Red version of what Christians call vacation Bible school. They included left-wing musical talents such as Joan Baez and Stalinist minstrels Pete Seeger and Paul Robeson. Radosh, in fact, personally learned to play banjo from Seeger. He attended school at the Little Red Schoolhouse.[1]

Radosh's pilgrimage into and out of Marxism-Leninism is a gripping one that merits fuller attention, but, for our purposes here, deserves focus for what it likewise confirms about the New Left's pairing of the sexual revolution and communist revolution. Radosh details the sexual anarchy he witnessed in the 1960s, where he said that few thought twice about hopping into bed on the first date. Radosh wrote, "Some of the things I did were questionable, but in the period when smashing monogamy was the new standard of the Movement, I could always rationalize my behavior as helping to free society from bourgeois definitions of reality."

Radosh is commendably candid about those experiences, and one of them is notably symptomatic of the New Left's sexual-cultural Marxism. In the summer of 1970, Radosh and a female companion trekked across the country to Washington State and then to Berkeley. There they met Bob Scheer, who would become a well-known left-wing columnist. Scheer had been a founding editor of the radical *Ramparts*. He enthusiastically invited Radosh and his girlfriend to a commune that he helped found and led.[2]

The commune was called the "Red Family." And it was just that: a modern, New Left, "Red" version of the family. It was a full-fledged ideological colony fitted to cultural Marxist specifications—Owen and Fourier on steroids (actually, hallucinogens).

One famous member of the Red Family had been Tom Hayden, SDS founder and eventual mate to Vietcong go-go girl Jane Fonda, who won his heart as she mounted the artillery of the communist Vietnamese, which countless Vietnam vets construed as a giant ideological middle finger to their sacrifice. The gesture turned on Tom Hayden. He left his wife and other recent women he had hooked up with at the Red Family commune to exchange ideological vows with Henry Fonda's daughter.

The Red Family was not just about sexual revolution or a revolution in family life, however; it was about armed insurrection. It maintained its own arms depot. The family was gunned up and ready for action at the Red homestead.

While arming for the revolution, much of the Red Family's time was spent rolling around in beds together, exchanging political love and (of course) STDs. Such activity was necessary in purging society of its bourgeois infestations. Said Radosh: "The commune had been practicing with firearms in the Berkeley hills, but most of its attention was directed to sexual politics and to questions such as whether or not it was 'bourgeois' to want to close the bathroom door while using the toilet."[3] Such were just some of the pressing questions to be resolved in the new world.

"You've got to come and see what we're up to," Radosh was urged by Scheer, who was head teacher at the California collective. "You need to see what we've created."

Radosh and his girlfriend found utter chaos at the family collective. One woman was groaning in the midst of childbirth. Other women, plus kids and various men, stood or walked around. Scheer excitedly shared information on the Red Family, and he also spent two hours raving to Radosh about his return from a recent pilgrimage (that same year, 1970) to Kim Il-sung's North Korea, which the future *Los Angeles Times* star columnist found inspiring. This was a North Korean regime which, for the record, smashed the family as soundly as anything the Bolsheviks ever did. By Radosh's description, Scheer discovered "paradise in Pyongyang."[4]

And now, if only Scheer and the New Left could bring that paradise to America.

In subsequent years, as Scheer become a popular writer at the huge-circulation *Los Angeles Times*, once a publication of respectability before it became a blatantly biased mouthpiece for the Democratic Party, the former Red Family big daddy seemed reticent about discussing his past. He was not exactly vocal about his earlier radical notions, of which David Horowitz says he seems to have had no second thoughts.[5] This includes his embarrassing affection not just for the Red women of the Red Family but for the Red man, Kim Il-sung, the real-life Big Brother of the world's most repressive Stalinist state.

Radosh's notes on Scheer's time with the Red Family and admiration of Kim's North Korea has also been told by David Horowitz in a number of his books, including his autobiography *Radical Son* and *Destructive Generation*, coauthored by fellow former radical Peter Collier, as well as one of his books in his series on *The Black Book of the American Left*.[6] Scheer had apparently attempted to dispute some of Horowitz's memory, but what Horowitz recorded matches Ron Radosh's accounts.[7] Before considering that, a few words on Horowitz's path:

David Horowitz was likewise raised by communist parents in New York, both dedicated Party members. They, too, had the requisite connections to Columbia University and Columbia Teachers College. They were members of the same communist union as Bella Dodd when Dodd was a Red working for New York public schools. The Horowitzes sent their son to the predictable left-wing places, including Camp Wo-Chi-Ca, an Indian-sounding name that was an acronym for "Workers Children Camp," a summer commie camp for kids of CPUSA parents. There, David buddied with boys like Billy Gerson and Freddy Jerome, whose parents were major players in the American Communist Party, and who went to school with Margaret Mead's daughter.[8]

David's parents would remain on the left and politically active throughout their lives. For his mother, her Marxism led her to the Planned Parenthood–abortion movement. She became a skillful, prominent Planned Parenthood activist and a Margaret Sanger protégé who was even feted with the Margaret Sanger Award.[9]

David followed his parents' footsteps into the movement. One of the distinctives about Horowitz's path is that though he was part of the '60s, he was a little older than many of the new radicals. He was married. And like his communist parents, he was faithful in marriage, moral, honest, and did not pursue the sexual hedonism relished by others of the age and ideology. In *Radical Son*, Horowitz wrote about wanting to remain faithful to his wife amid the torrent of sexual expressions all around him, especially by young women who flaunted themselves. Regardless of the sexual politics of the New Left, he considered adultery to be wrong. He recalled the tensions around the office at *Ramparts*, where he and Collier worked with Robert Scheer.

Horowitz was appalled by Scheer's sexist attitude toward women and laissez-faire feelings about intercourse. By the time they worked together at *Ramparts*, Scheer had a second wife, and Horowitz details well-known episodes of Scheer's infidelity, including a tryst in Fidel's Cuba with the leftist journalist who had secured Che Guevara's diaries for publication.[10]

Eventually, Horowitz and Scheer parted ways, as Scheer (in 1969) was removed at *Ramparts*, fired by Horowitz and Collier. But vestiges of his work remained. One day a box of books addressed to Scheer arrived at the offices. Nestled inside were the collected works of Kim Il-sung.

Scheer had taken a delegation to North Korea, where they were wined and dined and duped with lavish spreads of food and booze and fed the usual Stalinist state agitprop (agitation and propaganda) about the glories of the collective and its cornucopia of wondrous feats for the masses. As usual, the otherwise cynical left gobbled up each and every bite, always willing to swallow whatever mouthful of nonsense spoonfed by whichever murderous communist regime. One wonders if they witnessed the Kim sexism that came with the rest of the hoorah of hedonistic pleasures. The men of the Kim family, especially Kim's son, Kim Jong-Il, were notorious for their rampant sexual appetites, evidenced by their well-supplied and meticulously stocked and groomed harems of sex slaves and massive private pornography collections. No one knows the number of North Korean women the Kims have impregnated during their sixty-plus years of hideous rule.

Either way, Robert Scheer was reportedly taken. He came back to the United States ready to dish out propaganda for Kim Il-sung.[11] Horowitz and Collier were told by their copy editor at *Ramparts*, Jan Austin, who had joined the North Korea delegation, that Scheer had intended to write an introduction to Kim's thought for American audiences. That was why the box of books had arrived.[12]

By that time, Scheer had absconded to Berkeley for the Red Family, which Horowitz described as "an urban guerrilla commune" that the future syndicated columnist formed with Tom Hayden, SDS founder, and Scheer's soon-to-be ex-wife, Anne. The commune was not about nonviolent resistance. It embodied Hayden's vision as an armed force on the domestic front to engage police (i.e., "pigs") and law-enforcement agencies and officials. Shotguns were propped up in the corners of rooms. According to Horowitz, the New Marxist family had its own "minister of defense" who trained family members at firing ranges and schooled high school children in the art of explosives.[13]

Horowitz noted that the Red Family, Kim-like, was run on Maoist principles. The walls of its headquarters on Bateman Street were adorned with giant glowing portraits of their favorite Asian communist despots: Ho Chi Minh and (of course) Kim Il-sung. These were displayed alongside pictures of Huey Newton and Geronimo, the Apache.[14]

Horowitz confirmed the Red Family's deliberations of vexing taboos, such as whether it was too "bourgeois" to close the bathroom door when using the toilet—and whether underwear should be shared, that is, redistributed among the collective. He also detailed the show-trial antics that could ensue among the family. In one sordid, almost laughable case, Scheer convened a kangaroo court and orchestrated charges of "bourgeois privatism" between Tom Hayden and Anne. Such action was verboten at the Red household. Hayden was purged, exiled. It was a very Mao-ish, Cultural Revolution–like kind of thing.[15]

Hayden fled and found and married his Hanoi heartthrob, Jane Fonda.

Finally, the remembrances of both David Horowitz and Peter Collier (in their *Destructive Generation*) on the SDS-Weathermen gang are likewise revealing of these communist revolutionaries' sexual politics and views on marriage. As historians of the period who also lived through and personally observed a good deal of it, they confirm what Mark Rudd recollected in his memoir.

For Bernardine Dohrn especially, sex was a revolutionary tool. Greg Calvert, SDS president, recalled to Horowitz and Collier the first time he saw her. Whereas other SDS protesters were wearing buttons that said things like "Stop the War," hers said: "Cunnilingus Is Cool, Fellatio Is Fun." The self-described "revolutionary communist" from Milwaukee dressed the part and played the part, exhibiting herself to numerous men throughout the movement. "She used sex to explore and cement political alliances," said Jim Mellen, one of the members of the inner circle. "Sex for her was a form of ideological activity."[16]

Like their pal Tom Hayden's Red Family, the Weathermen's revolution required arms. They purchased and stockaded weaponry and practiced their usage in remote areas. Their so-called "bodyguards" carried concealed .38 pistols while covering the likes of Dohrn during her various public appearances and Marxist diatribes.[17]

But the mass of arms was nothing compared to the intertwining mass of body parts that Weathermen guys and gals laid upon one another in their collective group-sex efforts (sometimes called "animal meeting") to advance their sexual politics and to "smash monogamy." Collier and Horowitz wrote, "They initiated a 'smash monogamy' campaign to destroy bourgeois sexual hang-ups in the same way that street fighting was meant to 'smash' bourgeois prohibitions against violence."[18]

One of Dohrn's beaus, Bill Ayers, who would eventually become her lifelong spouse, gave a speech articulating the rationale for the group's anti-monogamy campaign. "We have to destroy that notion in order to build a collective," said Ayers. They needed "to destroy the notion that people can lean on one person and not be responsible to the entire collective."[19] Here we see the absolute link between the anti-marriage views of these people and their Marxist revolutionary views. And here, too, there was no waiting for any sort of Marxist "transcendence" or "sublation" of traditional marriage. These '60s comrades were waiting for nothing; they were smashing it then and there at full force.

The comrades were so insistent about not waiting for some gradual abolition of marriage or monogamy that they hassled and harangued would-be faithful couples into admitting their "political errors" and splitting apart. It was as if the faithful were committing political sins in the Church of Marx and had to be called out for their heresy, of which they had to repent or be excommunicated. And with smashing monogamy a first step, the next logical step was group sex—i.e., orgies. On this, Collier and Horowitz, like Rudd, provided lurid details from the participants.[20]

All restraints were being thrown to the wind by these cultural communists. What Reich and Marcuse and the Freudian Marxists had railed against was being fulfilled in reams by their ideological children. They were indeed totally smashing all bourgeois conventions.

The role of women in all of this is intriguing.

Once upon a time in America and the West, women were the gatekeepers who kept a lid on the unquenchable urges of men. They were the ones in the culture who said no. As the would-be child bearers in the equation, they enforced the boundaries. Bishop Fulton Sheen upheld them as the "custodians of life," who served as both physical and spiritual examples of motherhood. "The level of civilization is always the level of its womanhood," said Sheen.[21]

Such an ennobling view of women espoused by the likes of Sheen was dismissed by the Bernardine Dohrns of the world as a bunch of fascistic bourgeois claptrap.

In fact, amazingly, Collier and Horowitz reported that the campaign against monogamy by the Dohrn-Ayers gang was actually initiated by the women in the collective. Their twisted New Left ideological mindset allowed them to convince themselves that sexual monogamy led to sexual exclusivity that led to sexual "inequality" among the genders. This was just fine, of course, for the men in the group, who did what came much more natural to them than it does for women: they happily had sex with as many different partners as possible. For the men, the women were not paragons of purity to be coveted and protected but willing receptacles and pleasure units. In the new world ushered in by this new form of cultural revolutionary, the Weathermen women—all along trumpeting greater respect for women—would be the vanguards in lowering their sexual guards and opening the gates to their exploitation.

Of course, the supreme facilitator to this madness was a gift bequeathed by progressive sisters from an earlier generation: birth control. Everything changed with "the pill," the birth-control revolution that Margaret Sanger had so badly wanted. The advent of the pill in (of all times) the '60s, in lockstep with the cultural politics of the New Left and its Marxism and Freudianism and whatever else, generated an eruption in premarital and extramarital sex. The pill sought to separate reproductive organs from their reproductive purpose; sex became an end toward seemingly anything but its primary biological intention. And when those pills would occasionally fail to deliver their promised contraception, the culture that couldn't say no would demand and get the revered *Roe v. Wade* that would enable the frolickers to abort the undesired by-product of their wanton sexual activities. They were five decades behind the Bolsheviks, but they were at last getting their abortions and divorces by the bucketload.

Finally, Collier and Horowitz affirm what Mark Rudd remembered about the next sexual taboo that the Weathermen's sexual politics sought to knock down: homosexuality. They, too, report that this was one taboo too hard to break, especially for the boys, who just did not seem pumped up about "doing it" with their buddies.[22]

But not all the boys: The dedicated Bill Ayers spoke of his willingness to cross the bridge. In the glowing profile of him in (ironically) the September 11, 2001, *New York Times*, where Ayers expressed "no regrets" about his and his allies' earlier bombings in New York City and at the Pentagon, he openly spoke of the Weathermen's bisexual experimentation as they smashed monogamy. He described the Weathermen as "an army of lovers" that, for him, included his best male friend.[23]

The radicals were way ahead of their time in seeking to shatter male-female monogamous marriage and taboos against same-gender sexual activity. American culture would need about forty years to catch up with these '60s communist revolutionaries.

Notably, Horowitz, in other works, has detailed a similar militancy about smashing monogamy among the gay left. This has been likewise endemic (if not epidemic) to the gay-rights movement since the 1960s. The number of sexual partners for the average gay man utterly dwarfs the number for a heterosexual man. For gays, that lack of exclusivity is also typical of many of their partnerships.[24] This lack of monogamy is, of course, unhealthy as well as unfaithful, just as it is for heterosexuals—though much worse for gays because of AIDS. When Horowitz during a debate on politics and AIDS broached the advantage of monogamy, a gay activist shouted at him: "You see, you *see*! He said *monogamous*. That's his prejudice, his homophobia coming out!"[25]

The sexual revolution was spouting all sorts of fronts against traditional ways of thinking. Monogamy was being smashed to smithereens.

In all, wrote Collier and Horowitz, sex for the Weathermen and their comrades was a "bourgeois conceit that had to be attacked. . . . Sex was always part of politics."[26]

It sure was. That had been the intention all along. Freudian Marxism had conceived its bastard children. Its ideological offspring had been born.

The Frankfurt School gang that John Dewey yearned for at Columbia was at long last reaping what it had sown—total nihilism and the takedown of the culture, with American marriage in smoldering ruins, like those downed American aircraft in Vietnam. In both cases, whether downed marriage or downed aircraft, communist enemies had been the perpetrators.

Ultimately, many of these '60s children as grown adults would flock into the university system, the ongoing academic laboratories. Ayers went to John Dewey's and Kate Millett's and the Frankfurt gang's Columbia University, where he got his doctorate in education and sought to become an effective "change agent." He became a professor of education at the University of Illinois–Chicago. He and his wife, Bernardine, would come to know and work with a young, rising Chicago politician named Barack Obama, serving on boards with him in Chicago and infamously giving him (in a moment even reported by the *New York Times*) their political blessing from their Hyde Park living room in 1995.[27]

In 2008 many of these old SDS-Weather Underground radicals were reunited in a group called Progressives for Obama, spearheaded by Mark Rudd and Tom Hayden.[28] Hayden's own '60s onetime monogamous marriage went down in flames when he was smitten with Vietcong cheerleader Jane Fonda, another official Progressive for Obama. Tom and Jane married, only to divorce later. In the 1960s, as a student at the University of Michigan, Hayden had drafted the Port Huron statement, the founding document for SDS. In 2008, he drafted the founding document for Progressives for Obama, a group he started with Barbara Ehrenreich, who is also a signatory to the Beyond Marriage campaign. Obama was the first Democratic nominee for president that Hayden, Rudd, Ayers, Dohrn, and the other '60s communists finally found to their liking. Here was a presidential candidate, at long last, that they could enthusiastically support.

It would be a new president and a new dawn for those who had fancied themselves at the frontier of a new form of Red family.

16

THE GAY-MARRIAGE PRESIDENT— AND HIS MENTOR

SPEAKING OF BARACK OBAMA, I WOULD be remiss to neglect him and the influence of his mentor, a man on whom I wrote a full biography,[1] and who serves as a compellingly relevant case during this period. Frank Marshall Davis was a hard-core communist, an actual card-carrying member of Communist Party USA, who spent time with a young Barack Obama throughout the 1970s, right up to the moment that Obama left Hawaii for Occidental College in 1979.

Davis (1905–87) was a writer, journalist, poet, and activist. His politics were so extreme that he joined the Communist Party in Chicago in the early 1940s. As we know from his declassified six-hundred-page FBI file (and other sources), his card number was 47544. He became very engaged in Party circles. In 1946 he became the founding editor in chief of the *Chicago Star*, the Party-line newspaper for Chicago. There, Davis shared the op-ed page with the likes of Howard Fast, a "Stalin Prize" winner, and Senator Claude "Red" Pepper, who, at the time, sponsored the bill to nationalize health care in the United States.

Davis left the *Star* in 1948 for Hawaii, where he would write for the communist organ there, the *Honolulu Record*. His politics remained so radical that the FBI had Davis under continued surveillance. More than that, the federal government placed Davis on the Security Index, meaning that in the event of a war between the United States and the USSR, Barack Obama's mentor could be placed under immediate arrest.

Davis's targets were Democrats more than Republicans, given that it was Democrats such as Harry Truman who, from the White House, opposed Stalin's Soviet expansion. In December 1956, the Democrat-run Senate Judiciary Committee called Davis to Washington to testify on his activities. Davis pleaded the Fifth Amendment. No matter, the next year, the Democratic Senate published a report titled "Scope of Soviet Activity in the United States," where it listed Davis as "an identified member of the Communist Party."

Frank Marshall Davis would meet a young Obama in 1970, introduced by Obama's grandfather, Stanley Dunham, for the purpose of mentoring. The nine-year-old's grandfather felt that the fatherless boy was in need of a black male role model. For that, Dunham chose one of the most politically radical figures in all of Hawaii. He introduced the two in the fall of 1970. An eyewitness, a woman named Dawna Weatherly-Williams, who knew Davis so well that she called him "Daddy," was present the first time Obama and Davis met. She described the relationship as very influential, with Davis impacting Obama on "social justice," on "life," on "what's important," and on "how to use" his "heart" and "mind." Her account, and Obama's own, reveals a Davis who advised Obama on social-cultural matters, from attitudes on race and America, to education and women, to much more.

Stanley Dunham seemed to hope that Obama would find in Davis the father figure and role model he lacked. So deep was the impression that Obama, in his huge, best-selling memoir, *Dreams from My Father*, would cite "Frank" dozens of times over thousands of words and in each and every section of his memoirs.

Much more could be said on all of this, but the theme in this book is marriage, family, sexuality, and communist/far-left politics. To that end, one aspect of Davis that I barely mentioned in my biography of the man, but which others have dug into quite a bit, was his sexually adventurous lifestyle, both during the time he was married to his wife and later, after their divorce, when Davis was in his sixties and seventies but was nonetheless vigorous, promiscuous, and decidedly nontraditional.

The Internet is rife with scandalous accusations of Davis's various sexual escapades and preferences, and (most scandalous) how those choices might have impacted his literal relations with Obama and Obama's family. Some have done articles, books, and full-fledged documentaries arguing that Davis is Obama's real father. (I have no conclusive evidence to support that claim.) Even more scandalous, some have gone so far as to consider whether Davis had sexual relations with a young Obama, a bold assertion that has been out there for years and which I certainly cannot substantiate.[2] This kind of sensational material is often the first information that pops up in web searches on Davis and Obama.

Liberals offended by speculation on Davis's sordid adventures and how they might relate to Obama need to understand that the thoughts are not totally unjustified. Davis himself is at least partly responsible. At the height of the sexual revolution in the late '60s, when Davis was in his sixties, the old communist penned a quasi-pornographic novel called *Sex Rebel*, under an alias, "Bob Greene."[3] Bob's sexual exploits, from bisexuality to seducing barely teenage girls (including a thirteen-year-old named "Anne," which, as many have noted, happens to be the name of Obama's mother), are revealed frankly. They are shared without shame, even boasted about. Davis's own memoirs, *Livin' the Blues*, conceded his authorship of *Sex Rebel*.[4] He happily admitted "[I] could not truthfully deny that this book, which came out in 1968 as a Greenleaf Classic, was mine."[5] The only question is to what extent the exploits are fictional or nonfictional, desired experiences or actual experiences, partly or fully autobiographical.[6]

Author Jack Cashill has studied *Sex Rebel*, a book almost impossible to purchase, track down, and even borrow via interlibrary loan. Cashill noted that in *Sex Rebel*, the Davis persona, the narrator, insists that the protagonist's sexual adventures are all "taken from actual experiences." The narrator also concedes that "under certain circumstances I am bisexual." The mock introduction to the book, written by an alleged PhD named "Dale Gordon," goes further still, describing the pseudonymous author, Bob Greene, as possessing "strong homosexual tendencies in his personality."[7]

Tellingly, the book was conceived, documented, written, published, and perhaps lived while Frank Marshall Davis was still married. He and his wife, Helen, divorced in 1970, after twenty-four years of marriage and five children together. That marriage was a major struggle for years. Davis's huge FBI file includes claims that he once intended to divorce Helen as far back as May 1957. It features some highly personal information on their marital struggles and preferences for others outside their bed.[8] Helen, too, it should be noted, was a communist, who Davis met at the communist Abraham Lincoln School in Chicago in the 1940s, where he taught and she was a pupil. Helen's Communist Party USA number was 62109.[9]

Davis's *Sex Rebel* is an alarming and quite graphic and disturbing book written by a decidedly unconventional individual. Sharing and discussing that material is not necessary here, but it is important to understand that Davis's sexual life and practices were not unrelated to his communist philosophy.

If Barack Obama's liberal admirers and protectors in the media were not so biased in ignoring any information that could redound negatively to Obama, they would pause to read Davis's wide-ranging and prodigious written work, equally radical in its ideological as well as sexual content. They would be quickly outraged by Davis's objectification of women, his candid and prideful braggadocio about luring very young girls into bed, and his lush enjoyment in photographing nude women.[10] In his memoirs (not his novel), which are easily available, Davis referred to women as "babes" and "broads" and "fine young foxes" and "dykes" and "luscious ripened plums," and blithely made statements like "I have impregnated only three women." He never informed us who the other two women were (aside from his wife). He never acknowledged the existence of any child beyond those to Helen.

In that memoir, Davis was unapologetic in graphically thrilling over women's private parts, which he described in language too crude and vulgar to repeat here.[11] And again, to repeat, there appear to be clear indications of same-sex interest by Davis in his writings.

Did Barack Obama, our first Gay Marriage President, learn any of these unconventional notions of sex from Frank Marshall Davis? The two of them met together many times (at least ten to fifteen, according to Obama biographer David Maraniss), sometimes one-on-one and late into the evenings, and Davis always offered the underage teen whiskey, which they drank together until they were drunk.[12] Obama himself wrote of drinking whiskey with Davis in *Dreams from My Father*. He also talked of discussing women with Davis, which, as we know from Davis's own writings, could be a dreadfully obscene exercise.

We do not know if and precisely how Davis influenced Obama's thinking in this regard. Again, the media has never asked—and dares not ask—Obama anything about Davis.

As for Obama's views on homosexuality and the American family, for a president they have been as revolutionary as the Communist Party that Frank Marshall Davis joined and the sexuality that animated the old communist. Most significant has been Obama's support for gay marriage, on which important new information has just been reported as this book is being completed. Consider the following:

David Axelrod has known Barack Obama better than any adviser other than perhaps Valerie Jarrett. Axelrod, who shaped the Obama "hope and change" message, is the man responsible for making Obama president. It is hard to imagine Obama being elected in 2008 and reelected in 2012 without the masterful campaign hand of David Axelrod.[13]

In his long-awaited and just-released memoirs, Axelrod wrote about Obama's early views on gay marriage. Editor and columnist George Neumayr has carefully compared what Axelrod has reported and Obama's various statements and positions. In all, it paints an intriguing and disturbing picture. Contrary to Obama's claims that he is only a recent convert to gay marriage, it looks as though he supported gay marriage as far back as the mid-1990s, when he was an aspiring Chicago politician living near (and meeting and working with) the likes of Bill Ayers and Bernardine Dohrn. Obama apparently supported legalization two decades ago, but publicly suggested otherwise (meaning he lied) in order to get votes, especially from African Americans who rejected gay marriage in higher numbers than white Americans.[14]

According to Axelrod, in 1996, as a candidate for state senate from left-wing Hyde Park, Obama signed a questionnaire promising his support for legalization of same-sex marriage. "I had no doubt that this was his heartfelt belief," states Axelrod today. By 2011, adds Axelrod, President Barack Obama was "champing at the bit to announce his support for the right of gay and lesbian couples to wed." In May 2012, a year after his Justice Department announced it would not support the Defense of Marriage Act, Obama summoned ABC's Robin Roberts to the White House to publicly make his support of redefining marriage clear to all of America.[15]

Axelrod's account is quite remarkable. Even the most liberal Democrats were not supporting gay marriage as far back as 1996. If Obama was indeed behind same-sex marriage at that point—and Axelrod would know—then something earlier in his ideological formation might have been a factor. Was it Frank Marshall Davis? I cannot say. Davis might possibly have influenced a more open view toward sexuality by Obama, but it is hard to imagine that the old communist would have touted gay marriage—though step one could have arguably eventually helped soften and lead Obama toward step two.

And what of the many moves in between steps one and two?

Barack Obama's pro-gay overtures as president have been unprecedented. Aside from his crucial public endorsement to Robin Roberts of same-sex marriage, there were numerous actions from the outset of his presidency. In June 2009 Obama met with more than 250 gay leaders in the East Room of the White House to commemorate the fortieth anniversary of the Stonewall uprising, considered the Independence Day of the gay-rights movement. There, Obama gave special recognition to gay-rights icon Franklin Kameny. Kameny's radical sexual politics were captured in a remark he gave the year before: "Let us have more and better enjoyment of more and better sexual perversions, by whatever definition, by more and more consenting adults. . . .

If bestiality with consenting animals provides happiness to some people, let them pursue their happiness."[16]

Kameny's thoughts prompt recollections of Wilhelm Reich and other Frankfurt School sexual-cultural radicals. They might have made Herbert Marcuse blush (well, maybe).

As for Barack Obama, such sentiments did not deter him from honoring Kameny, or, for that matter, from other eye-opening actions on the gay front.

Among them, as Obama was holding the Stonewall event at the White House, he was also in the process of appointing Kevin Brett Jennings to be his so-called safe schools czar in the US Department of Education. Jennings had his own Stonewall connections, having recently been nominated for a Stonewall Book Award. Previously, he had received the Lambda Literary Award for best book in the category of children/young adult. The graduate of Columbia Teachers College had founded the Gay, Lesbian, and Straight Education Network (GLSEN), which was aggressive in sponsoring Gay/Straight Alliance clubs in schools, anti-bullying days, and other methods to foster "safety" and acceptance of gays in schools. Now, the new president, Barack Obama, wanted Jennings for his Department of Education. As safe schools czar, Jennings would have at his command a $100-million-plus budget that would, among other things, dispense grants to schools to proliferate more "anti-bullying" and other programs.

This was a major controversy at the time, but what is worth highlighting in this treatment is not merely Jennings's gay activism or connection to education or (naturally) to Columbia University, but his connection to figures like Harry Hay and Bill Ayers.

As journalist Robert Knight shows in an arresting exposé, Jennings in an October 1997 GLSEN conference held at a New York City church pointed to the original gay-communist pioneer as a literal inspiration: "One of the people that's always inspired me is Harry Hay," said Jennings (more on Hay in the next chapter). "In 1948, he tried to get people to join the Mattachine Society. It took him two years to find one person to join. Well, [in] 1993, Harry Hay marched with a million people in Washington, who thought he had a good idea forty years before. Everybody thought Harry was crazy in 1948."[17]

Obama-like, Kevin Jennings sees Harry Hay as an inspiring model for "change." All of them—Obama, Jennings, and Hay—styled themselves as, to borrow from one of Bill Ayers's favorite terms, "change agents."

As for Ayers, Robert Knight flags the 1999 book *Queering Elementary Education*, which (according to Knight) included an essay by a lesbian who taught her seven-year-old daughter how to masturbate. This lesbian mother openly talked of how she and her daughter were attracted to the same twelve-year-old girl. She reportedly described "queerly raised children" as "agents" in the area of "resistance and subversion." No doubt, those words—"resistance" and "subversion"—would have turned on the Weather Underground crew, who smashed such sexual boundaries in service to their resistance and subversion. And indeed, Dr. Bill Ayers, who after his years as a Weather Underground terrorist bomber and fugitive who escaped jail time, and who then went to Columbia Teachers College to get his master's degree and doctorate in education, endorsed *Queering Elementary Education*. With a strong blurb on the back cover, Ayers called it "a book for all teachers and parents," and happily conceded, "And, yes, it has an agenda." Ayers, following his years of sexual experimentation in the Weather Underground, including with his best male friend, now pushes for "social justice" in sexual orientation and gender-identity issues in K–12 public schools.

As for Kevin Jennings, he one-upped Bill Ayers's endorsement of *Queering Elementary Education*: He wrote the foreword to the book.[18]

So much more could be said here about Kevin Jennings, but a final word is especially telling. Robert Knight quoted Jennings from a March 2000 speech on "tolerance" at a church, where Jennings, in classic Marcusean name-calling and framing the opposition as having views that should not be tolerated, nonetheless made an incisive observation: "Twenty percent of people are hard-core, fair-minded [pro-homosexual] people. Twenty percent are hard-core [anti-homosexual] bigots. We need to ignore the hard-core bigots, get more of the hard-core, fair-minded people to speak up, and we'll pull that 60 percent [in the middle] over to our side."

This is an insightful point by Jennings. His assessment of the numbers is exactly right. And right now, gay activists are winning that 60 percent in the middle. It explains their ongoing gay-marriage triumph among the masses. In fact, their success and confidence are such that right now they are not ignoring the 20 percent who oppose them but taking them to court, boycotting them, demonizing them, and seeking to destroy them.

In short, this was the individual that Barack Obama appointed as his safe schools czar and a deputy at the US Department of Education. There was clearly a new man in the Oval Office, who, just as promised, had a new view toward "fundamental transformation" of America.

Again, how much (if any) of Obama's accommodation of gays and their political-cultural agenda might be an outgrowth of Frank Marshall Davis's impact is something we do not know, and that only Barack Obama himself could explain to us. With Obama's protective liberal media, we cannot expect any questions that would prompt any such clarification of Davis's influence. And even if Davis were a key early influence on Obama, he would have been only one factor.

Finally, sexual matters aside, we should consider the strictly Marxist element of Obama's early years.

There is no question that Barack Obama knew about and pondered and even debated the words of the cultural Marxists at Occidental College and Columbia, the institutions he attended right after leaving Hawaii. Obama stated in *Dreams* that just before he left the island for college, he paid a final visit to Frank Marshall Davis, where Davis dispensed more words of wisdom that Obama recounted in his memoir. Not only was Columbia a radical college, but Occidental was one of the most radical campuses on the West Coast.

Obama openly wrote in *Dreams* of "hanging out" with Marxist professors and attending socialist conferences in these college years. He also spent time at Occidental with John Drew, who had headed the campus Marxist organization. Drew went to Occidental because it was so pro-communist. "It was considered the Moscow of southern California when

I was there," Drew told me. "There were a lot of Marxist professors, many of whom I got to know pretty well."

I have interviewed Drew at length several times for books and various writings.[19] He knew Obama as a fellow Marxist at the time, with the young Obama introduced to him as precisely that by a mutual close friend (Drew's girlfriend). The three of them debated Marxist ideas at length, with differing perspectives on the feasibility of actual revolution in America—with the young Obama being much more optimistic.

"I was kind of more [from the] Frankfurt School of Marxism at the time," Drew told me. "I felt like I was doing Obama a favor by pointing out that the Marxist revolution that he and Caroline [Drew's girlfriend] and Chandoo [Obama's close friend] were hoping for was really kind of a pipedream, and that there was nothing in European history or the history of developed nations that would make that sort of fantasy—you know, Frank Marshall Davis fantasy of revolution—come true." Drew points to Marcuse: "I was more with Herbert Marcuse and others who were puzzled at why he didn't see Marx's predictions come true, and were interested in maybe the role of psychology in preventing—or false consciousness in preventing—a revolution from happening. So I was still a card-carrying Marxist, but I was kind of a more advanced, East Coast, Cornell University Marxist, I think, at the time."[20]

Drew would go on to get his PhD at Cornell and establish himself as a professor at Williams College. His long recollections on Obama from the time are extremely valuable in understanding Obama's thinking at that point in his life and perhaps even (to some degree) today, where Drew still perceives "the Marxist mental architecture" in the way Obama thinks and talks about certain things.

Unfortunately, those recollections are limited. They do not tell all we would like to know about our current president for this book. Nonetheless, we see here eyewitness evidence (from a Marxist contemporary) of Obama's familiarity with Marcuse, Marx, and other revolutionary ideas pertinent to this discussion.

What is fascinating is that all of these anti–traditional marriage and family forces would come to a fore, historically, under President

Barack Obama, certainly the juggernaut that same-sex marriage suddenly became by the end of his first presidential term. It was then, in his fourth presidential year, that he gave his historic interview with Robin Roberts endorsing gay marriage. Not only is Obama our first Gay Marriage President but (in all seriousness) our first Red Diaper Baby President, the product of parents and mentors who literally were pro-communist—in Frank Marshall Davis's case, a literal member of CPUSA in the Stalin era.[21]

Again, we can overstate things in this discussion, but it would also be a mistake to understate or ignore them. Surely, none of this seems irrelevant.

Perhaps most fitting, when we finally step back to appraise Obama's presidency, we may see his greatest impact not in economics, not in foreign policy (areas that subsequent presidents are more able to reverse), nor in persuading a nation to want bigger government, but in the pivotal cultural issues, like same-sex marriage and taxpayer funding of abortion, where he has dramatically moved the "progressive" ball forward. Symptomatic of the New Left and the cultural Marxists, Barack Obama's most enduring legacy may be on American culture.

17

COMMUNISTS AND HOMOSEXUALITY

AS COMMUNISTS OVER TIME BROKE DOWN barriers in sexual relations and the covenant of marriage, many moved toward acceptance and advocacy of homosexuality and bisexuality. "Smashing monogamy" was merely one manifestation of blowing up coveted traditions. Some of these cultural Marxists practiced what they preached. Kate Millett's "sexual politics" had translated into a lesbian lifestyle for her personally, and the New Left politics of guys like Mark Rudd and Bill Ayers at least dictated that they give bisexuality a shot (even when it didn't work).

As for the larger communist establishment, views toward homosexuals were more complex and usually considerably less enthusiastic. The Soviets were viscerally anti-gay, as were despots like Fidel Castro. The Russians were not stumping for gay marriage. Joe Stalin was no gay-rights crusader. President Richard Nixon's colorful Oval Office assessment of the Russians and homosexuals, caught on tape for posterity, is revealing: "The Russians. Goddamn it, they root them [homosexuals] out, they don't let 'em hang around at all. You know what I mean? I don't know what they do with them."

Who knows what, exactly, the Russians did with homosexuals? We do know, however, what Fidel Castro did with them. He had them locked up as public enemies, putting them in prison or lunatic asylums. In fact, as an amusing example of hypocrisy among American leftists, observe how they hail Cuba for its allegedly glorious educational system and "free" health care while ignoring Fidel's vigorous persecution of gays. For Fidel, health care for gays meant quarantining gays. *Washington Post* columnist Richard Cohen, a liberal, has called this double standard toward Castro, "Hollywood's Darling, Liberals' Blind Spot."[1]

Closer to home, recall that David Horowitz and Ron Radosh, both Red diaper babies raised by communist parents in the 1950s, experienced sexually traditional upbringings, with their parents fairly "bourgeois" in their attitudes. Another case in point is Mike Shotwell, likewise reared as a Red diaper baby in the same period.

Shotwell's father-in-law, Orville E. Olson, was a dogmatic Marxist, a dedicated Soviet patriot, exalting Stalin's Russia above all else. Orville had no tendencies toward such sexual radicalism; quite the contrary, he possessed highly negative attitudes toward gays. When Orville heard rumors of J. Edgar Hoover's questionable sexuality (for the record, many of these allegations were spread by communists), Orville loved it, gleefully mocking the anticommunist-crusading FBI director with epithets such as "fag" and "fairy." "My remembrances of Orville's statements about Hoover," says Mike Shotwell, "were pretty much in line with his derogatory statements about American ballet dancers who he considered laughable fairies in comparison to the more manly Russian dancers that [in Orville's view] were much better trained and all married." Says Shotwell: "I recall some of that type of conversation from the early to mid '50s, but prior to my turning 10 or so (1952), I'm not sure I knew exactly what a homosexual was. Let's say it was a vague concept. From the mid '50s on (this also could have been earlier), I recall Orville made open fun of Hoover as a 'pantywaist' who had affairs and sex parties with his boyfriend and the close knit circle around him."[2]

Interestingly, Shotwell adds that Adolf Hitler, who, for communists, was the ultimate fascist enemy, "was described in the same way" by Orville in their household. "In a way, the two [Hitler and Hoover] were linked in the same manner. It was a way of describing to us that crazy, anti-communist people were screwed up vicious monsters who went to all lengths to disguise their insanity. . . . To describe it another way, anyone who was against communism and the great world-wide proletarian revolution was either insane, an unbalanced person such as a gay, ignorant, or just plain stupid."

This is quite telling. J. Edgar Hoover has been the long-running victim (still to this day) of a vicious Communist Party smear/disinformation campaign, which included, among many other things, claims that he was an unbalanced, prancing, dancing, cross-dressing, pink-bow-in-the-hair, gay-lover-loving transsexual.[3] As befitting American communists—and, really, the left generally (especially Saul Alinsky acolytes)—there were no limits to the demonization permissible when the opponent stood in the way of their political goals. The left could engage in the most strident gay-bashing when it satisfied an ideological agenda.

So, here we see in the remembrances of Shotwell, and the less-off-color behavior of the parents of Horowitz, views of homosexuals in the 1950s that were hardly advancing gay rights. Sure, the Communist Party was not bereft of homosexuals (recall Whittaker Chambers's bisexualism), but those homosexuals were not embraced for their homosexuality or for what homosexual politics offered in furtherance of CPUSA's goals—quite the contrary.

Professor Harvey Klehr, one of America's foremost historians of the Communist Party, added support for this view, stating that the Party "was certainly suspicious of gays. And it went back quite a ways." He noted that many of the immigrant communities that formed the backbone of the American Communist Party from early in the century into the 1930s were "quite traditional in their views of morality." Klehr recalled coming across a document in the Moscow archives where members of the Greek section of the Party wrote a letter to the Control Commission, blasting an editor of the Greek Communist Party newspaper with an epithet crudely describing a man who gives oral sex to another man. These Greek comrades insisted that the editor's sexual proclivities should disqualify him from being in a position of authority.

Klehr acknowledged that the American Communist Party "did have a bohemian core in the early 1920s, but that was pretty much limited to NYC and Greenwich Village."[4]

Klehr added a critical point on one of the reasons for CPUSA's non-acceptance of gays in the 1940s and 1950s. "Not only was the CPUSA not supportive of homosexuality," he stated, "it actively opposed it. In the late '40s and early '50s, the Party expelled gays as security risks."[5]

Gays were security risks because they were subject to blackmail, precisely why homosexuals were likewise considered a risk by US government agencies and the military. It would take the Soviets or communist Chinese a mere nanosecond to exploit a gay man's sexual orientation for purposes of blackmail. The Chinese had already mastered the so-called "honey trap" technique for blackmailing married heterosexual men; to blackmail a homosexual no doubt would have been deemed great fun as well as very effective.

A contemporary eyewitness to this was Frank Meyer, one of the more prominent mid-twentieth-century converts from communism to conservatism, going on to join William F. Buckley Jr. as one of the founding editors of *National Review*. Meyer stated that "sexual perversion" (the language of the day for homosexuality) was a "vice" that "may or may not interfere with Party demands," but it did "endanger the Party" by making the individual "subject to blackmail" and "exposing the Party to attack."[6]

A classic case of a homosexual not fitting in with CPUSA at the time is Harry Hay. As Klehr noted, "That is when Harry Hay, who went on to found the Mattachine Society, was booted out."

This is precisely right. Formed in 1950, the Mattachine Society was created by Harry Hay and some gay communist friends and associates out of the Los Angeles area. They came together through the Progressive Party presidential bid of Henry Wallace in 1948, which was a rallying point for American communists (including Mike Shotwell's father-in-law, Orville, who was Wallace's chief campaign organizer in Minnesota). Originally conceiving their group as something called "Bachelors for Wallace," these communist homosexuals sought to organize themselves not so much to promote "gay rights" as understood today, but to address basic persecution. There is much more to their story and what happened, but for the purposes of this treatment, the group (to my knowledge) did not have the expressly stated goal of abolishing the traditional family or advancing same-sex marriage—which, again, was unthinkable even to gays at the time. Only a crazy man would have argued for a redefining of marriage to accommodate something called "gay marriage." Even gay people did not think that was remotely possible; they, too, deemed it absurd.

And Harry Hay, of course, was far from America's only gay communist. There were certainly others in the period, many of them acknowledged and detailed at glbtq.com. They, too, however, were not stumping for or even thinking about gay marriage; most were not even out of the closet.

So, for communists, where did the slow shift toward gay marriage today start? To be sure, it is a completely new phenomenon, but some of the fissures in sexual identity and practice leading America toward that break can be traced to the radicalization of the 1960s sexual revolution and the New Left. As this book has shown, it seems to have begun to change with the '60s sexual and political revolutions, which later hooked up with a wider cultural acceptance. Those revolutions pulled the communists even further left—not economically but culturally, socially, sexually.

We can see in this book a gradual evolutionary progression toward considering, accepting, and practicing homosexuality, from the Frankfurt School to Kate Millett, from the Mattachine Society to the bedtime ruminations of Mark Rudd and Bill Ayers, from Whittaker Chambers (who ultimately rejected the behavior) to perhaps the bisexuality of Frank Marshall Davis.

A pivotal moment that might have signaled a concrete, permanent shift in Communist Party USA's thinking is evidenced by a November 1983 document from CPUSA's twenty-third national convention, held November 10–13, 1983. Titled *Convention Resolutions Adopted & Resolutions Committee Report,*" it provides a very brief "Resolution on Homosexuality." Page 26 states, "The 23rd Convention of the CPUSA asks the Political Bureau to establish a committee to study whether our policy with respect to homosexuality and membership of homosexuals in the Party . . . needs changing and in what way and to make recommendations to the new Central Committee for disposition."

The pertinent section in the document is understated and anticlimactic, but such was typical of CPUSA protocol. After years of government surveillance of their activities, the comrades learned to keep sensitive things like this close to the vest. The fireworks came not on paper but in the dialogue and discussion. They wanted no incriminating paper trail that critics could follow and use against the comrades; they knew better.

Thus, what is more important is the interpretation of the document. A contact in the communist movement and within CPUSA's orbit contends that it signaled a marked, permanent tactical shift by CPUSA toward gays, making the Party pro-gay and co-opting the gay left and its agenda for the purpose of advancing CPUSA's communist agenda. If that is indeed the case, then this might have been a significant moment in ultimately bringing CPUSA to its noticeably pro-gay-marriage leanings today.

One can see an evolving change in tune on gays, as if perhaps communists could sense that maybe the gay-rights movement offered a glistening opportunity to finally take down essential traditions and institutions they had been assaulting for over a century, from Marx to Marcuse to Millett. That gift, it turns out, was just around the corner, with a corollary gift that communists could scarcely have imagined: the support of not just the gay movement but everyday Americans.

18

THE GIFT OF GAY MARRIAGE

ALAS, THEN CAME GAY MARRIAGE.

Despite so much battering of traditional-natural-biblical marriage, from self-inflicted wounds to the pummeling provided by '60s radicals, by communists, by the Bolsheviks and Chinese, by Karl Marx and Herbert Marcuse, and by all else, the universal core notion of marriage as a special, unique, exclusive bond between one man and one woman remained intact in America and the wider West. It was the ideal, the standard. It was the definition of marriage. It hung on. It prevailed. Battered and beaten, it was not defeated.

Could anything break it? Could anything cut it down?

Yes, the answer is finally upon us. The wider political left, in the West generally and America specifically, has found its hammer and its sickle to smash and undercut marriage. Under the banner of gay rights and slick slogans such as "tolerance," "freedom," "marriage rights," and "equality," and, on the flip side, Marcusean accusations of intolerance, bigotry, "hatred," and "homophobia" slung at opponents, the left has seized upon gay marriage with a relentless abandon. The left has its wrecking ball, and it is swinging it far and wide, without a moment of hesitation whatsoever. It did not invent gay marriage, but it has there found a permanent partner.

The far left at long last has a workable Trojan horse for its longtime goal of taking down traditional marriage and the traditional family. Advocates of gay marriage, the vast majority of whom never have been advocates of communism, are now dupes to that deeper process, whether they know it or not.

And sadly, it is so unnecessary. As one thoughtful liberal responded to one of my articles on this subject, if gays and their supporters had simply pushed for some form of civil unions or partnerships, rather than insisting on literally redefining marriage—smashing and changing its very literal meaning—none of the acrimony that America is seeing now in a bitter culture war between gay-marriage proponents and faith-rooted opponents would be occurring. This is all so unnecessarily divisive. Yet, such is what the Marxists and radicals have always done: divide and destroy. From Kremlin smear campaigns of disinformation and agitprop to Saul Alinsky's advice that political-cultural opponents be isolated and demonized, today's left is attacking traditional marriage defenders with a stunning ferocity. And now, they have a much wider array of gay-rights supporters (well beyond merely the political-cultural left) unwittingly enlisting in their mission.

Gay marriage also means gay adoption and the raising of children in nontraditional, nonnatural households. And here, for communists especially, gay marriage offers all sorts of other rich opportunities, such as the takedown of religious institutions. Consider the extraordinary example of Catholic Charities in Massachusetts, the nation's oldest adoption agency, which has now shut its doors and stopped doing adoptions because gay-marriage liberals have ordered Catholic Charities—in the name of "tolerance" and "diversity," ironically—to arrange gay adoptions of children, with no permissible objection on the grounds of religious rights and freedom of conscience. For the communist left, which has long despised the Roman Catholic Church more than any other institution, gay marriage and gay adoption are blessed vehicles for undercutting its great adversary, the Catholic Church, from continuing to perform one of its most commendable and successful functions over the centuries: the fostering and placement of children in adoptive homes. No communist hater of the Church could have imagined that gay marriage could have been so perfect in allowing such a powerful possibility. Had Marx and Lukács foreseen this prospect for their despised religious foes, they might have pushed for gay marriage long ago.

Just think: the Roman Catholic Church has long considered the male-female matrimonial bond to be so sacred as to be a literal sacrament. Catholic Canon Law and Magisterial teaching deems marriage "an irrevocable pact between man and woman."[2] For the secular left to have a hammer against no less than a Church sacrament is heady wine for modern religion haters.

Even more delicious than ending adoptions by Catholic Charities, gay marriage is proving a magnificent tool for the communist-atheistic left to pound Christians generally and rob them of critical First Amendment religious freedoms. Gay-marriage advocates—who, again, pride themselves on their "tolerance" and "diversity"—have been utterly relentless in denouncing, demonizing, boycotting, attacking, picketing, prosecuting, suing, fining, and even threatening to jail people who (in the name of their religious faith) disagree with them on same-sex marriage. At the time of this writing, Cynthia and Robert Gifford, a Christian family that owns a barn in New York but declined to rent it to a gay couple for a wedding ceremony because such an arrangement violates the family's religious beliefs and freedom, was fined thirteen thousand dollars.[3] Elane Photography in New Mexico, which pleaded with liberals not to be compelled by the state to photograph a same-sex wedding, was sued by gay-marriage advocates and is being prosecuted by the state. It was not enough for gay-marriage activists to simply find another photographer and leave Elane Photography alone. Nor was the same mercy granted to the Klein family in Oregon. The Kleins are bakers who pleaded the right not to be forced to make a cake for a same-sex ceremony; in turn, they were picketed, harassed, hauled before state commissions, and forced to shut their doors, with Aaron Klein now driving a garbage truck to provide income for his family.[4]

Jack Phillips, a baker in Colorado, faced possible imprisonment for declining to service a gay ceremony. The same harassment and state coercion is being applied in any number of states to florists and bakers and photographers who beg not to service same-sex events because such services contravene their religious principles.

The Chick-fil-A franchise, which is so loyal to its Christian beliefs that it is closed on Sundays—forgoing sizable profits—has been viciously targeted by gay-marriage brigades. What is the "sin" of this business? Chick-fil-A's owner dared to say that he opposed redefining his faith's teachings on marriage. When the owner and founder, S. Truett Cathy, a World War II veteran, died at age ninety-three in September 2014, the self-anointed liberal champions of "tolerance" flocked to websites to insist he was going to hell for being a bigoted "homophobe" and "Christian-trash-bag." "Let US All Celebrate One LESS Bigot on the Planet," one gay-marriage supporter wrote. Another added: "Bigotry is bigotry. He can RIH [Rest in Hell]."[5]

We could go on and on with examples of pro-gay-marriage intolerance against religious people who believe they have no right to redefine something that their God ordained, or who simply disagree with gay marriage for whatever reason. Consider the well-publicized situations with Mozilla, or ESPN's Craig James, or the owner of Barilla pasta, or the governor of Arizona, etc., etc.[6]

In short, revolutionary communists would have absolutely loved this radical rupture in the culture. They would have admired not so much the demonization, which they could do better than anyone, but the astonishing reality that everyday noncommunist Americans are doing the demonizing without them. They could have never counted on such support in the past. Now they are getting it compliments not of the public agreeing with them, the communists, on, say, abolition of all rights of inheritance or Stalin's objectives in Berlin, but through this completely odd and unexpected modern phenomenon called "gay marriage."

And these examples of targeting Christians for their beliefs on marriage are merely examples from within the boundaries of the United States of America. The situation for believers in parts of Western Europe and especially in Canada, where the dictatorship of secular relativism has become fully ingrained, is much more ominous and has been for quite some time.

Again, the startling irony is that these gay-marriage crusaders fancy themselves champions of tolerance, diversity, and "equal rights." That has never been accurate, and they are proving it now with special uncompromising rigidity. They are pursuing the fatuous contradictions they have always pursued: *selective* tolerance, *selective* diversity, and *selective* equal rights. Religious rights are not among their select. Thus, religious believers are not to be tolerated among their categories of diversity.

A quotation that sums up this thinking comes from gay activist, law professor, and President Obama's EEOC commissioner Chai Feldblum, cited at the beginning of this book for her support of the Beyond Marriage campaign. When asked about the conflict between gay rights and religious rights, Feldblum said, "I'm having a hard time coming up with any case in which religious liberty should win."[7] That is no surprise. Feldblum's assessment is made all the more astonishing given that religious freedom is actually the first freedom in the First Amendment of the Constitution.

Those still mystified by all of this need to understand that liberals/progressives operate according to a hierarchy of rights that they themselves are not even really aware of. Consistent with progressivism, their idea of rights, and especially which rights rise superior to others at any given time or period, is always progressing, or changing, or evolving. Right now, for liberals/progressives, sitting atop the totem pole in this hierarchy are so-called marriage rights and abortion rights, which, remarkably, did not even exist ten or fifty years ago (respectively). In the past, they called these things not rights but "gay marriage" and "freedom of choice." Quite shrewdly, however, they have now framed these "freedoms" as "rights," along the lines of "civil rights." Equally shrewdly, they push them forward under the mantra of "tolerance." It is a brilliant move that is working extremely effectively with millions of Americans.

But here is the main point: for today's liberals/progressives, the likes of "marriage rights" and "abortion rights" rise superior to other rights, certainly religious rights and property rights. We see this in the examples of intolerance by gay-marriage proponents listed earlier. It is also endemic in the Obama HHS mandate requiring religious believers to fund abortion drugs, which has become another culture-war crusade by today's left. In all these cases, there is one commonality: liberals/progressives angrily disregard the religious rights and property rights that they steamroll in the name of gay marriage and abortion. Religious rights and property rights are subjugated to a kind of liberal/progressive gulag. They are deemed bottom-of-the-barrel, and in no way nearly as important or worthy of consideration. In fact, those rights are held in contempt; they are bottom-dwellers. For religious believers who disagree, too bad. Progressives will see them in court.

This tolerance of only their own ideas of marriage (and of certain new "rights") and their refusal to tolerate the millennia-old definition held by others, is something that Herbert Marcuse would have not only endorsed but advised. Recall that Marcuse's New Left "liberating tolerance" urged "intolerance against movements from the Right, and toleration of movements from the Left."[8] Here again, Marcuse and the neo-Marxists were way ahead of their time. Of course, it is downright bizarre that those who today support natural-traditional-biblical marriage as it has always been supported by 99.999-plus percent of all who have ever lived can somehow be derided as holding a "right-wing" position, but such is the kind of maneuvering that the left always engages in, with its own ideas always progressing and ever changing, and always in a more nonnatural, nontraditional, nonbiblical direction.

In sum, what could be a better development for revolutionary communists? There has never been anything they hated as much as religion. Marx had dubbed religion the "opiate of the masses," and opined that "Communism begins where atheism begins."[9] In the *Communist Manifesto*, he declared that "Communism abolishes eternal truths, it abolishes all religion, and all morality."[10] Vladimir Lenin said far worse. Speaking on behalf of the Bolsheviks in his famous October 2, 1920, speech, Lenin stated matter-of-factly: "We do not believe in God." Lenin insisted that "all worship of a divinity is a necrophilia."[11]

He wrote, "There can be nothing more abominable than religion."[12]

Thus, for communists in particular, with hatred of religion central to their ideology, gay marriage could be the gift that keeps on giving. There is magic for them under the gay-rights rainbow. Not only is it a powerful tool for taking down the family, but it can also be heartily employed to bring into submission the most loathsome of communism's longtime foes: the Christian faith. If communists were not atheists, they would joyously resound in a loud chorus of "Hallelujah!"

19

ALL ABOARD! COMMUNISTS EMBRACE GAY MARRIAGE

WITH GAY MARRIAGE HAVING SUDDENLY GAINED seemingly insurmountable momentum in the culture, armed with political and legal backing, and thus finally offering communists the long-dreamed-of vehicle to take down traditional marriage, the family, and much more, communists are—not surprisingly—suddenly gung ho for gays and same-sex marriage. Any previous reticence about homosexuality in the Harry Hay days has been tossed out the window. Communists who once purged gays are now aboard the gay-marriage bandwagon. Two examples particularly stand out: Communist Party USA and (amazingly) Fidel Castro's Cuba.

Communist Party USA and its flagship publication, *People's World*, the successor to the Soviet-funded *Daily Worker*, have become cheerleaders for the gay-rights movement, and now consistently tout gay marriage. This can be seen on almost any given week in the headlines at *People's World* and in a perusal of the CPUSA website. Here are just some examples:

Consider Communist Party USA's statement in anticipation of its June 2014 national convention, held in Chicago.[1] The gay agenda was seamlessly integrated within the Party's language and purposes. The CPUSA statement began by demanding that the masses unite to "put people before profits" and then pledged to "transform" America. It stated:

> We live in a capitalist system where the 99% of people struggle every day to survive and the richest 1% control the vast majority of wealth and power. Capitalism cannot meet the needs of the vast majority. . . . Our schools are underfunded and essential public services are strapped and slashed. Home foreclosures are everywhere and millions of people are homeless and hungry in the richest country in the world. Racism, sexism, homophobia and all kinds of discrimination are commonplace.

Who knew that communists cared about "homophobia"? Well, they do, or (more accurately) they have found the issue handy for advancing their goals. We see here an unhesitant molding of Marcusean cultural Marxism with the orthodox economic/class goals of Marx-Engels communism. Once upon a time, these branches of communism were separate. Not anymore. They now serve one another.

Further on in the statement, CPUSA made its enemy crystal clear, as well as (again) seamlessly identifying with gay rights:

> The main obstacle to progress today is right-wing extremism. Right wing spokespeople and groups represent and are funded by the most conservative sections of the rich and powerful.
>
> The extreme right, which now dominates the Republican Party, is seeking to roll back all the social and economic rights that working people fought for and won. They want to take the country back to a time before marriage equality, before voting rights, before women's reproductive rights, before the right to a union. It seems at times that they want to take us back to the days of slavery.
>
> Democracy itself is under attack from this far-right group and their servants in the Washington and statehouses around the country.
>
> It's increasingly clear to millions of people: another world is possible and necessary. Another U.S. is possible too. Capitalism cannot solve these problems, we need a socialist USA. . . .
>
> The Communist Party of the United States of America has a 95

year history of fighting for democracy, jobs, equality and socialism.

Our party reflects the diverse working class of our country. Our members are of all the races, ethnicities and nationalities that make up the rich fabric of US society. We are native born and immigrant. We are men and women. We are young and old. We are straight and gay. . . .

Onward to Chicago!

Again, it is remarkable to see how the pro-gay and "marriage equality" language of the wider progressive left has so fluidly become part and parcel of Communist Party USA's platform and objectives.

Another example is the keynote address given at the national convention by CPUSA's general secretary, Sam Webb, the modern Party's version of Gus Hall, Earl Browder, and William Z. Foster. In his remarks, which were posted as the lead at *People's World*, Webb incorporated the words "gay" and "LGBT" and "sexual orientation," twice condemned "homophobia," and also trumpeted "marriage equality"—all to raucous applause from the Party faithful. In what must have had the gay-bashing Nikita Khrushchev rolling over in his grave, Sam Webb announced that he sees gays and LGBT people (he left out "Q" people) as part of Communist Party USA's plans for a "modern, mature, militant, and mass party."[2]

In a very Marcusean-like adaptation of Marxism, Sam Webb's modern CPUSA views gays and transgender people as integral to the modern Marxist agenda as labor unions. That is truly an eye-opening development. In fact, one article at CPUSA's website heralded bringing gays and transgender people and unions together. It was tellingly titled "Unions celebrate LGBTQ progress, say challenges remain." It noted the work of the AFL-CIO (among other unions) in celebrating "Gay Pride" and "advancing LGBTQ rights."[3]

How times have changed. How soon before unionized steel workers and coal miners and auto workers are asked to march arm in arm with gay men at Gay Pride parades, and denounced as intolerant "fascists" if they feel uncomfortable and refuse? CPUSA no doubt would laud the prospect.

Within roughly two weeks after Sam Webb's convention remarks,

People's World published at least three articles promoting gay rights and "marriage equality":

- "Obama continues to expand rights for LGBT Americans" (June 24, 2014)

- "Unions celebrate LGBTQ progress, say challenges remain" (July 1, 2014)

- "Texas Democrats set progressive platform" (July 1, 2014)

Three articles on this one hot-button cultural subject within just eight days is notable, given that *People's World* does not post a lot of new daily content. Some of these articles remained as leads in the rotating window of the website for over a week.[4] They were an unmistakable priority.

The first of these three articles lauded the gay-marriage efforts of the first Gay Marriage President. The article is a revelatory tutorial on what today's communists find so appealing about gay rights: once again, the reason goes back to altering the fundamental, traditional understating of marriage, family, and religion. The article noted approvingly: "Three years ago, the Obama administration stopped defending the legality of the Defense of Marriage Act [DOMA]. His [Obama's] Justice Department is also on the verge of announcing the completion of a review of federal law to determine what legal benefits can be extended to LGBTQ families. . . . The White House said some benefits can't be extended to LGBTQ families because federal law prohibits it. Obama is calling on Congress to eliminate those provisions from law."

The article also pushed for passage of the Employment Non-Discrimination Act (ENDA), which prohibits employers from firing lesbian, gay, bisexual, and transgender employees. In itself, that appears (and is) a noble goal, but the secular left wants to apply that prohibition to religious employers as well, meaning that an employer cannot invoke a religious reason for discharging an employee. A church, for instance, might want to not hire or perhaps remove a youth minister or religious education director who is pushing sexual beliefs or behaving in a way that violates the church's teachings on marriage and family and basic Judeo-Christian morality.

Here again, with a sweeping and aggressive ENDA that does not provide religious exemptions, the enemies of organized religion may have found another handy club to wield against religious foes. For communists, the gay issue provides yet another delicious dividend.

It is hard to pinpoint when exactly CPUSA openly and publicly embraced both homosexuals and gay marriage. At CPUSA's website at the time of this writing, there are many statements that are retrievable on the topic. Among them is an official June 21, 2006, statement from CPUSA titled "Gay Pride Month: Communists stand in solidarity." Released by Communist Party USA and the Young Communist League, it states: "The month of June has been designated as Pride Month in celebration of the struggles and achievements of lesbian, gay, bisexual and transgender people in the United States. . . . In 2006, we still have a long ways to go."[5]

Typical of CPUSA, it then tagged the usual enemies: conservatives, religious people, and George W. Bush. The 2006 article also, notably, referred to gay marriage. And also typical of the communist movement, again with the Frankfurt School and early communists and progressives in mind, it emphasized the need for the educational system to step in to advance the proper sexual agenda:

> In our schools, the ultra-right and religious conservatives deny students access to scientifically accurate sex education while more young people are becoming infected with HIV every year. In our schools, in our workplaces and in our streets, LGBT people are faced with discrimination, hatred and violence. . . . In Australia, the president overturned a law that would allow same-sex marriage and the conservative government now in power in Canada is also seeking to overturn its law that allows gay marriage.

Here, CPUSA had to go as far away as Australia to uphold gay marriage, since in 2006 it was still a pipe dream even in America, when

Barack Obama, Hillary Clinton, and virtually all of Washington's elected Democrats still publicly supported historic male-female marriage. Nonetheless, CPUSA found an example to advance its longtime antifamily cause, even if it had to go to Australia to get one.

The article went on, zeroing in on George W. Bush, as if Bush's opposition to gay marriage had made him some kind of political freak, suggesting that Bush favoring what had always been humanity's position made him some sort of ultra-right, Mussolini-esque demagogue: "Here at home, Bush and the ultra-right continue to push the anti-gay button in order to drum up support in the 2006 elections. Just as in 2004, Bush is using gay marriage as a rallying cry for his conservative base that has started to turn against him because of his disastrous handling of the Iraq war and domestic issues."

This framing of George W. Bush as supposedly seizing gay marriage to rally "ultra-right" (read: Christian/religious) voters was pure fiction. In 2004, I finished and published a long book on the faith of George W. Bush, and gay marriage was a nonissue.[6] It was not being advocated anywhere near like it is now. Bush, who, contrary to liberal caricature and ignorance, was not a fundamentalist, not an evangelical, and had a highly tolerant New Testament–oriented faith, even citing Jesus Christ as the motivation for his amazing and extraordinarily generous and expensive global AIDS initiative,[7] was against gay marriage (as was his fellow Methodist, Hillary Clinton), and that was that. He never engaged in any gay bashing or exploiting of the issue politically. He simply held the same position every president had ever held. To suggest otherwise is fantasy. This was, however, the kind of crass agitation and propaganda that CPUSA had mastered over the decades.

I could fill these pages with similar examples that exist at *People's World*. Because of limited space, I will briefly summarize another recent example that appears as one of the four lead articles in the rotating window of the publication. Written by one of the communist publication's most popular reporters, it calls for a renewed strategy for the 2016 election, an "inclusive" one applied to all fifty states to avert another damaging loss to Republicans. This strategy includes harnessing gay marriage as a winning issue for the far left and for communists. The article notes that "over the past few years a sea change has taken place in people's thinking toward marriage equality and LGBTQ rights."[8]

Indeed it has. The communists have that right. Thus, for communists, it is high time to ride that wave, to bring their deeper agenda to shore along with the help of the enlightened cultural masses of America.

Lastly, here is a stark example of how communist thinking has so dramatically changed on gay issues. It comes from one of the most oppressive and anti-gay regimes abroad, from one of the most trenchant bastions of Third World "homophobia." In 2012, a rather curious fan of Barack Obama's sudden embrace of gay marriage was no less than a Castro from Cuba: Mariela Castro, niece of ailing and aging Cuban tyrant, Fidel Castro, and daughter of current despot, Raul Castro.[9]

Comrade Mariela heralded President Obama's endorsement of gay marriage. She called his statement "humane" and "understanding," said it had "great value" and "influence," and wished that the American president's "words will be taken seriously in the political and legislative decisions made in different states and in the whole world." She expressed hope that such statements from Obama would be followed by "concrete actions."

This is quite striking. Here was a high-level Cuban communist publicly pushing not only for gay rights but gay marriage. She did so freely, with no threat of reprisal from the regime—quite the contrary.

As reporter Ben Johnson noted, Mariela, a Red diaper baby and communist-state-"trained sexologist," heads something called the Cuban National Center for Sex Education (CENESEX). Her group calls to mind earlier such pioneering sex-communist efforts, such as neo-Marxist Wilhelm Reich's Association for Proletarian Sexual Politics and America-based Orgone Institute. Mariela is carrying on the tradition of such Frankfurt School cultural Marxists. And she is just as boldly nontraditional.

In Havana, in broad daylight, Mariela Castro led an LGBT activist parade, where, as Johnson reported, "Some 400 transvestites sashayed behind Castro, doing a conga line through the streets, to celebrate the

Fifth Cuban Day Against Homophobia, observed elsewhere on May 17. Marchers shouted, 'Down with homophobia! Long live sexual diversity!'"[10]

This is not just extraordinary; it is utterly unprecedented in Cuba's tyranny. To repeat: a *Fifth* Cuban Day Against Homophobia. The day is celebrated just after May Day, the high holy day for the communist state. Mere decades ago, this absolutely would not have been accepted in Cuba. The marchers would have been immediately jailed, without question—and handcuffed and beaten and carted straight to the loony bin.

Raising more eyebrows still, Mariela maintains that her uncle, the grand old gay-basher-in-chief, actually favors same-sex marriage, "but he has not made it public." More than that, Fidel, according to his niece, is a closet gay-rights advocate. She further reports, "He has done some advocacy work, speaking of the need to make progress in terms of rights based on sexual orientation and gender identity."

This is breathtaking. It was truly once unimaginable in Cuba. Call it Fidel's "progress."

The Castros appear to be going all the way, not content with merely stomping out the "homophobia" that, in Cuba, once meant stomping on gays as they were tossed into nuthouses. To hasten the move toward "gay marriage," Mariela says that Cuba will be changing its "Family Code" and its "constitution." This is not a complicated legislative process on the island. It requires simply an executive fiat akin to President Obama's HHS mandate on contraception and abortion drugs, but even more powerful on the island dictatorship.

All of this seems completely puzzling. What is going on in Cuba?

As for Mariela, her enthusiasm could stem from an addiction to social media and American sitcoms, thus making her hot for gay marriage, hopping upon the latest fad and fashion of the cultural bandwagon. But what about this reported sudden conversion by her uncle and his communist tyranny? Does it make any sense?

Yes, it does. The root of the answer, once again, is the much older Marxist/communist assault on marriage. Wittingly or unwittingly, intentionally or unintentionally, led either by the spirit of the times or by more sinister forces that have long led communists, the communist priority is less gay rights than it is a continued assault on the family. The assault means a rejection of older and more established and despised enemies for communists: morality, tradition, religion, God.

For a devout atheistic communist like Fidel Castro, who spent his first thirty years in power labeling his island's Catholics "social scum" and banning their churches, their Christmas, their holy days, and everything in between, this is another opportunity to strike at the heel of his most reviled foe. The Catholic Church that he devoured in Cuba considers male-female marriage a literal holy sacrament. Why would Castro side with that? No way. He would rather trample upon what is deemed holy by an adversary he long considered unholy. If the Church is against it, he's for it.

For Cuba's communists, faced with a conflict between their penchant for persecuting the family/marriage and for persecuting gay people, the communist war on traditional morality and faith and the family wins out, thus dictating a sudden embrace of gays. As long as the traditional family is reversed, Marxism is advanced. That is the overriding priority. Communists will do whatever they need to destroy the family; "gay marriage" is an ideal, handy device. Even in Castro's Cuba, it works nicely for their purposes.

Just as Karl Marx characterized the communist goal of "abolition of the family" as revolutionary, as "the most radical rupture with traditional relations," Mariela Castro speaks of this new Cuban-communist cause as "revolutionary." In the spirit of earlier Marxist feminists, like Betty Friedan and Kate Millett, she will break the patriarchal family model. "It's a hugely important first step," says Castro.[11]

It certainly is. It is one that President Barack Obama favors. As he does, he is cheered by and allied with the Castros, who see him as taking a crucial global lead on behalf of their cultural Marxism.

To that end, there is an interesting Obama administration coda to this story: Ben Johnson reported that this "revolutionary process" in Cuba has been aided by the American taxpayer, even well before Obama's historic action in December 2014 to normalize relations with Cuba. Johnson says that in 2011, the US State Department spent three hundred thousand dollars promoting homosexual activism in Cuba. The funds went "to strengthen grassroots organizations to create the conditions that allow meaningful and unhindered participation by members of the lesbian, gay, bisexual, and transgender (LGBT) community in all aspects of Cuban society."[12]

More than that, in another telling move, President Obama's gay-rights comrade, Mariela Castro, was granted a visa to visit the United States for an academic conference in San Francisco. The visa was granted by Hillary Clinton's State Department.[13] For decades, the Castros have been denied visas to enter the United States. Not this time. Something has changed.

When first hearing the news of the visa, some anticommunists figured it was merely another example of the Obama administration going soft on communist regimes. Now, however, given the later news of Mariela's close kinship with Barack Obama on "gay marriage," maybe there was more to the story.

This is indeed revolutionary, made possible by Americans who voted for "hope and change" in November 2008 and 2012. This is part of Barack Obama's "fundamental transformation," even if the everyday Americans who hysterically applauded that phrase had not the vaguest idea what it entailed.

20

WITH GRATITUDE TO MR. AND MRS. MAINSTREET

SPEAKING AT THE NATIONAL PRAYER BREAKFAST in January 1979, not long before he died, the legendary Bishop Fulton Sheen asked his audience how one defines a football field. The answer, he said, was by its boundaries.[1] So, too, has been our definitional understanding of marriage, with boundaries set by nature and nature's God, by natural law and biblical law, by biology and tradition. As the once-unshakable boundaries that have always undergirded marriage are removed—beginning with its redefinition as no longer one man and one woman—the whole edifice will collapse. Any honest, rationally thinking pro-gay-marriage liberal will admit that once marriage is redefined as anything but one man and one woman, with the only standard being that consenting adults who love one another should be permitted to marry, there will be no end to the redefinition: multiple wives, group marriages, sibling marriages, fathers and stepfathers marrying daughters and stepdaughters, uncles marrying nieces, you name it. Shocked liberals screaming that they would never support such arrangements will be inured to them once they come, happily ready to "progress" and to "evolve" to this next new step or "change" taking us "Beyond Marriage."

Anyone who pays attention to these things knows that they are already beginning to happen, especially in Europe but also in Asia and in "progressive" courts in the United States. In fact, as I complete this final chapter, what is being billed as the world's first three-man (nonmonogamous) gay marriage has just occurred in Thailand, with the adoption of children for the triple (not couple) no doubt just around the corner.[2] With the advent of gay marriage, the breach has been opened, large enough that one day you will be able to drive a truck through it—a truck with a sign on the back that says "Just Married," with all sorts of nontraditional couples and triples and quadruples and whatever else housed inside. It is the fast track to the new road for a new America and an altogether new form of human arrangements and civilization heretofore uncharted in the long, ancient history of men and women and their families. Even its redefiners have no idea what it will ultimately entail, and yet they are in one hell of a hurry to get there. Those who dare suggest a pause before the culture takes this literally unprecedented leap are immediately denounced as irredeemable bigots who obviously hate homosexuals and cruelly want to stop people from loving one another.

The takedown of marriage has arrived, with the boundaries that always defined it removed. Most of all, the notion of a God, a Designer who set those boundaries, had to be removed and is being removed.

The old Marxists and neo-Marxists would be thrilled. They would be shocked, but thrilled. And they would understand completely the big picture and the momentous fundamental transformation under way. Most of the rest in modern society have no clue. It is crucial for everyone, including gay Americans, to know they have signed on to something extraordinarily radical and quite sinister—namely, a long-time extremist/communist left effort to undo the family as we have always known and understood it.

Marriage between a man and a woman predates Christ. It is a position with roots as deep as the garden of Eden. Male-female marriage has been far and away the dominant position of all peoples and cultures and societies since the dawn of humanity, at no time of which was the idea of homosexual marriage remotely on the map. Even the ancient

Greeks and Romans, long held up as the dubious model of degenerate sexual perversity, would not go that far. Robert Reilly, author of *Making Gay Okay*, notes that although some ancient Greeks did write paeans to homosexual love, "it did not occur to the celebrants of this kind of love to propose homosexual relationships as the basis for marriage in their societies." The only homosexual relationship that was most publicly accepted, said Reilly, was between an adult male and a male adolescent as a "largely pedagogical relationship."[3]

Of course, that in itself is wicked, though enlightened progressive Americans will probably warm to that someday as well, particularly if the adult and adolescent claim to be in love and are engaging in sex consensually (especially in a culture that cheerfully accepts widespread premarital sex, including among youth). Nonetheless, notes Reilly, this male-male relationship in ancient Greece was to be temporary, as the youth was expected to get married—that is, a *heterosexual* marriage (there was no other kind)—and start a family as soon as he reached maturity. Such was the cultural expectation. Reilly says that the idea that someone was a "homosexual for life" or gay "as a permanent identity" would have struck the Greeks as extremely odd. Reilly says that there was not even a word for "homosexuality" in Greece at the time (or in any other language until the late nineteenth century). He says that homosexual relationships between mature male adults were not accepted by Greek culture.

Fast-forward several thousand years to the home of homosexuality in America, San Francisco: even leading gay voices such as Harvey Milk, the pioneering gay politician in San Francisco, just two decades ago could not imagine an America of men marrying each other.

Americans and Europeans today, in the twenty-first century, are breaking entirely new ground, and yet with no hesitation whatsoever by millions in their cultures. Quite the contrary, those who suggest caution are accused (incredibly) of holding "extreme" viewpoints, as sort of statistical outliers, even as they agree with well over 99.999 percent of human beings who have ever walked the earth, and agree with tens of millions of Americans still.

This has changed only in the last handful of years. The entire Democratic Party and both Bill and Hillary Clinton were on board for the Defense of Marriage Act just a decade or two ago. Barack Obama publicly opposed same-sex marriage merely four years ago. But now, suddenly, those who support the accepted view of marriage since the start of humanity are considered the radicals. It is a stunning development, being fundamentally transformed before our very eyes. The extreme/communist left is delighted.

Advocates of gay marriage have no idea how what they want to do so closely conforms to today's communist agenda. I would implore them not to get angry at me for pointing out what is happening. I see it because I have long studied the communist/far left. Others who do not know that movement do not see. They are blind to the historical-ideological machinations at work. These forces are not discernible to Mr. and Mrs. Mainstreet, who are unwitting and unknowing participants to this longer process. They are being duped by other forces. They are not intending harm, nor do they realize how and where they are part of something bigger, a larger movement using and exploiting them for a purpose they cannot imagine.

Sure, they and gay Americans come to gay marriage for what they perceive as positive and entirely un-sinister forces: their notions of love, freedom, tolerance, equality. I understand this completely. I respect their positive motivations. I do not agree with their applications and interpretations of these things, but I absolutely and fully understand that their intentions are anything but malicious. They do not see themselves as hell-raisers on the same page as communists or whatever other type of left-wing radicals. Nonetheless, the far left couldn't care less how the rest of the culture and everyone else gets there, with whatever slogans or well-intended notions, so long as they get there and assist the grand takedown.

Some time ago, I received an e-mail from a *Townhall* reader responding to one of my articles on gay marriage. He was once part of the "gay left." He told me that most gay people, who are either not political at all or nowhere near as political as the extreme left, have no idea how their gay-marriage advocacy fits and fuels the far left's antifamily agenda, and specifically its longtime takedown strategy aimed at the nuclear family.

The e-mailer is exactly right (and inspired me to begin collecting this material). Most of the gay people I have known are Republicans, not leftists. Generally, I have had no problem easily dialoguing with gay people, though it is now getting more difficult, as liberals have done their usual excellent job convincing a certain group (this time gays) that I as a conservative Republican hate them. Even when socially liberal—and, even then, mainly on matters like gay rights—the gay people I have met have been economic conservatives, not to mention pro-life, which I have always especially appreciated. But in signing on the dotted line for gay marriage, they have also, whether they realize it or not (actually, they do not), enlisted in the radical left's unyielding, centuries-old attempt to undermine the family. They are being used, duped. For that matter, so are Republicans and "conservatives" who support gay marriage, so are libertarians (who suffer from an idolatry of freedom fully decoupled from faith), and so are the independents/"moderates" swimming (as they usually do) with the cultural tide.

Unlike the communists who sought new forms of marriage and wife/mother "emancipation" in order to deliberately undermine the traditional family, the vast majority of today's proponents of same-sex marriage have friendly motives. Their goal is not to tear down traditional-natural-biblical marriage but to expand (and thus redefine) marriage to a new form of spousal partner. They do this not with intended malice toward the family but with the intent of providing a new "freedom" and "right" to a new group of people (homosexuals). Yet, that is the fatal conceit. In truth, marriage is not ours to redefine. Christians like myself (a Roman Catholic) would note that we do not have that right, that such would blaspheme and anger God, and that words have meanings. A cat is a cat, a dog is a dog, a tree is a tree, and marriage is marriage. If gay-marriage advocates would like, they can call their new spousal arrangements something else, but I personally and religiously cannot concede to join them in calling the new configurations marriage. To me and billions before me, marriage is a male-female creation determined by nature and nature's God. It isn't mine to redefine.

Not surprisingly, both today's supporters of same-sex marriage and yesterday's communists who hoped to destroy marriage insist on excluding God from the process, which is indeed a necessity to the possibility. They insist that organized religion and traditional biblical and natural law arguments have no merit and nothing to do with their new conceptions of marriage. Both sides recognize the absolute need—as atheistic communism always has—to expunge God from the equation. They are united in communists' historic-ideological appeals to atheism. This is a crucial but profoundly disturbing area of commonality that should send chills down the spines of many modern same-sex marriage supporters, if they ever come to think of it.

In this, Joe Merlot and his soccer-mom wife, and their apolitical gay friends from college, certainly are not conscious participants dutifully taking marching orders from Marxist ringleaders at Communist Party USA headquarters. They never have been and never will, especially because gay Americans are all over the map politically and ideologically. They sure as heck are not communists. If any of them are, it is surely a tiny percentage. But that is what being duped is all about—not comprehending the deeper, darker forces at work, which you are unknowingly aiding and abetting.

An utterly fascinating aspect of the general public's support of same-sex marriage is that this is the only time that a majority of everyday Americans have agreed with communists in one of their sharp, atheistic stances against marriage and the family. When Marx and Engels and Kollontai and Trotsky and Lenin and Lukács and Marcuse and Millett and Mao and Castro and Reich and Ayers and Dohrn and their assorted comrades pushed fringe ideas on infidelity and free love, on new motherhood, on full-time nursery care for children as wards of the state, on polymorphous perversity, on smashing monogamy, and so forth, they were far outside the mainstream. At its height in the 1930s, Communist Party USA never had more than about a hundred thousand members, less than 1 percent of the overall population, and the Weathermen had an infinitesimal membership. Susie and Joe Q. Public were never with communists on anything, least of all their incendiary marriage views. Not anymore. Today, CPUSA and the American majority at long last finally agree, and they agree on a nontraditional marriage/family matter that does nothing less than irreversibly redefine marriage. It is a breathtaking development to behold.

Today, gay marriage is an absolute cultural juggernaut, steamrolling to a sudden surge of majority acceptance, and steamrolling those who dare to dissent. Where did the kindling that lit this fire start? Anyone who lived through it will tell you: It began germinating in the petri dishes of our universities and their grand cultural-social laboratories, just as Georg Lukács and the Frankfurt gang envisioned. There, leftist professors long after Lukács and Marcuse, many of them disciples of their thought, argued for same-sex marriage under the banner of diversity and tolerance, and later with assertions of "marriage equality." They certainly were not all communists, but they were leftists, and they certainly were not Christian conservatives. Any millennial educated in modern classrooms will tell you that a prime breeding ground for same-sex marriage has been the university. For at least two decades now, colleges have offered courses like "Queer Citizenship" and "Exploring Homophobia" within departments and disciplines and majors and minors and certificates in programs like (to name just one) the University of Maryland's Lesbian, Gay, Bisexual, and Transgender Studies Program.[4] On today's campus, these programs are commonplace, and raise nary an eyebrow among students whose sex-saturated culture is leading them to think that one in two or three of their classmates is gay.[5]

It is truly a Marcusean-polymorphous dreamworld come true. Wilhelm Reich was way before his time. Today, Reich would be chairing an academic department on LGBTQ studies at a major university. He would be sharing his ideas with an openness and ease that would have blown away his contemporaries. The Frankfurt School cadre sought to reshape cultural views of sexuality via education, and that is exactly where they have succeeded and continue to make astonishing progress. That is where the gay-marriage phenomenon truly has been hatched.

Again, needless to say, few to none of the early Marxists cited herein would have raised the prospect of gay marriage. The mere thought of male-male or female-female "matrimony" would have left nearly all of them speechless. Questions like, "Can a man marry a man?" would have once been a test question to gauge a person's level of sanity. But regardless, they helped start the germination.

Such is precisely the kind of cultural adaptation of Marxism that the Frankfurt School had in mind when it redirected Marx's and Engels's economic-based communism to cultural applications, from income/class equality to sexual adaptations. I cannot say that a modern neo-Marxist with careful training in the Frankfurt School coined the term "marriage equality" (I have no idea of the term's origins), but the concept makes perfect sense from the viewpoint of the modern cultural/neo-Marxist. I would not be surprised if a modern Marxist did develop the term.

And moreover, for whatever reasons, the young people enrolled in our monolithic ideological indoctrination centers known as "American universities" lapped it up—or at least enough of them did. Those who did now pervade other cultural institutions critical to changing society's opinions: media, television, films, education, and, the greatest influencer of all (which the Frankfurt crew could never have imagined), the Internet, where they commandeer engines like Google and Yahoo! and Facebook and Mozilla, where they are a constant, relentless, fierce force in the eyes and ears of everyone all the time with their new understandings and new (albeit ever-evolving) sacred cows, many of which (they do not realize) are in full harmony with the objectives of the neo-Marxists. The Internet troops have an enormous ability to shape perception by the minute.

In a widely reported comment, columnist George Will remarked that the opposition to gay marriage is literally dying, because it is older people who oppose it far more than younger people. That is absolutely correct. It is the youth who will change marriage and family via their enthusiastic embrace of gay marriage and gay adoption, thus abolishing the traditional understanding of marriage and the family—precisely as neo-Marxist Georg Lukács and friends like Herbert Marcuse had hoped. In turn, with their university training and through their cultural portals—media, television, film, education, and Internet—they will also change the minds of the vast silent majority in the remainder of the culture at large, an American majority that was never radical in its tastes, but which no longer holds fast to the traditional-religious boundaries that navigated the lives of their ancestors.

And so, all of these non-radical actors, whether they realize it or not, are unwitting dupes to a much longer and older effort by the radical, extreme left to alter marriage and the family. That change, thanks to this wider support, is finally upon us. Its radical forebears are smiling and laughing from their graves.

What is so shockingly different about today is that gay marriage is not being advocated on the remotest margins of society by angry, crackpot German and Austrian and French atheistic philosophers in European cafés but by everyday mainstream Americans, by Mr. and Mrs. Mainstreet. And what they are not only advocating but vigorously and often militantly pushing, to borrow from Marx's language, is the most radical rupture of traditional relations of all—so radical that Marx and his more anti-marriage comrade Engels would be dumbfounded at the mere thought of where America and the West stand today. We are breaking entirely new ground in the long, long sweep of human history, and the groundbreakers act as if it is no big deal whatsoever; to the contrary, they portray those against gay marriage as the extremists, and, of course, as the "hatemongers."

Everyday Americans now stand with their shovels and plow at the ideological colonies of their own making. They do not know it, but they stand on the sunken, shaky shoulders of the ideological colonists, utopians, and pioneers who preceded them: Owen and Fourier and Noyes, Engels and Marx and Marcuse and the Weathermen and the Red Family. The ghosts of New Harmony and Oneida eerily beckon them to join them in their failures. Today's ideological colonists think they are doing something new and exhilarating, but their current form of *progress* really is nothing new under the sun.

Nonetheless, the "progressive" left apparently had to "progress" itself and its culture to this point. And now that it has arrived to this current (albeit always-evolving) spot, this is an especially exciting time for extreme leftists. One is almost tempted to congratulate them. They are no doubt dizzied by their success and, even more so, by their unexpected allies. They are genuinely transforming human nature. And they are doing it with the unwitting support of a huge swath of oblivious citizens and voters. It has been a long time coming.

APPENDIX

POST-CONVENTION
STUDY & APPLICATION
23rd NATIONAL CONVENTION, CPUSA

COMMUNIST PARTY, U.S.A.
235 WEST 23rd STREET, NEW YORK, NY 10011 · (212) 989-4994

CONVENTION
RESOLUTIONS
ADOPTED
&
RESOLUTIONS
COMMITTEE
REPORT

RESOLUTION ON SOME PROCEDURAL STEPS TO BE TAKEN IN CONNECTION WITH THE DAILY WORLD BECOMING A MASS CIRCULATION PAPER ON THE WEST COAST

In order to further the effort to expand the Daily World into an effective national daily newspaper and to raise the level of Party press work in general, the 23rd Convention:

1. Welcomes enthusiastically the Daily World Hi Tech Fund Campaign and hails its successful conclusion.

2. Commends and congratulates all districts, all Party members and friends of the Party who contributed to the $600,000 Hi Tech Drive and made it possible to go over the top, including those in California and the West who generously supported the drive while maintaing the People's World

3. We applaud the fact that it is becoming possible with our new technology to extend the mass circulation of the Daily World to become a national paper with regional editions.

4. Resolve that the Party will help in the coming period as much as possible to strengthen, maintain and expand the People's World with a regional united front character.

5. Agree that when it becomes a practical possibility to extend the mass circulation of the Daily World to the West Coast, then the national leadership will be glad to participate in a discussion with Party and other People's World supporters on any new problems which the People's World may face.

*   *   *

RESOLUTION ON HOMOSEXUALITY

The 23rd Convention of the CPUSA asks the Political Bureau to establish a committee to study whether our policy with respect to homosexuality and membership of homosexuals in the Party stated in the Central Committee Resolution of July 1978 and in the "Declaration on Communist Party Standards" adopted by the Central Committee Dec. 1981 needs changing and in what way and to make recommendations to the new Central Committee for disposition.

*   *   *

ALSO BY THE AUTHOR

ABOUT THE AUTHOR

PAUL KENGOR, PHD, IS AUTHOR OF over a dozen books, including several bestsellers. Kengor is an internationally recognized authority on the presidency, the Cold War, and communism, with extensive experience in Soviet archival research, particularly the Comintern Archives on Communist Party USA.

Dr. Kengor's articles have appeared in numerous publications: the *New York Times*, *USA Today*, CNN.com, FoxNews.com, *Washington Post*, *American Spectator*, *Wall Street Journal*, *The Guardian*, *Christianity Today*, *World*, *National Catholic Register*, *Crisis*, *Jewish Press*, *Jewish World Review*, and many others. He has published articles in top refereed, scholarly journals, such as *Political Science Quarterly* and *Presidential Studies Quarterly*, and has been an editor or contributed chapters to books published by Harvard University Press, Columbia University Press, Oxford University Press, and other academic houses.

Kengor has appeared on MSNBC, C-SPAN, NPR, BBC, and FoxNewsChannel, and has done many TV and radio shows, including "The O'Reilly Factor," "Hannity," Mark Levin, Michael Medved, Glenn Beck, and Bill Bennett.

Kengor received his doctorate from the University of Pittsburgh's Graduate School of Public and International Affairs and his master's degree from American University's School of International Service. He holds an honorary doctorate from Franciscan University (Steubenville, Ohio).

NOTES

CHAPTER 1: FUNDAMENTAL TRANSFORMATION

1. See Paula Ettelbrick, "Since When Is Marriage a Path to Liberation" in William B. Rubenstein, ed., *Lesbians, Gay Men, and the Law* (New York: New Press, 1993), 398-405.

2. This quote is widely available on the Internet. Among others, see Robert P. George, "What Few Deny Gay Marriage Will Do," *First Things*, April 16, 2013.

3. For a quick overview of some of the literature on this subject in light of the current gay-rights movement, see chapter 8 of Robert R. Reilly, *Making Gay Okay* (San Francisco: Ignatius Press, 2014).

4. "Obama's Father's Day speech" (transcript), CNN's Election Center 2008, upd. June 27, 2008, http://www.cnn.com/2008/POLITICS/06/27/obama.fathers.ay/.

5. "Beyond Same-Sex Marriage: A New Strategic Vision for All Our Families and Relationships," July 26, 2006, beyondmarriage.org, http://www.beyondmarriage.org/full_statement.html.

6. When later under scrutiny by the US Senate for confirmation of her EEOC position, Feldblum attempted to backtrack from her original signature to the Beyond Marriage petition, which to this day retains her endorsement. See "Obama EEOC nominee calls support for radical marriage manifesto 'a mistake,'" Catholic News Agency, November 20, 2009, http://www.catholicnewsagency.com/news/obama_eeoc_nominee_calls_support_for_radical_marriage_manifesto_a_mistake/. Feldblum said she had problems with some elements of the sweeping statement, but certainly not all of them.

7. Pope Francis, "Address of His Holiness Pope Francis to the People of Sri Lanka and the Philippines," Mall of Asia Arena, Manila, Philippines, January 16, 2015.

8. A popular source often cited by right-of-center commentators is W. Cleon Skousen's very popular 1958 book, *The Naked Communist*. A widely circulated list from the book is commonly cited, usually without attribution to the book itself. On pages 259–62 (1961 edition), Skousen listed forty-five "Current Communist Goals" endemic to the "Communist conspiracy." Several of these involve marriage, family, and sexuality (though certainly not gay marriage). They include: 26. "Present homosexuality, degeneracy and promiscuity as 'normal, natural, healthy'"; 40. "Discredit the family as an institution. Encourage promiscuity and easy divorce"; and, 41. "Emphasize the need to raise children away from the negative influence of parents. Attribute prejudices, mental blocks and retarding of children to suppressive influence of parents." Skousen does not give a source for these goals, which, in his defense, are largely accurate in a more general sense; he does not clarify that different types of Marxists differed on these goals (such as the Frankfurt Marxists versus traditional Marxists). The list appears to be a product of Skousen's crafting, developed from his prodigious research. He spent sixteen years working for the FBI in one of its divisions. Some dismiss Skousen and his work, whereas others do not. (One of his detractors is Ernie Lazar, an honest, careful, and skilled veteran researcher of archival work.) Skousen's list of goals were taken seriously enough that Congressman Albert Herlong, a Florida Democrat, appears to have had them officially inserted into the *Congressional Record* on January 10, 1963. I believe that Skousen's list has been influential enough that it should at least be addressed somewhere in this book, even if in the notes. Unfortunately, the remainder of his well-organized book does not give much useful information on the communist attack on marriage and family.

9. Joseph Ratzinger (Pope Benedict XVI), *Christianity and the Crisis of Cultures*, transl. Brian McNeil (San Francisco: Ignatius 2006), 36.

CHAPTER 2: EARLY COMMUNIST AND SOCIALIST MOVEMENTS AGAINST FAMILY AND MARRIAGE

1. Many communists and socialists themselves used these labels interchangeably, including the Soviets. Today, we tend to view socialists as milder, less-intrusive versions of communists, advocating more property rights and not as much government intervention.

2. Quoted in Daniel J. Flynn, *A Conservative History of the American Left* (New York: Random House/ Crown Forum, 2008), 19.

3. Ibid., 23, 26–29, 32.

4. Ibid., 19.

5. Ibid., 30-32.

6. Ibid., 34–37.

7. Daniel Flynn has a full chapter on Noyes and the "Bible Communists." See ibid., 52–62.

8. David S. Reynolds, "Complex Marriage, to Say the Least," *New York Times*, October 24, 1993, http://www.nytimes.com/1993/10/24/books/complex-marriage-to-say-the-least.html.

9. Richard Weikart, "Marx, Engels, and the Abolition of the Family," *History of European Ideas*, vol. 18, no. 5 (1994): 657.

10. Ibid., 657–58.

11. Ibid., 661.

12. Ibid., 664.

13. H. Kent Geiger, *The Family in Soviet Russia* (Cambridge, MA: Harvard Univ. Press, 1968), 15–16.

14. Karl Marx and Friedrich Engels, *The Communist Manifesto*, Signet Classics ed. (New York: Penguin, 1998), 72. This edition contains an excellent introduction by Martin Malia, the longtime professor at the University of California–Berkeley. As Malia notes, the "principal author" of the 1848 book was Marx. In this treatment, I'll refer mainly to Marx rather than Engels when quoting from the *Manifesto*.

15. Weikart, "Marx, Engels, and the Abolition of the Family," 668–69.

16. Dr. D. Vance Smith, e-mail message to author, November 26, 2013. I thank Dr. Smith for permission to quote from his emails in a last-minute request prior to publication of this book.

17. *Wikipedia* definition retrieved March 7, 2015, https://www.google.com/?gws_rd=ssl#q=Aufhebung+.

18. Weikart, "Marx, Engels, and the Abolition of the Family," 664.

19. Geiger, *The Family in Soviet Russia*, xi.

20. Ibid., 15, 20.

21. Marx, *The Communist Manifesto*, 71.

22. Ibid., 71–72, 75.

23. See my long and in-depth discussion in chapter four of Paul Kengor, *Dupes: How America's Adversaries Have Manipulated Progressives for a Century* (Wilmington, Delaware: ISI Books, 2010), 80–91.

24. V. Yazykova, *Socialist Life Style and the Family* (Moscow: Progress Publishers, 1984), 7.

25. Weikart, "Marx, Engels, and the Abolition of the Family," 664.

26. See: David Horowitz, *The Black Book of the American Left*, vol. 2, *Progressives* (Los Angeles: Second Thoughts, 2013), 138.

27. Weikart, "Marx, Engels, and the Abolition of the Family," 665.

28. Geiger, *The Family in Soviet Russia*, 40.

29. See, among others, Geiger, *The Family in Soviet Russia*, 11; and Weikart, "Marx, Engels, and the Abolition of the Family," 657.

30. Weikart, "Marx, Engels, and the Abolition of the Family," 665–66.

31. Friedrich Engels, *The Origin of the Family, Private Property and the State* (New York: International, 1942), 67.

32. Geiger, *The Family in Soviet Russia*, 20–21, 33.

33. Weikart, "Marx, Engels, and the Abolition of the Family," 665–67.

34. One of the most influential early accounts of Marx's family life was Otto Rühle, *Karl Marx: His Life and Works* (New York: Viking, 1929). Among more recent works, see Francis Wheen, *Karl Marx: A Life* (New York: W. W. Norton, 2001). Here, I rely in particular on Paul Johnson's excellent chapter (3) on Marx in his book, *Intellectuals* (New York: HarperCollins, 1989).

35. Johnson, *Intellectuals*, 74.

36. Ibid., 77.

37. Some sources claim three daughters committed suicide, but I believe the correct number is two.

38. Johnson, *Intellectuals*, 62, 78–79.

39. Weikart, who quoted this letter, argued that despite Marx "probably father[ing] an illegitimate child," he was nonetheless "apparently a model husband and remained faithful to his wife." Weikart wrote this in 1994, perhaps before knowing of more recent research on Marx's woefully poor conduct as a husband. Of course, a husband who fathers an illegitimate child to the family's young nanny is not a model or faithful husband.

40. Quoted by Weikart, "Marx, Engels, and the Abolition of the Family," 668. It is possible that Marx in this instance was speaking tongue in cheek, given the exorbitant cost of a man financially supporting a large family (as opposed to a single man with no such obligation). On the other hand, Marx may well have meant it in a different way, a way that would be a profoundly significant insight into his views on family.

41. There are different translations of this quote. This one is used by Robert R. Reilly. Another (longer) translation is this: "And since innovations [also translated as "revolutions" or "revolutionary changes"] creep in through the private life of individuals also, there ought to be a magistracy which will have an eye to those whose life is not in harmony with the government, whether oligarchy or democracy or any other" (Aristotle, *Politics* 1308b20–21, Jowett translation). The Irwin/Fine translation is, "And since people's private ways of life also lead them to revolution . . ." A strict Greek translation would be "on account of private lives." I thank my Grove City College colleagues in the Department of Philosophy for their assistance with this.

CHAPTER 3: MARX'S DISCIPLES

1. See James Thrower, *God's Commissar: Marxism-Leninism as the Civil Religion of Soviet Society* (Lewiston, NY: Edwin Mellen Press, 1992), 64; Jennifer McDowell, "Soviet Civil Ceremonies," *Journal for the Scientific Study of Religion* 13, no. 3 (1974): 265–79; and Powell, "Rearing the New Soviet Man," in B. R. Bociurkiw et al., eds., *Religion and Atheism in the USSR and Eastern Europe* (London: MacMillan, 1975), 160–65.

2. W. Bruce Lincoln, *Red Victory: A History of the Russian Civil War* (New York: Simon and Schuster, 1989), 476–77.

3. Geiger, *The Family in Soviet Russia*, 253–54.

4. Ibid.

5. Vladimir Lenin stated this in *Pravda*, June 16, 1913, republished according to the original *Pravda* text in *Lenin, Collected Works*, vol. 19 (Moscow: Progress, 1977), 235–37.

6. See Geiger, *The Family in Soviet Russia*, 254. The figure on some Soviet women having as many as twenty abortions is breathtaking but no doubt accurate. I have read published claims of as many as forty abortions by some Russian women, an astronomical figure that seems impossible and which I cannot substantiate—though I imagine there have been such rare occasions.

7. John Riddell, "1921–26: The Communist Women's Movement," *International Socialist Review*, January–February 2013, 37.

8. John King Fairbank and Merle Goldman, *China: A New History* (Cambridge, Mass.: Harvard University Press, 2006), 371–81.

9. Li Zhisui, *The Private Life of Chairman Mao* (New York: Random House, 1994).

CHAPTER 4: THEORISTS AND PRACTITIONERS

1. John Riddell, "1921–26: The Communist Women's Movement," *International Socialist Review*, January–February 2013, 38.

2. Alexandra Kollontai, "International Women's Day," *International Socialist Review*, January–February 2013, 29-34.

3. Aleksandra M. Kollontai, *Communism and the Family* (New York: Andrade's Bookshop, 1920), 10, cited in H. Kent Geiger, *The Family in Soviet Russia* (Cambridge, MA: Harvard Univ. Press, 1968), 51.

4. Alexandra Kollontai, "Communism and the Family," *Komunistka*, no. 2, 1920 (Russian); *The Worker*, 1920 (English), available online at https://www.marxists.org/archive/kollonta/1920/communism-family.htm.

5. Ibid.

6. Hollie McKay, "Critics slam MSNBC host's claim that kids belong to community, not parents," Fox News, April 9, 2013, http://www.foxnews.com/entertainment/2013/04/09/critics-slam-msnbc-hosts-claim-that-kids-belong-to-community-not-parents/.

7. Ibid.

8. Geiger, *The Family in Soviet Russia*, 44.

9. Ibid., 48.

10. Ibid.

11. Ibid.

12. Bella V. Dodd, *School of Darkness* (New York: Devin-Adair, 1954), 3, 33–35, 39–41, 42–43. On George Counts's Moscow pilgrimage with John Dewey, see Kengor, *Dupes*, 66, 102.

13. Ibid., 47, 60, 159.

14. Ibid, 153–62.

15. Testimony of Bella V. Dodd, United States Senate, *Committee on the Judiciary, Subcommittee to Investigate the Administration of the Internal Security Act and Other Internal Security Laws*, March 10, 1953, 511–46.

16. See the very revealing book by CPUSA head William Z. Foster, *Toward Soviet America* (New York: Coward-McCann, 1932).

17. Sheen also brought back to the faith Louis Budenz, bringing the *Daily Worker* editor—whose name at the time of his reversion was still on the masthead—into the Church, along with his wife and three daughters. Thomas C. Reeves, *America's Bishop: The Life and Times of Fulton J. Sheen* (San Francisco: Encounter Books, 2001), 170–73.

18. See, among many others, Daniel J. Flynn, *A Conservative History of the American Left* (New York: Random House/Crown Forum, 2008), 180. The movie on Reed, *Reds*, includes a scene with Reed in prison, urinating the color red, which equally could have been related to his kidney disease. He was racked with health problems, some of them related to his sexual exploits and others not.

19. Benjamin Gitlow, *I Confess: The Truth about American Communism* (New York: E. P. Dutton, 1940); and Benjamin Gitlow, *The Whole of Their Lives* (New York: Scribner's, 1948).

20. Gitlow, *I Confess*, 316.

21. David Horowitz, e-mail message to author, November 13, 2014.

22. Ron Radosh, e-mail message to author, November 14, 2014.

CHAPTER 5: "COMMUNIST MARRIAGE"

1. Whittaker Chambers, *Witness* (New York: Random House, 1952), 205–6.

2. Ibid.

3. Sam Tanenhaus, *Whittaker Chambers* (New York: Random House, 1998), 61.

4. Ibid.

5. Meyer A. Zeligs, *Friendship and Fratricide: An Analysis of Whittaker Chambers and Alger Hiss* (New York: Viking, 1967), 118.

6. Tanenhaus, *Whittaker Chambers*, 65.

7. Ibid., 65–66.

8. Chambers, *Witness*, 264–68.

9. Ibid.

10. Tanenhaus, *Whittaker Chambers*, 65, 342–44.

11. Ibid., 345.

12. Ibid., 342–45.

13. This became a favorite anecdote of Ronald Reagan, who recounted it frequently in his many invocations of Chambers.

14. Tanenhaus, *Whittaker Chambers*, 393.

CHAPTER 6: MARGARET SANGER'S RUSSIAN ROMANCE

1. Madeline Gray, *Margaret Sanger* (New York: Richard Marek, 1979), 61.

2. This is an aspect of Woodrow Wilson that is not appreciated today by either his progressive supporters or his conservative detractors. See my lengthy analysis in Kengor, *Dupes*, 39–52.

3. See Gray, *Margaret Sanger*, 58–59; and Donald De Marco and Benjamin Wiker, *Architects of the Culture of Death* (San Francisco: Ignatius Press, 2006), 290–94.

4. See Michael Sherbone, *H. G. Wells: Another Kind of Life* (London: Peter Owen, 2010), 256-63; Norman and Jeanne MacKenzie, *H. G. Wells* (New York: Simon and Schuster, 1973), 331-33; and Anthony West, *H. G. Wells: Aspects of a Life* (New York: Random House, 1984), 83–88.

5. H. G. Wells, *An Experiment in Autobiography: Discoveries and Conclusions of a Very Ordinary Brain (Since 1866)* (New York: Little, Brown, 1984), 215, 667, 687–89. Wells made several trips to the USSR in the 1920s and 1930s. See H. G. Wells, *Russia in the Shadows* (New York: George H. Doran, 1921), 160–62.

6. De Marco and Wiker, *Architects of the Culture of Death*, 294.

7. For my analysis, see Paul Kengor, "Obama's Racial Eugenics Award?" *American Spectator*, December 3, 2013. De Marco and Wiker, both of whom are anti-Sanger conservatives, charitably state, "Of course, outright extermination was not their goal." De Marco and Wiker, *Architects of the Culture of Death*, 313.

8. See Margaret Sanger, "The Pope's Position on Birth Control," *Nation*, January 27, 1932, 102–3, http://www.thenation.com/article/popes-position-birth-control.

9. See Kengor, *Dupes*, 10, 54–55.

10. George Bernard Shaw wrote this in 1928 for his book *The Intelligent Woman's Guide to Socialism, Capitalism, Sovietism and Fascism*. A 1937 edition by Pelican Books is posted at https://www.marxists.org/reference/archive/shaw/works/guide3.htm. Random House also published an edition in 1971.

11. Devin Dwyer, "Planned Parenthood at Center of Budget Shutdown Threat," ABC News, April 8, 2011, http://abcnews.go.com/Politics/planned-parenthood-center-budget-shutdown-threat/story?id=13328750.

12. Devin Dwyer, "Planned Parenthood Cuts Draw Filibuster Threat from Senate Dems," *The Note* (blog), April 7, 2011, http://abcnews.go.com/blogs/politics/2011/04/planned-parenthood-cuts-draw-filibuster-threat-from-senate-dems/.

13. Carmen Cox, "Democrats Use Planned Parenthood Debate to Raise Funds," ABC News Radio, April 8, 2011, http://abcnewsradioonline.com/politics-news/democrats-use-planned-parenthood-debate-to-raise-funds.html.

14. Paul Kengor, "Reflections on Roe: When Margaret Sanger Spoke to the KKK," American Spectator, January 22, 2015, http://spectator.org/articles/61552/reflections-roe-when-margaret-sanger-spoke-kkk.

15. Catalina Camia, "Understanding the shutdown fight over women's health," USA Today, April 10, 2011, http://content.usatoday.com/communities/onpolitics/post/2011/04/planned-parenthood-abortion-government-shutdown-/1#.VQNXJilCSAB.

16. Mike Lillis, "GOP using Planned Parenthood as 'whipping boy' in health debate," The Hill, February, 19, 2011, http://thehill.com/blogs/blog-briefing-room/news/145227-pelosi-gop-using-planned-parenthood-as-whipping-boy-to-cloak-family-planning-disdain.

17. Josh Richman, "Boxer fires back against GOP budget plan," Oakland Tribune, March 23, 2011, http://www.insidebayarea.com/breaking-news/ci_17683204.

18. Sanger, "The Pope's Position on Birth Control," *Nation*, January 27, 1932, 103.

19. William Martin, ed., *What Liberals Believe* (New York: Skyhorse, 2012), 1.

20. Margaret Sanger, "Birth Control in Soviet Russia," *Birth Control Review*, June 1935, 3.

CHAPTER 7: MARGARET MEAD AND FRIENDS

1. A key clarification on Kinsey: He was perhaps the nation's most famous (and infamous) sex researcher, who suffered from (among other things) masochistic and chronic masturbatory behavior. His influence on the sex revolution, gay movement, and feminism is undeniable. He was also a marriage professor before launching his huge area of research. Some readers of this book will wonder why I have not included Kinsey. The answer is that he cannot be easily politically classified or even easily placed on the political left, let alone the communist left. He had been raised a strict Methodist and harbored certain conservative views. When it came to economics and big government, he seemed conservative; whereas when it came to cultural and social behaviors, he was clearly much more "progressive" and bucked standard notions of morality. One of his leading biographers, James Jones, said that Kinsey called himself a political independent throughout his life and usually voted Republican, consistent with the Indiana heartland where he settled and did his research at Indiana University. "Dr. Kinsey was a conservative," Jones quoted one Kinsey colleague as saying. "He had no use for FDR." Nor did he have any use for the New Deal or for Keynesian economics (which he reportedly "despised"), and saw Soviet communism (in the words of his biographer) as a "bankrupt philosophy" that was "doomed to failure." See James H. Jones, *Alfred C. Kinsey: A Life* (New York: W. W. Norton, 1997), 195. In short, Kinsey was many things, but he was no communist pursuing New Left cultural Marxism to take down marriage and the family.

2. Paul C. Mishler, *Raising Reds* (New York: Columbia University Press, 1999), 100–2; Susan Braudy, *Family Circle: The Boudins and the Aristocracy of the Left* (New York: Knopf, 2003), 40–42, 390n; and Kengor, *Dupes*, 330–31.

3. Eugene Taylor, *The Mystery of Personality* (New York: Springer, 2009), 204.

4. *Encyclopedia of Marxism* Glossary of People, s.v. "Kurt Lewin," on the Marxists Internet Archive, https://www.marxists.org/glossary/people/l/e.htm, accessed March 9, 2015.

5. Ralph de Toledano, *Cry Havoc! The Great American Bring-down and How it Happened* (Washington, DC: Anthem, 2006), 138–39.

6. See Zoe Burkholder, *Color in the Classroom: How American Schools Taught Race, 1900–54* (New York: Oxford Univ. Press, 2011), 206n; Mary Bowman-Kruhm, *Margaret Mead: A Biography* (Westport, CT: Greenwood Press, 2003), 78; John Van Willigen, *Applied Anthropology: An Introduction* (Westport, CT: Greenwood Press, 2002), 78.

7. Toledano, *Cry Havoc!*, 139–40.

8. De Marco and Wiker, *Architects of the Culture of Death*, 250–57.

9. Ibid.

10. Ibid., 257.

11. Ibid., 261.

12. Ibid., 257.

CHAPTER 8: FIGHTING THE "SATANIC SCOURGE" OF COMMUNISM

1. H. Kent Geiger, *The Family in Soviet Russia* (Cambridge, MA: Harvard Univ. Press, 1968), 21, 37, 77, 82–83.

2. See Robert S. Barker, "Natural Law and the United States Constitution," *Review of Metaphysics* 66 (September 2012): 105–30. The text and also Barker's July 2013 presentation to the American Founders Lecture Series hosted by the Center for Vision & Values at Grove City College are posted at http://www.visionandvalues.org/2013/07/natural-law-and-the-united-states-constitution-2/.

3. See Matthew 19:4–6 (New Testament) and also the Genesis account in the Old Testament.

4. Quoted in the *Catechism of the Catholic Church*, par. 1955, http://www.scborromeo.org/ccc/para/1955.htm.

5. Quoted in Martha Vinson, *St. Gregory of Nazianzus: Select Orations* (Washington, DC: Catholic University of America Press, 2003).

6. See: Catechism of the Catholic Church, par. 2357, http://www.scborromeo.org/ccc/para/2357.htm; and the June 2003 statement by the Congregation for the Doctrine of the Faith, "Considerations Regarding Proposals to Give Legal Recognition to Unions Between Homosexual Persons," http://www.vatican.va/roman_curia/congregations/cfaith/documents/rc_con_cfaith_doc_20030731_homosexual-unions_en.html.

7. Quoted in Pope Piux IX, *Qui Pluribus* (On Faith and Religion), November 9, 1846, available at Papal Encyclicals Online, http://www.papalencyclicals.net/Pius09/p9quiplu.htm.

8. The following quotes are from Pope Leo XIII, *Quod Apostolici Muneris* (On Socialism), December 28, 1878, http://www.saint-mike.org/library/papal_library/leoxiii/encyclicals/quod_apostolici_muneris.html.

9. These are all cited in Pope Pius XI, *Divini Redemptoris* (On Atheistic Communism), March 19, 1937, available at Papal Encyclicals Online, http://papalencyclicals.net/Pius11/P11DIVIN.HTM. The quotations that follow are also from this encyclical. (I have not listed the dire, dramatic warnings of Our Lady of Fatima in 1917. For this chapter, I have adhered to official Church documents and statements.)

10. President Ronald Reagan, "Address to the National Association of Evangelicals," March 8, 1983.

11. The remaining encyclical quotes in this chapter are from Pius XI, *Divini Redemptoris*.

12. The reference to the encyclical on marriage is alluding to the December 31, 1930, encyclical *Casti Connubii*.

13. A reference to the serpent's promise to Eve if she would eat the forbidden fruit. See Genesis 3.

CHAPTER 9: THE VOICE OF SHEEN

1. For Schwarz's warnings on communism's threat to faith, family, and marriage, see his best seller: Fred Schwarz, *You Can Trust the Communists (to Be Communists)* (Englewood Cliffs, NY: Prentice-Hall, 1960), 33–35, 55, 154–55, 171, 179.

2. Billy Graham is rightly known much more for his evangelism than for strident anti-communism, but he was certainly a dedicated anti-communist who was especially appalled by the aggressive atheism of international communism.

3. See the excellent biography by Thomas C. Reeves, *America's Bishop: The Life and Times of Fulton J. Sheen* (San Francisco: Encounter Books, 2001).

4. Ibid., 1–2.

5. Whittaker Chambers, "Peace and the Papacy," *Time*, August 16, 1943.

6. Fulton J. Sheen, *Communism and the Conscience of the West* (Indianapolis and New York: Bobbs-Merrill, 1948), 140–41.

7. Ibid., 141.

8. Ibid.

9. Ibid., 142.

10. Howard Spodek, *The World's History* (n.p.: Prentice-Hall, 1998), 618.

11. Sheen, *Communism and the Conscience of the West*, 142–43.

12. Ibid., 143.

13. Ibid., 146–47.

14. Sharon LaFraniere, "Russians Feel Abortion's Complications," *Washington Post*, February 22, 2003.

15. The other book that Clark cited was Thomas Merton's *The Seven-Storey Mountain*, published about the same time. See Paul Kengor and Patricia Clark Doerner, *The Judge: William P. Clark, Ronald Reagan's Top Hand* (San Francisco: Ignatius, 2007).

16. Fulton J. Sheen, *Peace of Soul* (New York: McGraw-Hill, 1949), 147–49.

17. Ibid., 149.

CHAPTER 10: CULTURAL MARXISM AND THE FRANKFURT SCHOOL

1. Traditionally this quote has been attributed to Dostoyevsky. Often attributed to his *Brothers Karamazov*, the wording is slightly different, perhaps due to translation issues.

2. See Fulton J. Sheen, *The Church, Communism and Democracy* (New York: Dell, 1954), 156–65.

3. Corliss and Margaret Lamont, *Russia Day by Day: A Travel Diary* (New York: Covici-Friede, 1933).

4. This fact is well established. Among other sources, see H. Kent Geiger, *The Family in Soviet Russia*, 94.

5. Martin Jay, *The Dialectical Imagination: A History of the Frankfurt School and the Institute of Social Research: 1923–50* (Berkeley: University of California Press, 1973), 84–85.

6. Nearly every Lenin quotation seems subject to dispute nowadays, but this one has been commonly cited for years, is seemingly legitimate, and (at the least) is indeed reflective of his cynical views of humanity and education. Like so many Lenin statements, pinning down the exact remark is elusive because of the differing translations.

7. Jonah Goldberg, *Liberal Fascism* (New York: Doubleday, 2008), 227.

8. Ibid., 287.

9. Ralph de Toledano, *Cry Havoc! The Great American Bring-down and How it Happened*, 46, 156.

10. Jonah Goldberg, *Liberal Fascism*, 377.

11. Toledano, *Cry Havoc!*, 179.

12. Different sources give different dates (in a 1923–24 time frame) for the start of the Institute. Ralph de Toledano says that the institute opened its doors on June 22, 1924, as an "adjunct" to the University of Frankfurt. Toledano, *Cry Havoc!*, 31.

13. For an early document on the founding of the Marx-Engels Institute, see "L.B.," "The Marx-Engels Institute," translated from *La Critique sociale*, no. 2 (July 1931): 51–52, online at http://www.marxists.org/archive/riazanov/bio/bio02.htm.

14. The Committee on Un-American Activities and the U.S. House of Representatives, *Guide to Subversive Organizations and Publications (and Appendices)*, rev. (Government Printing Office, 1957; 1961), 1. Hereafter referred to as *Guide to Subversive Organizations and Publications*.

15. For more on the founding of the Marx-Engels Institute, see "L.B.," "The Marx-Engels Institute."

16. Toledano, *Cry Havoc!*, 8–9.

17. Douglas Martin, "Ralph de Toledano, 90, Writer Known as a Nixon Friend, Dies," *New York Times*, February 6, 2007, http://www.nytimes.com/2007/02/06/obituaries/06toledano.html?_r=0.

18. Toledano, *Cry Havoc!*, 115–25.

19. Ibid., 38–39.

20. Toledano does not provide an exact date for the meeting, but he is a trustworthy source. For a Marxist source on the founding of the Marx-Engels Institute in 1920, which likewise provides only the year, see "L.B." "The Marx-Engels Institute."

21. Toledano, *Cry Havoc!*, 23.

22. Ibid., 25.

23. Ibid., 95, 190.

24. Ibid., 94–95.

25. Ibid., 25.

26. Ronald Reagan, "Radio Address to the Nation on the American Family," December 3, 1983; Reagan, "Proclamation 5513—National Family Reunion Weekend, 1986," July 29, 1986; Reagan, "Proclamation 5570—National Adoption Week," November 13, 1986; Reagan, "Remarks at a White House Briefing for Supporters of Welfare Reform," February 9, 1987; and Reagan, "Proclamation 5912: National Family Week, 1988," November 19, 1988. When Reagan called the family "the nucleus of civilization," he was quoting Will and Ariel Durant. Reagan, "Radio Address to the Nation on Family Values," December 20, 1986.

27. Reagan, "Radio Address to the Nation on Family Values," December 20, 1986.

28. Reagan, "Proclamation 4999—National Family Week, 1982," November 12, 1982.

29. Reagan, "Proclamation 4882—National Family Week, 1981," November 3, 1981.

30. The dates on this move vary. Some report it as 1935; others as 1938. On Berlin as Babylon, see Toledano, *Cry Havoc!*, 62–63.

31. Ibid., 78–83.

32. I detail this at length in my book *Dupes*. See chapters 4–6 on John Dewey, 80–109.

33. Toledano, *Cry Havoc!*, 79–84.

34. Ibid., 85–86, 187–88.

35. Ibid., 148.

36. Ibid., 27.

37. Ibid.

38. Ibid., 96, 105.

CHAPTER 11: THE WORLD OF WILHELM REICH

1. See Wilhelm Reich, *Passion of Youth: Wilhelm Reich: An Autobiography* (New York: Farrar, Giroux, and Strauss, 1988), 4–46; and Colin Wilson, *The Quest for Wilhelm Reich* (New York: Doubleday, 1981), 29.

2. See Kengor, *Dupes*, 92-100.

3. *Encyclopedia of Marxism* Glossary of People, s.v. "Wilhelm Reich," on the Marxists Internet Archive, at http://www.marxists.org/glossary/people/r/e.htm#reich-wilhelm.

4. Donald De Marco and Benjamin Wiker, *Architects of the Culture of Death* (San Francisco: Ignatius, 2006), 228.

5. Ralph de Toledano, *Cry Havoc! The Great American Bring-down and How it Happened* (Washington, DC: Anthem, 2006), 38, 96.

6. Christopher Turner, *Adventures in the Orgasmatron: How the Sexual Revolution Came to America* (New York: Farrar, Straus & Giroux, 2011).

7. Quoted in Toledano, *Cry Havoc!*, 91.

8. Wilhelm Reich, *The Sexual Revolution: Toward a Self-Governing Character Structure* (New York: Pocket Books, 1975), 28.

9. De Marco and Wiker, *Architects of the Culture of Death*, 227.

10. Ibid., 227–28.

11. The quotations that follow are from Wilhelm Reich, *The Function of the Orgasm*, vol. 1 of *The Discovery of Orgone* (New York: Farrar, Straus, and Giroux, 1973).

12. Christopher Turner made this argument in his book *Adventures in the Orgasmatron*. I find Turner's argument fully convincing because I have always had this belief myself, always assuming that Woody Allen got his idea from Reich's orgone.

13. Harvey Klehr, e-mail message to author, November 30, 2014.

14. Ariel Levy, "Novelty Acts," *New Yorker*, September 19, 2011. Another source who merits this title is arguably Alfred Kinsey, whose sexual anarchism was possibly to the left of even Reich.

15. De Marco and Wiker, *Architects of the Culture of Death*, 222, 231–32.

16. "Morals: The Second Sexual Revolution," *Time*, January 24, 1964.

17. While the title "Father of the Sexual Revolution" is shared with Alfred Kinsey, Wilhelm Reich coined the phrase in the 1930s.

CHAPTER 12: HERBERT MARCUSE'S NEW LEFT

1. See Jonah Goldberg, *Liberal Fascism* (New York: Doubleday, 2008), 175.

2. Ralph de Toledano, *Cry Havoc! The Great American Bring-down and How it Happened* (Washington, DC: Anthem, 2006), 48.

3. These two pronunciations are both provided at the Marcuse website, http://www.marcuse.org/ herbert/. One person at the site wrote, "I'd write it phonetically (in US-English) [mahr KOO zeh], with the emphasis on the middle syllable. That is the standard German pronunciation." Another wrote: "As a member of Herbert's son Peter's family, we grew up in the US with an anglicized pronunciation (which you'd hear on my answering machine, phonetically [mar "QU"SS] (with the 'cu' pronounced like the letter "Q") and the emphasis on the second syllable."

4. On this, see especially M. Stanton Evans and Herb Romerstein, *Stalin's Secret Agents* (New York: Threshold, 2012).

5. Among the best literature on this, see Evans and Romerstein, *Stalin's Secret Agents*; M. Stanton Evans, *Blacklisted by History: The Untold Story of Senator Joe McCarthy and His Fight against America's Enemies* (New York: Crown Forum, 2009); Herbert Romerstein and Eric Breindel, *The Venona Secrets: Exposing Soviet Espionage and America's Traitors* (Washington, DC: Regnery, 2000); Alexander Vassiliev and Allen Weinstein, *The Haunted Wood* (New York: Random House, 1998); John Earl Haynes and Harvey Klehr, *Venona: Decoding Soviet Espionage in America* (New Haven and London: Yale Univ. Press, 1999); Harvey Klehr, John Earl Haynes, and Fridrikh Igorevich Firsov, *The Secret World of American Communism* (New Haven and London: Yale Univ. Press, 1995); and Toledano, *Cry Havoc!*, 44, 71, 116, 126–37, 209–10. Among the most recent works, Diana West mentions Marcuse's alarming connections on pages 287 and 364n of her book *American Betrayal* (New York: St. Martin's Press, 2014).

6. Ibid.

7. Herbert Marcuse, *Eros and Civilization: A Philosophical Inquiry into Freud* (Boston: Beacon, 1955; 1967), 54. Citations are to the 1967 edition.

8. Ronald Aronson, "Marcuse Today," *Boston Review*, November 17, 2014, http://www.bostonreview. net/books-ideas/ronald-aronson-herbert-marcuse-one-dimensional-man-today.

9. Ibid.

10. Ibid.

11. Kevin Slack, "Liberalism Radicalized: The Sexual Revolution, Multiculturalism, and the Rise of Identity Politics," Heritage Foundation, First Principles Series, no. 46, August 27, 2013, http://www.heritage.org/research/reports/2013/08/liberalism-radicalized-the-sexual-revolution-multiculturalism-and-the-rise-of-identity-politics.

12. On page xv of the preface to the 1966 edition of *Eros and Civilization*, Marcuse wrote that "polymorphous sexuality" was "the term which I used to indicate that the new direction of progress would depend completely on the opportunity to activate repressed or arrested organic, biological needs: to make the human body an instrument of pleasure rather than labor. The old formula, the development of prevailing needs and faculties, seemed to be inadequate; the emergence of new, qualitatively different needs and faculties seemed to be the prerequisite, the content of liberation." If that explanation is unsatisfying, it is also typical Marcuse.

13. The GLBTQ website provides a hyperlink to "polymorphous perversity," which defines it thus:

"Polymorphous perversity is a Freudian term referring to unfocused, infantile sexuality. In Freudian terms, as individuals mature, the focus of their sexuality passes from polymorphous perversity through oral and anal stages to culminate in adult, genitally focused sexuality. More generally, the term is used to indicate the ability to derive erotic pleasure from any part of the body." http://www.glbtq.com/glossary.php?id=25.

14. *glbtq: An Encyclopedia of Gay, Lesbian, Bisexual, Transgender, and Queer Culture*, s.v. "Marcuse, Herbert," accessed March 10, 2015, http://www.glbtq.com/social-sciences/marcuse_h.html.

15. Ibid.

16. Aronson, "Marcuse Today."

17. To read Marcuse's original 1965 piece, titled, "Repressive Tolerance," visit the website, www.marcuse.org. For commentary, see Daniel J. Flynn, "The Sixties' Road to Rutgers and Beyond," *American Spectator*, May 9, 2014; Toledano, *Cry Havoc!*, 151–53, 159, 188, 191; and also Goldberg's *Liberal Fascism*.

18. Toledano, *Cry Havoc!*, 28.

CHAPTER 13: THE '60S AND THE NEW LEFT MARXIST FEMINISTS

1. David Horowitz, e-mail message to author, November 13, 2014.

2. David Horowitz, *The Black Book of the American Left*, vol. 2, *Progressives* (Los Angeles: Second Thoughts, 2013), 29.

3. See my discussion of this in Kengor, *Dupes*, 61–64, evidenced by a declassified December 2, 1920, letter in Comintern archives that I reproduce and discuss at length.

4. Ibid., 58–68.

5. Ibid., 245, 304–6.

6. Kudos to Spyridon Mitsotakis for connecting dots on Friedan–Wolff between my book *Dupes* and the biography by Daniel Horowitz. See Spyridon Mitsotakis, "The Marxist Roots of Feminism," *Front Page Magazine*, August 29, 2011, http://www.frontpagemag.com/2011/spyridon-mitsotakis/the-marxist-roots-of-feminism/.

7. Daniel Horowitz, *Betty Friedan and the Making of "The Feminine Mystique": The American Left, the Cold War, and Modern Feminism* (Amherst, MA: Univ. of Massachusetts Press, 2000).

8. David Horowitz, "Feminism's Dirtiest Secret," *Front Page Magazine*, June 9, 2000.

9. David Horowitz, "Betty Friedan's Secret Communist past," *Salon*, January 18, 1999.

10. See Kirsten Lise Fermaglich, "'The Comfortable Concentration Camp': The Significance of Nazi Imagery in Betty Friedan's the Feminine Mystique (1963)," American Jewish History 91, no. 2 (June 1, 2003), 205–32.

11. It has been said that even though she tried marriage and thus sex with men, she was really only sexually attracted to women. She had sexual relations with both genders. See Kenneth W. Mack, *Representing the Race: The Creation of the Civil Rights Lawyer* (Cambridge, Mass.: Harvard University Press, 2012), 211–15.

12. See Horowitz, *Betty Friedan and the Making of "The Feminine Mystique,"* 201, 313n; Carey Roberts, "The Untold Story of Betty Friedan," ifeminists.com, November 25, 2003, http://www.ifeminists.net/introduction/editorials/2003/1125roberts.html; and "Betty Friedan," DiscoverTheNetworks.org, accessed March 10, 2015, http://www.discoverthenetworks.org/individualProfile.asp?indid=1328.

13. Horowitz, *Betty Friedan and the Making of "The Feminine Mystique,"* 48, 96, 271n.

14. De Toledano, *Cry Havoc!*, 141-43.

15. See, among others, Toledano, *Cry Havoc!*, 142; and Horowitz, *The Black Book of the American Left*, vol. 2, *Progressives*, 169.

16. The page numbers for the following quotes from *Sexual Politics* refer to the 2000 reprint by the University of Illinois Press.

17. Mallory Millett, "Marxist Feminism's Ruined Lives," *Front Page Magazine*, September 2, 2014.

18. "The Liberation of Kate Millett," *Time* magazine, August 31, 1970.

19. Mallory Millett, "Marxist Feminism's Ruined Lives," *Front Page Magazine*, September 2, 2014.

20. Ibid.

21. Ibid.

22. Ibid.

23. *glbtq: An Encyclopedia of Gay, Lesbian, Bisexual, Transgender, and Queer Culture*, s.v. "Millett, Kate," http://www.glbtq.com/literature/millett_k.html, accessed March 10, 2015.

CHAPTER 14: SMASHING MONOGAMY: THE WEATHERMEN'S SEXUAL REVOLUTIONARIES

1. Mark Rudd, *Underground: My Life with SDS and the Weathermen* (New York: William Morrow, 2009), 189.

2. Ralph de Toledano, *Cry Havoc! The Great American Bring-down and How it Happened* (Washington, DC: Anthem, 2006), 33, 39, 49, 156–59, 227, 246.

3. An expert on the Weathermen consulted for this book (with the help of Ron Radosh) maintains that by their fugitive days they had "moved on" from Marcuse to Fanon. On Obama reading Fanon, see Barack Obama, *Dreams from My Father*, repr. ed. (New York: Crown, 2007), 100, and also my analysis in Paul Kengor, *The Communist* (New York: Threshold Editions, 2012), 247–48, 257.

4. Rudd, *Underground*, 5–21.

5. Ibid., 32–33.

6. Ibid., 41–42, 321.

7. Ibid., 146, 278–80.

8. Ibid., 214–15.

9. This quote has been reported countless times and is easily available for documentation. As horrible and unimaginable as it may seem, it is not disputed. For an example of it being reporting very recently by one of the participants, see Rudd, *Underground*, 189.

10. Ayers has been asked to comment on this episode many times. The best face that Ayers has tried to put on the episode is to claim that his sweetheart was being "ironic" or had employed "rhetorical overkill" or was speaking "partly as a joke" (but never *fully*). David Horowitz looked into the incident and reported: "In 1980, I taped interviews with thirty members of the Weather Underground who were present at the Flint War Council, including most of its leadership. Not one of them thought Dohrn was anything but deadly serious." David Horowitz, "Allies in War," *Front Page Magazine*, September 17, 2001, http://islet.org/horowitz/20010914.htm.

11. Rudd, *Underground*, 189.

12. Larry Grathwohl, *Bringing Down America: An FBI Informer with the Weathermen* (New Rochelle, NY: Arlington House, 1976), 145–53, 199–200. My edition is a second edition printed in 2013.

13. Grathwohl wrote about these things in his memoirs and talked about them very openly in a number of lectures decades later. I came to know Grathwohl and heard these accounts from him personally. He told me about the four-finger dance at a July 2012 event at the National Press Club, where we both were speakers (the second event where we spoke together). I have written about Grathwohl and the Weather Underground in my 2010 book *Dupes* and also in a tribute to Grathwohl published after his unexpected death in 2013. See Paul Kengor, "RIP, Larry Grathwohl, Weather Underground infiltrator," *American Spectator*, July 26, 2013.

14. Rudd, *Underground*, 166.

15. Rudd mentioned abortion in *Underground* on pages 123 and 267.

16. Rudd, *Underground*, 164–65, 183.

17. Ibid., 165–66.

18. Ibid., 166.

19. Ibid., 206–7.

20. Ibid., 121–22, 205–7.

21. Ibid., 208.

22. See David Horowitz, *Radical Son: A Generational Odyssey* (New York: Free Press, 1997), 175–76.

23. Michael Lerner, "Herbert Marcuse at 100," *Tikkun* Magazine, September/October 1998, 11. Also see Jonah Goldberg, *Liberal Fascism* (New York: Doubleday, 2008), 331; Jack Jacobs, *The Frankfurt School, Jewish Lives, and Antisemitism* (New York: Cambridge Univ. Press, 2015), 117 and 210-11; and "Scholars and Activists who were influenced by Herbert Marcuse," at the Marcuse website, http://www.marcuse.org/herbert/scholaractivists.htm, accessed March 10, 2015.

24. See Barbara Olson, *Hell to Pay* (Washington, DC: Regnery, 1999), 312–13; and Joyce Milton, *The First Partner* (New York: William Morrow, 1999), 283–84.

25. Rudd, *Underground*, 40.

26. Grathwohl, *Bringing Down America*, 144, 158–59.

27. Ibid., 158.

CHAPTER 15: THE RED FAMILY

1. Ronald Radosh, *Commies: A Journey Through the Old Left, the New Left and the Leftover Left* (San Francisco: Encounter, 2002), 41.

2. Ibid.; and Ron Radosh, "When the New Left Shilled for North Korea," PJ Media, March 7, 2013, http://pjmedia.com/ronradosh/2013/03/07/when-the-new-left-shilled-for-north-korea-an-unknown-story/.

3. Radosh, *Commies*, 106–7.

4. Ibid., 107–8. Radosh presents new information and attestation of Scheer's North Korean romance in his more recent article at PJ Media, "When the New Left Shilled for North Korea."

5. David Horowitz, *The Black Book of the American Left*, vol. 2, *Progressives* (Los Angeles: Second Thoughts, 2013), 206.

6. Ibid., 114, 206, 211–15, 220–22; and Peter Collier and David Horowitz, *Destructive Generation: Second Thoughts about the Sixties* (New York: Summit, 1989), 245, 259–60, 266–67.

7. Horowitz, *The Black Book of the American Left*, 221–22; and Radosh, "When the New Left Shilled for North Korea."

8. David Horowitz, *Radical Son: A Generational Odyssey* (New York: Free Press, 1997), 25–27, 64, 286.

9. Ibid., 69, 213–14.

10. Ibid., 173–75.

11. Radosh, who observed this firsthand, stated in his writings that Scheer spread North Korea's "propaganda line once he returned home" to the United States.

12. Horowitz, *The Black Book of the American Left*, 221.

13. Horowitz, *Radical Son*, 195–96; and Horowitz, *The Black Book of the American Left*, 114.

14. Horowitz, *Radical Son*, 195–96.

15. Ibid., 196.

16. Collier and Horowitz, *Destructive Generation*, 73–77.

17. Ibid., 85.

18. Ibid., 74, 85.

19. Ibid., 85–86.

20. For the intrepid of heart, see ibid.

21. Sheen said this in a 1953 broadcast of his TV show, *Life Is Worth Living*. This particular episode was titled, "Women Who Do Not Fail."

22. Collier and Horowitz, *Destructive Generation*, 87.

23. Dinitia Smith, "No Regrets for a Love of Explosives," *New York Times*, September 11, 2001.

24. See Robert R. Reilly, *Making Gay Okay* (San Francisco: Ignatius Press, 2014), 52–65.

25. Horowitz, *Radical Son*, 344.

26. Collier and Horowitz, *Destructive Generation*, 87.

27. See my extended analysis of this in Kengor, *Dupes*, 454–65.

28. See my chapter on this in *Dupes*, 466–80.

CHAPTER 16: THE GAY-MARRIAGE PRESIDENT—AND HIS MENTOR

1. Paul Kengor, *The Communist: Frank Marshall Davis: The Untold Story of Barack Obama's Mentor* (New York: Simon & Schuster, Threshold Editions/Mercury Ink, 2012).

2. On this, see the examination by Jack Cashill, *Deconstructing Obama* (New York: Threshold Editions, 2011), 283–84.

3. Bob Greene, *Sex Rebel: Black (Memoirs of a Gash Gourmet)* (San Diego: Greenleaf Classics, 1968).

4. *Livin' the Blues: Memoirs of a Black Journalist and Poet* (Madison, WI: University of Wisconsin Press, 1992), xxvi.

5. Ibid., 346. Also in *Livin' the Blues*, the introduction by Frank's biographer, John Edgar Tidwell, confirms the authorship. The authorship is so certain that even *Wikipedia*, which otherwise tiptoes around troubling claims like Frank's communist work, wrote that "Davis also authored a hard core pornographic novel, which was published in 1968 under a pseudonym. The book, titled, *Sex Rebel: Black (Memoirs of a Gash Gourmet)*, was written under the pseudonym, 'Bob Greene.'" *Wikipedia*, s.v. "Frank Marshall Davis," *Wikipedia*, retrieved March 17, 2011.

6. Here, too, see Tidwell's introduction in *Livin' the Blues*, xxvi. Tidwell likewise struggles with this.

7. See Cashill, *Deconstructing Obama*, 277, 284.

8. This is found on page 2 of Frank Marshall Davis's FBI file record #100-5082.

9. Frank Marshall Davis FBI file. This information is found on page 4 of Honolulu File 100-5082.

10. Davis, *Livin' the Blues*, 230.

11. Ibid., xxvi, 21, 42, 72, 84, 229, 241, 333, 347.

12. See my analysis of Maraniss: Paul Kengor, "On Davis Maraniss and Obama's Communist Mentor," *American Thinker*, July 9, 2012, http://www.americanthinker.com/articles/2012/07/david_maraniss_and_obamas_communist_mentor.html.

13. See my lengthy analysis of Axelrod: Paul Kengor, "The Quest for David Axelrod's Leftist Roots," *American Spectator*, April 2014, 46–47, http://spectator.org/articles/58116/quest-david-axelrod%E2%80%99s-leftist-roots.

14. George Neumayr, "Axelrod's Admission," *American Spectator*, February 18, 2015.

15. David Axelrod, *Believer: My Forty Years in Politics* (New York: Penguin, 2015), 446–47, 452–53.

16. Quoted in Reilly, *Making Gay Okay*, 3–4.

17. Robert Knight, "The Marxist Roots of 'Gay Liberation,'" October 27, 2010, posted at www.usasurvival.org/HOME/ck10.27.10.html.

18. Kevin Jennings, foreword, in William J. Letts, IV, and James T. Sears, eds., *Queering Elementary Education* (Lanham: MD: Rowman-Littlefield, 1999), ix–xi.

19. Among them, see Kengor, *Dupes*, 445–46; and Kengor, *The Communist*, 249–62.

20. Interview with Dr. John Drew, October 16, 2010, for *Glen Meakem on the Weekend* radio show. (I was the guest host for Meakem for this particular show. I knew Drew already and invited him on the show as a guest.) I began interviewing and corresponding with Drew via e-mails and phone conversations in April 2010.

21. See my article: Paul Kengor, "Our First 'Red Diaper Baby' President?" *American Spectator*, October 22, 2012, http://spectator.org/articles/34558/our-first-red-diaper-baby-president.

CHAPTER 17: COMMUNISTS AND HOMOSEXUALITY

1. Richard Cohen, "Hollywood's Darling, Liberals' Blind Spot," *Washington Post*, April 8, 2003.
2. Mike Shotwell, e-mail message to author, September 7, 2013.
3. I have been researching this Hoover campaign and will address it in a future work.
4. Harvey Klehr, e-mail correspondence with author, December 1, 2014.
5. Harvey Klehr, e-mail correspondence with author, November 30, 2014.
6. Frank S. Meyer, *The Moulding of Communists: The Training of the Communist Cadre* (New York: Harcourt, Brace, 1961), 80–81.

CHAPTER 18: THE GIFT OF GAY MARRIAGE

1. See Ion Mihai Pacepa and Ron Rychlak, *Disinformation* (Washington, DC: WND Books, 2013).
2. See Pope Benedict XVI, "Papal Address to the Roman Rota," Vatican City, January 28, 2013, http://www.zenit.org/en/articles/papal-address-to-roman-rota--2. Benedict here cited section 1055 of the Code of Canon Law.
3. Jessica Chasmar, "N.Y. farm owners fined $13,000 for refusing to host lesbian wedding," *Washington Times*, August 19, 2014.
4. Claire Healey, "Bakery Bullies," *American Spectator*, October 12, 2013, http://spectator.org/articles/56838/bakery-bullies.
5. See Paul Kengor, "Death of a Hell-Destined Homophobe," *American Spectator*, September 10, 2014, http://spectator.org/articles/60386/death-hell-destined-homophobe.
6. See my summary in Paul Kengor, "The Left's Evolving Hierarchy of Rights," on the website of the Center for Vision & Values, April 4, 2014, http://www.visionandvalues.org/2014/04/the-lefts-evolving-hierarchy-of-rights/.
7. See Maggie Gallagher, "On Chai Feldblum's Claim That I Misquoted Her," *National Review: The Corner* (blog), October 28, 2014, http://www.nationalreview.com/corner/391301/chai-feldblums-claim-i-misquoted-her-maggie-gallagher.
8. Daniel J. Flynn, "The Sixties' Road to Rutgers and Beyond," *American Spectator*, May 9, 2014.
9. The "opiate of the masses" remark is well-known. The source for the quote, "communism begins where atheism begins," is Fulton J. Sheen, *Communism and the Conscience of the West* (Indianapolis and New York: Bobbs-Merrill, 1948). Sheen, who spoke and read several languages, translated the quote into English from an untranslated Marx work.
10. Karl Marx and Friedrich Engels, *The Communist Manifesto*, trans. Samuel Moore (1848; New York: Penguin Classics, 2002), 242.
11. Lenin wrote this in a November 1913 letter to Maxim Gorky. See James Thrower, *God's Commissar: Marxism-Leninism as the Civil Religion of Soviet Society* (Lewiston, NY: Edwin Mellen Press, 1992), 39.
12. See J. M. Bochenski, "Marxism-Leninism and Religion," in B. R. Bociurkiw et al., eds., *Religion and Atheism in the USSR and Eastern Europe* (London: MacMillan, 1975), 11.

CHAPTER 19: ALL ABOARD! COMMUNISTS EMBRACE GAY MARRIAGE

1. "Announcing the Communist Party Convention, June 2014!" statement posted November 27, 2013, on the website of Communist Party USA, http://www.cpusa.org/announcing-the-communist-party-convention-june-2014/.

2.   Sam Webb, "Convention Keynote: For a modern, mature, militant, and mass party," remarks at the 30th national CPUSA convention, June 13, 2014, posted at http://www.cpusa.org/convention-keynote-for-a-modern-mature-militant-and-mass-party/.

3.   Kenneth Quinnell, "Unions celebrate LGBTQ progress, say challenges remain," *People's World*, July 1, 2014, http://peoplesworld.org/unions-celebrate-lgbtq-progress-say-challenges-remain/.

4.   See http://www.peoplesworld.org/obama-continues-to-expand-rights-for-lgbt-americans/; http://www.peoplesworld.org/unions-celebrate-lgbtq-progress-say-challenges-remain/; and http://www.peoplesworld.org/texas-democrats-set-progressive-platform/.

5.   "Gay Pride Month: Communists stand in solidarity," Communist Party USA, press release, June 24, 2006, http://www.cpusa.org/gay-pride-month-communists-stand-in-solidarity/.

6.   Paul Kengor, *God and George W. Bush* (New York: HarperCollins, 2004).

7.   I have written at length on this topic. Among others, see Paul Kengor, "A fundamental flaw in divining Bush's faith," *San Francisco Chronicle*, September 19, 2004; and Paul Kengor, "Bush Quietly Saves a Million African Lives," *National Catholic Register*, July 31, 2009, http://www.ncregister.com/site/article/bush_quietly_saved_a_million_african_lives/.

8.   John Bachtell, "Lesson from the 2014 elections: Inclusive 50-state strategy needed," *People's World*, December 1, 2014, http://peoplesworld.org/lesson-from-the-2014-elections-inclusive-50-state-strategy-needed/.

9.   See Ben Johnson, "Castro's daughter: Obama should legalize same-sex 'marriage,'" LifeSite News, May 14, 2012, https://www.lifesitenews.com/news/castros-daughter-obama-should-legalize-same-sex-marriage.

10. "Mariela Castro, Cuba President Raul Castro's Daughter, Backs Obama on Gay Marriage," *Huffington Post*, May 10, 2012, http://www.huffingtonpost.com/2012/05/10/mariela-castro-obama-gay-marriage_n_1507845.html.

11. "Cuba Mulls Legalising Gay Marriage," *London Telegraph*, May 11, 2012, http://www.telegraph.co.uk/news/worldnews/centralamericaandthecaribbean/cuba/9258978/Cuba-mulls-legalising-gay-marriage.html.

12. Matthew Cullinan Hoffman, "Under Obama admin pressure, Cuba considers recognizing homosexual unions," LifeSite News, January 24, 2012; and Ben Johnson, e-mail message to author, May 2012.

13. "U.S. Visa to Mariela Castro Sparks Controversy," *Miami Herald*, May 17, 2012.

CHAPTER 20: WITH GRATITUDE TO MR. AND MRS. MAINSTREET

1.   Fulton Sheen, Remarks at the Annual National Prayer Breakfast, Washington, DC, January 18, 1979.

2.   For my commentary on this, see: Paul Kengor, "'Progress!' The World's First Three-Way Gay Marriage," *Crisis Magazine*, March 12, 2015.

3.   Robert R. Reilly, *Making Gay Okay* (San Francisco: Ignatius Press, 2014), 22.

4.   For a long list of examples, see chapter 9 of Reilly, *Making Gay Okay*, 154–72.

5.   I am not at liberty to share the data, but a colleague at a conservative Christian college recently informed me of an internal campus survey in which students assumed that at least 33 percent of their country and classmates were gay. This was based not on actual observation of such sexual activity (the actual number on the campus was estimated to be closer to 2 percent) but on assumptions from media.

INDEX

Office of Strategic Services (OSS), 69, 98, 116
Office of War Information (OWI), 114
Olson, Orville E., 175
one-child policy (China), 36
One-Dimensional Man (Marcuse), 118–19, 120, 124–25
Oneida, New York, commune, 18, 113, 205
Orgone Institute, 193
Origin of the Family, The (Engels), 26, 28, 86, 131
Oughton, Diana, 149
Our Lady of Fatima, 82, 219n9 (chap. 8)
Owen, Robert, 8, 14–17, 22, 24, 38, 63, 153, 205

P

Padre Pio, 83
parental rights, Marx and Engels on, 27
"party marriages," 48
Passion of Youth (Reich), 106
patriarchy, 69, 132–33, 147
Peace of Soul (Sheen), 84, 90–91
Pelosi, Nancy, 59
People's World, 8, 187, 189, 190, 192
Pepper, Claude "Red," 163
Phillips, Jack, 183
pill, the, 140, 144, 160
Pipes, Richard, 120
Pio of Pietrelcina. *See* Padre Pio
Pius II (pope), 85
Pius IX (pope), 72, 74–76
Pius XI (pope), 78
Pius XII (pope), 85
Planned Parenthood, 39, 53, 55, 56, 58–60, 64, 144, 155
Political Affairs (Communist Party's theoretical journal), 67
Pol Pot, 15, 16, 31, 149
"polymorphous perversity," 122, 123, 202, 223n13 (chap. 12)
"polymorphous sexuality," 122, 222n12
population redistribution, 42
Prairie Fire: The Politics of Revolutionary Anti-Imperialism, 150
prisons, most common denominator among men in, 4
private property, 15, 16, 22, 25, 80, 84
Progressives for Obama, 162

prostitution, 39, 93, 133, 135
public schools, Marx's call for free education for all children in, 24, 25
Putin, Vladimir, 34

Q

Queering Elementary Education, 170
Qui Pluribus (On Faith and Religion), 72, 74–75
Quod Apostolici muneris (On Socialism), 76–77

R

racism, 127, 188
    of Karl Marx, 30
Radek, Karl, 97, 100
Radical Son (Horowitz), 155, 156
Radosh, Ron, 46, 152–55, 175, 224n3, 225n4, 225n11
Ramparts, 127, 153, 156, 157
Reagan, Ronald, 79, 82, 90, 100–1, 216n13 (chap. 5), 221n26
"red baptisms," 32–33
Redbook, 67
Red Butterfly Collective, 124
Red diaper babies, 25, 45, 46, 152, 173, 175, 193
Red Family, 8, 152–62, 205
Red Terror, 54
Reds (film), 45, 216n18
Reed, John, 44–45, 54, 216n18
Reich, Annie (Pink) (wife of Wilhelm), 108, 110
Reich, Cäcilie (née Roniger) (mother of Wilhelm), 105, 106
Reich, Leon, 105, 106
Reich, Wilhelm, 7, 12, 65, 69, 95, 97, 101, 104–15, 119, 120, 123, 146, 159, 169, 193, 202, 203, 221n12, 221n14
Reich, William, 113
Reid, Harry, 59
Reilly, Robert R., 119, 215n41
Revolution Betrayed, The (Trotsky), 35
Robespierre, Maximilien, 15
Rockefeller Foundation, 69, 101–2, 116, 117
Roe v. Wade, 34, 70, 89, 132, 160
Roman Catholic Church, 57, 72, 74–81, 82, 85, 89, 181–82, 195
    on Communism, 74–77, 78–79, 80
    definition of marriage by the, 81

"A brilliant analysis of the assault on the family."
—DAVID LIMBAUGH, LAWYER, SYNDICATED COLUMNIST AND
NEW YORK TIMES BESTSELLING AUTHOR

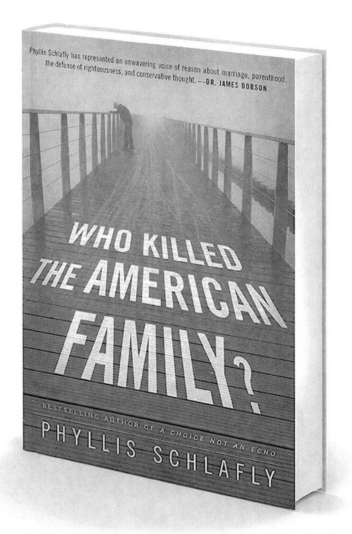

Phyllis Schlafly has represented an unwavering voice of reason about marriage, parenthood, the defense of righteousness, and conservative thought. —DR. JAMES DOBSON

WHO KILLED THE AMERICAN FAMILY?

BESTSELLING AUTHOR OF *A CHOICE NOT AN ECHO*

PHYLLIS SCHLAFLY

WHO KILLED THE AMERICAN FAMILY? reveals the concerted assault on the American nuclear family by many forces: feminists, judges, lawmakers, psychologists, school districts, college professors, politicians offering incentives and seeking votes, and more, each opposed to the traditional American nuclear family and each with its own raison d'être for wanting to abolish it. The wreckage of the American family leaves us with the inability to have limited government, because government steps in to perform tasks formerly done by the nuclear family.

WND Books • WASHINGTON DC • WNDFILMS.COM

"A compelling case that America's public education system must undergo radical change."

—RON PAUL, FORMER CONGRESSMAN AND PRESIDENTIAL CANDIDATE

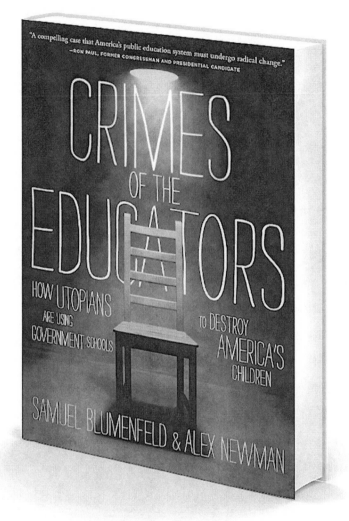

American author and veteran educator Samuel Blumenfeld and journalist Alex Newman have taken on the public education establishment as never before and exposed it for the de facto criminal enterprise it is. CRIMES OF THE EDUCATORS reveals how the architects of America's public school disaster implemented a plan to socialize the United States by knowingly and willingly dumbing down the population, a mission now closer to success than ever as the Obama administration works relentlessly to nationalize K-12 schooling with Common Core.

WND Books • WASHINGTON DC • WNDFILMS.COM

CPSIA information can be obtained at www.ICGtesting.com
Printed in the USA
LVOW10s2343270515

440032LV00007B/9/P